Concepts of Music and Copyright

Concepts of Music and Copyright

How Music Perceives Itself and How Copyright Perceives Music

Edited by

Andreas Rahmatian

School of Law, University of Glasgow, UK

Edward Elgar
PUBLISHING

Cheltenham, UK • Northampton, MA, USA

Published by
Edward Elgar Publishing Limited
The Lypiatts
15 Lansdown Road
Cheltenham
Glos GL50 2JA
UK

Edward Elgar Publishing, Inc.
William Pratt House
9 Dewey Court
Northampton
Massachusetts 01060
USA

A catalogue record for this book
is available from the British Library

Library of Congress Control Number: 2015943010

This book is available electronically in the Elgaronline
Law subject collection
DOI 10.4337/9781783478194

FSC www.fsc.org MIX Paper from responsible sources FSC® C013056

ISBN 978 1 78347 818 7 (cased)
ISBN 978 1 78347 819 4 (eBook)

Typeset by Columns Design XML Ltd, Reading

Printed and bound in Great Britain by
TJ International Ltd, Padstow, Cornwall

Contents

Contributors

John Butt

John Butt is Gardiner Professor of Music at the University of Glasgow and musical director of Edinburgh's Dunedin Consort. In 2006 he was elected Fellow of the British Academy. In 2013 he was awarded the medal of the Royal College of Organists and an OBE. His books include *Bach Interpretation* (1990), a handbook on *Bach's Mass in B Minor* (1991), *Playing with History* (2002), and a book on Bach's passions, *Bach's Dialogue with Modernity (*2010). He is also editor or joint editor of both the Cambridge and Oxford Companions to Bach and of the *Cambridge History of Seventeenth Century Music* (2005). John Butt's conducting engagements with the Dunedin Consort (2003–) have included major Baroque repertory and several new commissions. His recording of Messiah in its first performed version (Dublin, 1742) received the Gramophone award in the Baroque Vocal Category in 2007 and the MIDEM award for Baroque Music in 2008. In 2014 Butt and Dunedin won a Gramophone award in the Choral Category for a reconstruction of the first performance of Mozart's Requiem. John Butt has been guest conductor with a number of orchestras and he also continues to be active as a solo organist and harpsichordist.

Martin Parker Dixon

Martin Parker Dixon is Lecturer in Music at the University of Glasgow. He studied classical guitar and composition at the Royal Scottish Academy of Music and Drama in Glasgow and completed his PhD on T.W. Adorno at Cambridge University. He worked for many years with Cambridge Experimental Theatre and occasionally composes music. His research interests lie in post-war music and philosophy and in seeking to develop a radical hermeneutics of contemporary music. He has published especially on Adorno, John Cage, and technology in relation to music.

Alison Firth

Alison Firth is Emeritus Professor at the University of Surrey, and visiting professor of Newcastle University and Queen Mary, University of London. She is also Vice-President of BLACA (British Literary and Artistic Copyright Association). Alison Firth read physics at Oxford

University and later qualified and has practised as a barrister in intellectual property chambers since 1983. As an academic, first at the Centre for Commercial Law Studies, Queen Mary, University of London, and then as Professor of Commercial Law at Newcastle University before her present position, she researches and publishes in all areas of intellectual property law. Her books include (with G. Lea and P. Cornford) *Trade Marks: Law and Practice* (2006) and (with J. Phillips) *Introduction to Intellectual Property Law* (4th edition 2001).

Paul J. Heald
Paul Heald is the Richard W. and Marie L. Corman Professor of Law, at the College of Law of the University of Illinois at Urbana–Champaign. He is currently also a fellow and associate researcher at CREATe, the RCUK Centre for Copyright and New Business Models in the Creative Economy, based at the University of Glasgow. Heald earned his bachelor's and master's degrees in comparative literature from the University of Illinois. He earned his law degree *cum laude* from the University of Chicago. His recent publications have focused on economic aspects of IP law, including theoretical papers on optimal patent remedies, the role of transaction costs in patent law and the problem of patent pricing as well as empirical studies on best-selling fiction and musical compositions from 1913 to 1932 and the behaviour of famous trademarks in product and service markets.

Björn Heile
Björn Heile is Reader in 'Music since 1900' at the University of Glasgow. His first degree is in musicology and English and American literature from Technische Universität Berlin, and he obtained his PhD at the University of Southampton. His research interests are in new music, experimental music theatre, performance practice of experimental music, music and modernism and jazz studies, in particular jazz performance on screen. His books include *The Music of Mauricio Kagel* (2006), *The Modernist Legacy: Essays on New Music* (2009, as editor), *Watching Jazz: Encounters with Jazz Performance on Screen* (as co-editor, forthcoming) and *The Ashgate Research Companion to Modernism in Music* (as co-editor, forthcoming).

Andreas Rahmatian
Andreas Rahmatian is Senior Lecturer at the University of Glasgow, specialising in intellectual property law and commercial law. Originally from Vienna, he obtained a degree and a PhD in law and a second degree in musicology and history there, and continued his studies with an LLM at the University of London. He qualified as a solicitor in London before

he became an academic. His research interests comprise intellectual property law, property law and property theory, legal history, intellectual history and the law, and concepts of art and law, especially the relationship between music and copyright. His books include *Copyright and Creativity: The Making of Property Rights in Creative Works* (2011), which was shortlisted for the SLS Peter Birks Prize for outstanding legal scholarship in 2012, and *Lord Kames: Legal and Social Theorist* (2015).

Charlotte Waelde
Charlotte Waelde is Professor of Intellectual Property Law at the University of Exeter. Her work focuses on the interface between intellectual property law and changing technologies, the changes in the law wrought by those technologies, and the impact that those changes have on the way that the law is both perceived and used by the affected communities. She explores ways in which the law may be better calibrated to meet the needs of stakeholders. Professor Waelde regularly participates in policy-making processes and consultancy activities. She has also advised a range of international organisations including OPEC, ICSID and the European Parliament among others, and she has co-ordinated many academic responses to policy consultations. Among her publications are (with G. Laurie, A. Brown, S. Kheria, J. Cornwell), *Contemporary Intellectual Property: Law and Policy* (2013), and *Law and the Internet* (2009).

John Williamson
John Williamson is Research Associate in Music at the University of Glasgow. Previously he has worked, in various combinations, as a journalist, concert promoter/festival organiser and band manager. During that time he also completed a PhD on intellectual property, entrepreneurship and rent-seeking in the music industries in 2010. At the University of Glasgow he taught on the university's first Popular Music Studies courses. His research interests lie in popular music, popular music history, trade union history, copyright and intellectual property, entrepreneurship, music industries, popular music politics, journalism, and cultural and creative industries.

Introduction

Andreas Rahmatian

What is the relationship between copyright and music? How does copyright perceive music? How do musicians see the purpose of copyright for music?

This edited collection of chapters on music and copyright, with four musicians and musicologists and four copyright lawyers as contributors, grew out of an interdisciplinary workshop on music and copyright at the University of Glasgow that I organised on the occasion of the tercentenary celebrations of Glasgow Law School in 2013. This workshop, 'Artistry and Artificiality? Music and Copyright', took place on 6 September 2013. Its aim was to bring together musicians and musicologists with copyright law specialists, and to make musicians think about copyright and lawyers reflect about music.

This collection is truly interdisciplinary, a path often welcomed but less often followed. When lawyers do interdisciplinary work in intellectual property law, this tends to be cross-disciplinary within the law (for example, copyright and human rights) or it descends into a kind of law-and-economics study in which legal institutions and (hermeneutic) interpretative methods are remodelled as economic concepts and, where that proves difficult, a call for reforming (or deforming) the law is frequently put forward so as to bring 'positive' law more in line with the supposedly immutable, universal 'natural' laws of the all-encompassing market. In this intellectual climate the arts and humanities naturally fare badly, and the potential of philosophy and the humanities for interdisciplinary legal studies is too much neglected. This is particularly true of music, because, while many disciplines have considerable awareness of the existence of conceptual frameworks in philosophy, logic, linguistics or history which may inform their own, the rich legacy of music theory and thinking in musical conceptions as a *musica theorica* has long been forgotten outside music scholarship. But having some understanding of music was part of the general education well into the nineteenth century, and this knowledge could enrich the thinking in other areas. Today one has to be an anachronistic *uomo universale* if, for example as a lawyer, one studies the structure of a Bach fugue or a Mozart sonata to get some inspiration for solving an intricate problem of organisation and presentation of legal arguments in an article or in a pleading. Normally music is either irrelevant to lawyers or a pastime entirely unrelated to their 'proper job'. Where the nature of the subject-matter, copyright, inescapably binds law and music together, music is often only considered as some potentially valuable resource which can be sold and rented out, through assignments and licences. And this dealing with copyright, where the musical work is only an incidental object, is then within the focus of the lawyers' attention, of academics and practitioners alike.

In contrast, musicians, musicologists and sociologists of music are very much aware of the phenomenon of copyright, which plays an increasingly important role within their own disciplines. But copyright is then often viewed from the outside as a kind of undifferentiated, monolithic concept or as a tangle of uninteresting technical rules, unsympathetic to the idea of collaboration between performers/composers in favour of one single author-genius, struggling with the ideas of performance and of the process of creation, and being generally a threat to the unfolding of creativity, particularly through the commercialisation of music by the entertainment industries for which copyright provides the necessary legal vehicle. While these are all valid points of criticism, copyright nevertheless gives a more complex picture.

The principal idea of this book is to present the thoughts of music scholars who examine copyright and copyright lawyers who look at music, each from their own discipline and from their familiar conceptual framework. Copyright lawyers may be perplexed when they read how music scholars perceive copyright, as a phenomenon of intellectual history or as the subject-matter of a philosophical argument, with little reference to specific statutes or case law, and music scholars may be puzzled by the lawyers' extensive discussion of court decisions on copyright in musical works in which one may be able to discern only indirectly a notion of the art form of 'music'. The creation of such a possible bewilderment is intentional. A multidisciplinary approach starts with the appreciation as to how scholars in other disciplines think.

Specialists in music and musicology discuss the idea of the musical work and of performance, as well as the question of 'collective' authorship in collaboration processes, especially where they involve performance and improvisation. Specialists in copyright examine the formal system of copyright and the way in which musicians, singers and performers deal with the law in practice. Copyright lawyers will also look at the building blocks of 'musical works' in law, how they are translated into copyright and how they reflect (or not) the reality of music creation and music performance. The final chapters will discuss the socio-political role and economic effects of certain aspects of copyright on the music business. The contributions concentrate on the subsistence instead of the infringement of copyright, and on the nature of its subject-matter ('music', or the 'musical work'?). Concepts and ideas, and their social effects, rather than the technical legal rules of exploitation of copyright with regard to musical works, are of principal interest.

John Butt explores in his chapter the development of the 'work concept' in Western art music, being the intellectual foundation for the copyright category 'musical work'. Is there in any given period a phenomenological entity that can be defined as a 'work'? The idea of the 'musical work' is not only more closely related to Western art music, but is also associated with specific eras in the history of music. Butt presents the current discussion in musicology and adjacent disciplines in this regard, from around the sixteenth century to the present time. The more recent weakening of the classical work concept allows consideration of other factors implicit in the music, particularly performance. New media and methods of communication have also helped to draw attention to different ways of listening to music, contrary to a generally assumed passivity of the music listener. Music is no longer listened to as an impersonal object in its own right. This also means that the idea of 'musical works' as fixed and inviolable objects is gradually relinquished.

In the next chapter Charlotte Waelde discusses the performative aspect of music and the interpretation of musical works in performance, as well as the question of arrangement, which is in reality often closely connected with the performance of music. These are all complicated problems for copyright, as Waelde shows when she deals with the relevant case law on originality and (co-)authorship. Music cannot be captured in its entirety by copyright. And what actually constitutes the musical composition, or traditionally, 'the score'? Since much of experimental music escapes any institutionalisation and definition, policy intervention can hardly be directed at a specific object and becomes difficult. Waelde demonstrates in case studies – interviews with performing musicians/composers – what composition and performance really are for musicians.

Martin Parker Dixon takes a more philosophical approach in his piece. What does authorship in relation to a work of music mean? Is it a kind of (social and legal) entitlement to a 'musical work' and what is the justification for such an entitlement? Is it some 'herculean labour'? The ability, art and craft to make 'something'? To express 'deep feelings'? Theories relating to creativity may begin with a reflection on the nature of the thing being made. Dixon puts forward two theses to examine claims to paternity and integrity of the work, claims which are given legal effect by the two corresponding, and the two most important, moral rights: the 'auteur thesis' – the author as the singular, necessary and efficient origin of the work of art, and the 'artisanal thesis' – the author being (at best) co-responsible for the formation of a work of art. Dixon picks up a line of thought from Jean-Paul Sartre: it might be that fundamentally the artist makes artworks in order to possess them; to have not only a thing but also to have the work they 'put into' the object (be it constructive work, emotional work, spiritual work, etc). Can we leave aside speculation about creativity and address instead the experience of possessing, by asking what claims are being made to substantiate that possession?

In my own chapter I argue that copyright law has no genuine understanding of the nature of music as an art form; it attaches to certain aspects of music which it declares as normatively relevant and thus ascertains building blocks of the legal protection system. In this way music is considered as an object of legal transactions, especially as an object of transferable property. This is a result of the translation process of music into legal categories. The chapter looks at the elements and stages of this process, starting with sketching out a philosophical discussion of the phenomenon of music as a basis for copyright protection. It then discusses court cases of copyright on originality, co-authorship and on the 'idea–expression dichotomy' that demonstrate the legal categories with which the law encapsulates and re-interprets the elusive art of music.

Björn Heile approaches the question of authorship in music from a musician's and musicologist's perspective, with particular reference to jazz. In his chapter he analyses the contributions to Duke Ellington's famous song 'Mood Indigo' by Ellington himself, by his clarinettist Albany (Barney) Bigard, by the latter's teacher, Lorenzo Tio, and others. He reconstructs the creative contributions of various individuals in detail, evaluating their originality and significance for the final result. Although Ellington was by no means the sole creator of the song, Ellington did take most of the fundamental creative decisions. In his musical analysis Heile shows that the idea of authorship is also dependent on the kind of work or part of the work which it relates to: what is a memorable tune, what is musical material that is a 'standard', what are improvisations and what significance do they have for 'authorship'.

Alison Firth's chapter concentrates on the complicated question of copyright co-authorship and co-ownership in music. By way of an extensive analysis of the relevant case law in copyright, she shows how joint authorship is understood in UK law: joint authorship depends upon collaboration of musical co-authors, and on original contributions from them towards the finished work. The contributions must be merged, so that they are not distinct. The contributions must also be of the correct kind, that is to say, contributions towards the expressive form that is protected by copyright. But Firth's discussion also demonstrates that these principal rules on joint authorship cannot be extracted easily from the court decisions, as these are not always consistent and grapple with the performative and improvisatory nature of music.

In the next chapter John Williamson provides an insight into the lobbying of interest groups in the music industry and their influence on law-making in copyright. Williamson offers a possible new perspective for the character of performers' rights, by interpreting them as musical labour. He discusses the evolution of performers' rights in the UK with particular focus on the previously unrecognised role of the Musicians' Union. Although the Musicians' Union saw recorded music from the beginning as a threat to the live work undertaken by its members, it has been an important participant in the negotiations surrounding such rights, by simultaneously lobbying both on national and international levels while carving out deals with the record companies and broadcasters. Williamson provides a critical evaluation of the Musicians' Union's shifting role in relation to industrial and technological changes, as well as the evolution of copyright legislation.

The final chapter, by Paul J. Heald, is directed at the practical side of music 'consumption' by listeners and users. It is an empirical study that demonstrates that notice-and-takedown regimes can create a market for music on the video- and music-sharing website YouTube. According to transaction cost theory, notice-and-takedown regimes can lower transaction costs by facilitating communication between users and copyright owners, especially where content filtering provides the automatisation of much of the process. Heald's market study tests this transaction cost theory by tracking 90 songs on YouTube that reached No. 1 on the US, French, and Brazilian pop charts from 1930 to 1960. An analysis of the data demonstrates that the US Digital Millennium Copyright Act (DMCA) 'safe harbor' system as applied to YouTube helps maintain public access to many old songs by allowing those possessing copies (primarily infringers) to communicate with copyright owners at relatively low cost to satisfy the market of potential listeners.

I would like to thank the contributors to this edited collection for participating in the workshop and for agreeing to prepare their workshop papers for publication, and for delivering most stimulating book chapters, which made my work as editor a very enjoyable experience. I am also grateful to the peer reviewers, in the disciplines of music as well as of law, for reviewing the chapters. Furthermore, I would like to thank the Law School of the University of Glasgow for having given me the opportunity to host the workshop in autumn 2013, and the publisher Edward Elgar for making the publication of this book possible.

Finally, one may quote a passage from *Versuch über die wahre Art das Clavier zu spielen* (1753) by C.P.E. Bach (*Vorrede*, p. 4), which confirms and at the same time contradicts notions of copyright in relation to music and performance:

> Die vortrefflichsten Meister in der Ausübung [des Clavierspielens], denen man etwas Gutes abhören könnte, sind noch nicht in so grosser Anzahl zu finden, als man sich vielleicht einbilden dürfte. Das Abhören, eine Art erlaubten Diebstahls, aber ist in der Musik desto nothwendiger, da, wenn auch die Abgunst unter den Menschen nicht so groß wäre, viele Sachen aufstossen, die man kaum weisen, geschweige schreiben kan, und die man also vom blossen Hören erlernen muß.

> (The best masters in the exercise [of keyboard playing], from whom one could learn something good by way of listening, cannot be found in quantities as great as one may imagine. Listening, a kind of permitted theft, is, however, in music the more necessary (even if enviousness among humans were not so strong), since many matters come up which one can hardly explain, let alone write, and which one must learn from mere listening.)

Nantes, France, April 2015

1. What is a 'musical work'? Reflections on the origins of the 'work concept' in western art music[1]

John Butt

To many, it would still seem absurd to suggest that there is any argument to be had about how 'musical works' exist: the answer is surely obvious to anyone with an interest in the history of western classical music, since even the titles alone can conjure up a host of past and possible performances and, most importantly, experiences. Moreover, most musical works are associated with a documentary trace, the score, by which certain parameters are fixed, others suggested or left open, and the work can thus be identified as a document qualifying for copyright protection or authorial ownership, much in the manner of a verbal text.

Already though, this very brief sketch of assumptions is reliant on specific contexts of performance, authorship, title and documentation, which are all too easily naturalised across diverse types of music (witness a growing concern with authorship, ownership and varying levels of 'authenticity' in reproduction within the history of popular music). There is something definitely 'western' about this too. While there might indeed be canons of 'high' and 'low' music in the traditions of countless non-western cultures, very few of them are concerned with documentary precision or the intellectual property rights of individual, unique creators (of course, this is not to say that western-style music, in both 'art' and popular categories, cannot successfully be introduced or indeed created within these cultures).

If there is this synchronic observation to be made across contemporary cultures, might there not also be a diachronic one? In other words, if 'musical works' have more resonance in some parts of the world than others, might they not also thrive in specific eras of western history? The

[1] This chapter reworks several substantial passages previously published in Butt (2005) and Butt (2010).

historicity of musical works has long been a concern among German musicologists, most particularly Carl Dahlhaus and Walter Wiora.[2] Writers in this tradition tend to assume that in any given period there is a phenomenological entity that can be defined as a 'work' so long as our command of language and our intuition of the dynamics of music history are up to the task. In this view, if many works in the later stages of western music history acquired features that gave them a greater claim to autonomy (assuming that this is a useful criterion in defining a 'work'), this was more a matter of degree than of kind. Within the context of the European tradition, there is for many, therefore, an essential trans-historical unity implied by the concept of a work. Certainly, developments in music notation, tonal harmony and increasingly mechanised methods of reproduction helped produce a more solidly 'work-like' work from, say, the mid-eighteenth century onwards, and most specifically in western Europe. Music from previous times was not automatically devalued (although that might often have been the net result), but rather valued for the degree to which it provided an important precursor for the 'fuller' work, a sort of 'Old Testament' to ground the 'New'. Works here fitted into a progressive narrative (each new work having to represent a 'step further'), with faintly Whiggish pretentions.

But, in the decades following World War II it is not difficult to detect a slight unease about the direction of musical progress among both composers and historians. To put it simplistically: were we beginning to run out of notes? Were we producing music that might possibly not make any sense to the human ear and understanding? Most importantly, was classical music, just like other arts, becoming irrelevant in an increasingly connected world, in which 'high' and 'low' cultures had equal claims to value?

The 1960s saw the beginnings of the dissolution of the 'highbrow' in relation to the academic study of literature, and musicology was not that far behind. From the 1980s onwards, US scholars (some inspired by contemporary French and German thinkers) became increasingly irritated by the dryness and deference of traditional 'positivist' scholarship.[3] Soon the very basis of the 'academic canon' was called into question and even war-horses of the western tradition were becoming subject to various forms of 'deconstruction' (ranging from the colloquial sense of uncovering social and cultural norms concealed within them to the more

---

2 Dahlhaus (1983); Seidel (1987); Wiora (1983 (1988)).

3 This move is often conveniently, and justifiably, dated to the publication of Joseph Kerman's trenchant critique of contemporary 'positivist' musicology, Kerman (1985).

theoretical, Derridian approach). Scholars split roughly into those who wanted to save the classical canon from itself (and particularly from its devotees) by taking issues of culture, politics and gender head on, and others who wanted to see this music dethroned and – at best – as only one music among many within popular and world traditions. In all, the ground was extremely well prepared for the most influential English-language study of the musical work, which appeared in 1992, *The imaginary museum of musical works*, by Lydia Goehr.[4]

One of the most disarming aspects of Goehr's approach was the fact that she came from outside the usual circles of American/UK musicology, and seemed – at least in this book – unaware of the disputes currently underway (which usually came under the stirring, but ultimately facile, title of 'New Musicology'). Her targets were, rather, in another field entirely, one considerably more hermetic than the all-singing world of musicology: analytic philosophy. Philosophers in this tradition share something with music analysts (themselves very different beasts from historical musicologists) in considering musical works to subsist independently of their historical position and cultural context. Indeed these 'external' aspects could be seen as damaging distractions from the task of rendering the abstract structures of musical works much more latent.

Goehr's thesis was hardly radical in itself: not unlike German musicologists in the preceding decades, she asserted that the concept of the musical work is historically conditioned. More provocative was her view that the work concept did not develop until around 1800 and that, strictly speaking, no musical works were written before this time (not even, seemingly, by Monteverdi, Bach or Mozart). In Goehr's account, no analytic theory adequately accounts for the historical boundary of the music that it concerns. The notion of the work is, instead, a Wittgensteinian 'open concept', allowing for the subtraction or addition of defining characteristics provided that its continuity is preserved and that it is consistently recognisable over its period of operation. Open concepts are thus 'signposts' facilitating language use. The work concept is also a 'regulative' concept, one that defines certain normative and interrelating practices that are implied when we talk of musical works.[5]

Goehr seeks to show how the many strands constituting the work concept came together around 1800, so that it is, in fact, closely associated with early Romantic aesthetics of music. Defining features

4 Goehr (2007 (1992)).

5 *Ibid.*, pp. 89–101, quote from p. 93.

include the notion of the unique, original composer, a distinction between art and craft, a defining written score of the work, a sense of musical autonomy distinct from other aspects of the world (especially the everyday), a formalist move towards inner rather than outer significance, a co-option of religion by music, stronger copyright laws, the construction of concert halls as the principal premises for musical consumption, and, most importantly perhaps, disinterested contemplation on the part of the listener. While many of these strands are present before that date (thus certain pieces and composers show a superficial affinity with pieces and composers from the period in which Goehr's work concept became operative), in the strictest sense, only 'pieces of music' exist before 1800, not 'musical works'.

Inevitably, Goehr's book has engendered considerable discussion, not least the objections from scholars of earlier music, who clearly feel that their research would be devalued if the music concerned were no longer given the status of 'musical work'. But most of the discussion has ignored one of the more productive issues to be implied by Goehr's historicist approach. This is the notion that we should not just be discussing whether works as actual objects, or as idealised embodiments of pieces of music, existed at one time or another, but rather whether the interaction between ideas held about music, various social practices and the various musical objects or events at hand *together* generated the notion of the musical work. If some tend to assume that musical works are objects that are basically non-human and thus stable in character (those on the side of analytical philosophy and music analysis), others have surely gone too far in the direction of social constructivism and assumed that pieces of music exist only by virtue of the attitudes of a particular society – that there is nothing essentially 'there' beyond the cultural norms at hand. For a while, it was a moment for uncontrollable mirth and sarcastic put-down whenever any scholar unwittingly mentioned 'the music itself', since this clearly showed a refusal to admit the necessary human constructivist element into music and, at worst, evidenced an elitist, culturally normative attitude to western art. Yet the vertiginous attitude of social constructivists towards objects of art, while a stern lesson for those who underestimate the importance of human involvement at every level, is surely beginning to sound as tired as that argument of America's NRA (National Rifle Association), namely, that 'guns don't kill people, people do'. This would seem to suggest that guns are neutral, innocent objects that are constituted as weapons only through human agency; they cannot influence the human, or put evil ideas into one's head that are not there already. Here I am very much influenced by Bruno Latour's attitude to the findings and 'facts' of science: rather than opting for a natural order 'out there' on the one hand, or total social construction on the other, he sees a constant circulation between the human and the non-human. Facts and natural objects obviously have to be constructed or formulated in order to be recognisable and accessible to the human understanding, but they also acquire a little autonomy in return, influencing what appears as, and how we conceive of, the world around us.[6]

Pieces of music – whether remembered, composed in the mind, notated or sounded – are obviously human constructions through and through, but they also acquire an element of autonomy instantaneously. We cannot necessarily predict how we are going to react to, or conceive of, them at any point in the future. If we are somehow changed through our encounter with music, something must surely somehow be 'there' and not merely be constructed by us on the spur of the moment. But what the argument for social constructivism does indeed show us is that what is 'there' is not a stable entity that endures regardless of the energy we bring to it.

In examining the possibility of work concepts before that of the nineteenth century some, such as Reinhard Strohm, look for similarities linking one age to another. Therefore, the move towards the profiled composer and the perfection of individual works (as was happening in the fourteenth and fifteenth centuries, if not before) is precisely that which Strohm considers essential for the European tradition as a whole. It would thus be false to suggest that the western tendency to abstract art from its context and function, treating it as if it were a world in itself, is just a nineteenth-century invention.[7] But, according to Goehr, what render this later conception unique are the specific social, aesthetic and analytic practices attached to music, ones that resonate with earlier 'work concepts' but which do not necessarily constitute a more refined, perfected version of a consistent concept. As she later writes, the fact that the origins of the work concept can often individually be traced back to earlier periods does not mean that the fully fledged concept emerged then. To her, apparent similarities, such as the perfection of a notated musical text or a canon of commendable pieces of music, hide profound differences in culture in which the meaning of a perfected text or commendable exemplar was entirely different.[8]

---

6 Latour (1999).

7 Strohm (2000).

8 Goehr (2000).

Strohm correctly complains that Goehr tends to homogenise the incredibly complex and varied attitudes to pieces of music before 1800, blatantly ignoring factors that in some respect come close to elements of the later work concept. But she is surely right to insist that we critically examine the roots of our conceptions (a clear example of Nietzsche's 'critical' use of history).[9] While there is a very real sense in which we try to influence our successors – a crucial element in child-rearing for instance – most forms of significant artistic influence draw on the past and react to ideas that are already there. Crudely put, the processes of influence and development are characterised more by sucking than blowing. We cannot simply assume that any innovation of a past era was made with anything close to the forward-looking aim that we now might attribute to it.

This point is, of course, one of the central elements of Darwinian evolution, but the concept of evolution is more popularly associated with a process that is progressive and developmental, one in which there is some ideal end in mind even if earlier actors were not aware of this. This brings us back to the so-called Whiggish approach to history, in which aspects of the past are highlighted for their foreshadowing of a more perfect and enlightened present. It is against this concept of evolution and progress that I most take issue. There is nothing wrong with finding resonances in the past (granted that there is the danger of presentism) – this is, after all, one of the crucial functions of history, which serves to enhance our own sense of belonging to a broader culture of humanity. But this should not be confused with a sense of the past seeking resonances in the future. The Whiggish approach also tends to undervalue aspects of the past that do not conform to its particular model of progress; so it may well render us ignorant of alternative concepts, events, styles or pieces that were dropped from the historical or cultural canons, but from which we still might be able to learn. This is especially pertinent to music from the seventeenth century, for instance, when the very instability of concepts of music led to a degree of experimentation that was probably unprecedented. Many pieces from this time might well be undervalued or ignored if we merely judged them according to whether they were 'hot' or 'cold' in relation to the game of work-laden hide-and-seek.

Another crucial reason to resist the notion that composers and other musicians were aiming towards the work concept all along is that this attitude might ultimately be detrimental to the very institution of western

9 Nietzsche (1983).

art music as it exists today. Only by recognising the contingency of the work concept, only by recognising its historical boundedness, do we have a chance of planning for its survival and revival in a rapidly changing world. Blind belief in its universal validity will not by itself preserve the institution. As Latour remarks for the apparently far more robust field of scientific facts: 'It is always dangerous to imagine that at some point in history, *inertia* is enough to keep up the reality of phenomena that have been so difficult to produce', there is no such thing as a 'final' victory that requires no further work or action.[10] Even cherished near-universal values, such as democracy or fundamental human rights, need constant attention and effort; if these are taken as givens they may simply disappear over time.

In all, Goehr's study is particularly useful in showing how modern analytic theories of music are all beholden to the work concept, specifically in the guise in which it arose at the end of the eighteenth century, and thus tend to apply only to certain values and repertories of the nineteenth century and half the twentieth. Much can be disputed concerning her generalisations about nineteenth-century musical culture, in which the performative and improvisational could still be very important. But what I set out to do in the remainder of this chapter is to flesh out a little of the argument that Goehr leaves even less well supported, namely, the issue of how pieces of music were developed and conceived of during the three centuries before 1800. If everything did indeed fall into place at that latter point (and even if that point is negotiable, as it surely must be), what were the preconditions? My ultimate aim is to see whether such preconditions relate to any aspects of western history, culture or periodisation that can help explain the overall phenomenon of the western musical work in broad but non-universalist terms. My overall hypothesis is that the musical work in its more reified senses relates to the covering conditions of *modernity*.

Goehr's claim would seem senseless if we were to take at face value Listenius's statement (from the 1530s)[11] that the art of *musica poetica* results in a 'perfect and absolute *opus*' that survives the death of its maker. According to Heinz von Loesch, Listenius may not be referring exclusively or even primarily to individual pieces of music. Von Loesch argues that this formulation is one that early Lutheran music theorists

---

10 Latour (1999: 155, 168).

11 Listenius developed this definition from the opening of *Rudimenta musicae* (1533) to a fuller version in *Musica: Ab authore denuo recognita multisque novis regulis* (1537). For a comprehensive survey of these writings and the tradition that they engendered, see von Loesch (2001).

adopted from Aristotle and Quintilian to describe the activity of production in general, which could equally result in printed publications or theoretical treatises (even if Listenius's formulation was soon to become associated exclusively with musical compositions). Given that the essentially German theoretical tradition of *musica poetica* – of which Listenius was one of the founders – was to die out (together with the theoretical reliance on Aristotle and Quintilian) in the late seventeenth and early eighteenth centuries, it is unlikely that this was a significant component of later, progressively stronger concepts of work. On the other hand, one could argue that there is a sort of work concept, across most of the arts, right back in the ancient world. But if there is, it contains very few of the regulative conditions that Goehr claims became operative in 1800.

Therefore, in exploring the possibilities for a work concept in earlier centuries, much depends on the combination of characteristics that one considers necessary for a work. This might involve simply the identity and portability of notated musical pieces by famous composers as implied by Tinctoris (1477), or something closer to Goehr's open, regulative concept that requires a broad combination of conditions such as the separability of musical works from extra-musical environments, bourgeois concert-hall practice, and copyright. One way out of this impasse might be to take Gretel Schwörer-Kohl's distinction between a broader (and weaker) sense of 'work' and the narrower sub-category of 'opus-work' as a starting point.[12] The broader concept would cover compositions resulting from 'creative activity of the highest order', some form of self-contained formal structure, and some historical durability. But the concept of the 'opus-work' would demand more notational fixity, attribution to a specific author, and some degree of originality within the context of the age. The broader concept of work could be applied to a wide range of music, including much non-western music, while the 'opus-work' would refer mainly to the western classical tradition, more or less in Goehr's sense, and only to a limited number of non-western traditions.

Nevertheless, this distinction is not without its problems. The term 'opus' has a long history and was already well established in the sixteenth century. This might perhaps reflect the transfer of work concepts from other artistic fields, but it still does not necessarily evoke the individualised and unique connotations of Schwörer-Kohl's definition of the 'opus-work'. Moreover, her inclusion of 'creative activity of the highest order' as a principal definition of the broader sense of 'work'

[12] Schwörer-Kohl (1997).

begs a question of relative quality that cannot objectively be answered; it also raises the issue of whether the judgement is made from the standpoint of the composer's environment or of later reception. Perhaps the broader definition should be liberalised to include *any* musical entity (be it an event, a musical text, or just an idea) that can be perceived, remembered or discussed. Yet this would make the term 'work' virtually synonymous with 'piece of music' and thus more or less superfluous. The word 'work' works to the extent that it carries some sort of *charge* that 'music' on its own would not otherwise hold.

So significant is the charge associated with workhood in the western tradition that, to many, it is imperative to trace the roots of its corollary, compositional thinking, to its earliest stages and follow these through the subsequent centuries. Workhood can thus be thought of as something that develops in tandem with the very concept of western civilisation and the sense of 'universality' that this brings.[13] Strohm makes the point that there has always been a 'cohabitation' of functional elements with 'work-like significance' in music; thus it is a mistake to take the absence of a specific functional role as a crucial factor in defining any particular piece as a work.[14] From this perspective it is eminently possible to see musicians from the fifteenth to eighteenth centuries as playing their part in the creation of conditions that 'full' workhood co-opted during the nineteenth. Strohm notes Tinctoris's assertion (1477) that composers found fame in their works and also that commentators of the next generation likened the finest music of the Josquin era to the great works of pictorial and verbal art. While this latter point incidentally suggests that music culture does not lag so far 'behind' the other arts as we are often led to believe, it does raise the question of whether even the contemporary objects in other arts should be considered works in as strong a sense as they are often regarded. In all, though, it is clear that the idea of a musical work enjoying a public trajectory and bringing fame to an absent composer greatly expanded during the sixteenth century. Historians also observe a growing sense of canon formation and the predominance of single-author collections; these would suggest the notion of a 'great' composer standing above the merely skilled musician. This was marked by an adaptation of the traditional veneration of models from the past (covered by the notion of *Imitatio*), as encapsulated in general education by the commonplace book tradition, towards the notion that creators could be original and actually depart from the past. This

13 Strohm (1993: 1–5, 412–88).
14 Strohm (2000: 139).

shift was encapsulated by Descartes' constant call that past authority should be critically challenged and that all models should be treated with scepticism. Indeed, one important aspect of the development of stronger work concepts across all the arts must have lain in the fact that human originality actually became a possibility. The pre-modern view had largely been that, given God was the only true creator, any claim to originality must have counted as heretical.

Yet, time and again, the more one notes an apparent move in the direction of the work concept (at least in Goehr's sense), another move seems to go in the opposite direction – in opera for instance, the genre that is the first actually to be termed a 'work', it was well into the eighteenth century before the composer became celebrated on an equal footing even with the singers, and quite often the librettist had pride of place. Moreover, with the growth of instrumental performance it became customary to expect some degree of improvisation, and elaboration of existing notated pieces, thus weakening the absolute authority of notation. On the other hand, some genres specifically geared towards performance, such as those performed by the *concerto delle donne* at Ferrara in the 1580s, show evidence of the performers obeying the letter of the notation, diminutions and all,[15] although here it is almost as if the *concerto* were being celebrated for its unusual practice of *not* improvising embellishments – in any case, it may well be that the notation follows what the singers were accustomed to do rather than vice versa. It was perhaps a record of past performances, skilfully to be duplicated in the present and future performances.

In finding resonances between past and present – which is one of the crucial functions of history, and serves to enhance our own sense of belonging to a broader culture of humanity, and from which we can learn certain lessons – the satisfying discernment of similarities between past and present surely needs to be counterbalanced by an awareness of the profound differences. For instance, whatever new sense of individuality did indeed begin to evolve during the course of the sixteenth and seventeenth centuries, this was against the background of an overriding belief that music was still grounded in natural and universal rules governing all musicians, regardless of their local differences. To its adherents of the time (and perhaps some today), late Renaissance polyphony embodied assumed natural laws that connected music directly to the rest of creation; all systems belonged together under a sort of

[15] Newcomb (1980: vol. 1, 25–26, 55).

supernature.[16] At best, the aspect of nature increasingly embodied in the human passions, in the newer musical conceptions straddling 1600, would have been a lesser one. At worst, the growing emphasis on the heart rather than mind was to many the beginning of a slippery slope towards anarchy. This point demonstrates very clearly the way in which seemingly abstract and internally perfected *prima pratica/stile antico* music (i.e. the 'old' style of music as seen from the perspective of some of the newer ones of the seventeenth century) was so fundamentally different in conception from the more 'absolute' branches of music of the nineteenth century. The abstractness of perfected Renaissance counterpoint was testimony to its contiguity with the whole chain of being, which after all had never been immediately evident to the naked eye (or, in this case, ear). The abstractness of later, stronger, work concepts, on the other hand, was testimony to the separation from the world that could now be achieved by art, within the world itself.

The theoretical conception of 'disenchantment' is particularly relevant to the discussion of the development of stronger concepts of works. First formulated by Max Weber, disenchantment highlights the gradual move away from the magical significance of the world and human practices, still fully alive in the Middle Ages, along with the veneration of past ancestors and authorities, and reliance on beliefs in a wider macrocosmic order – what Adorno and Horkheimer call the 'extirpation of animism'.[17] Although the theory naturally generalises, it remains a useful tool for viewing the development of the modern world, beginning with the Renaissance and Reformation, by which assumed connections and resonances between the order of things and souls were gradually dismantled. But, with the concomitant move towards materialism, the control of nature and bountiful information, particularly with the scientific revolution straddling the turn of the seventeenth century, we became alienated from the objects disenchanted, precisely as these become more familiar and comprehensible within a rationalised taxonomic system.[18] 'Works' in the stronger sense, might then serve to shore up this loss by providing alternative worlds in which wholeness still pertains – part of what might sometimes be referred to as a process of 're-enchantment'.

Willem Erauw draws attention to a particular point made in Goehr's thesis concerning the development of musical works around 1800, namely that cultural activities assumed the transcendental function that a

---

16 Chua (2001: 18).
17 Adorno and Horkheimer (1997: 5).
18 Chua (2001).

declining religious practice could no longer provide.[19] He sees essential practices in reception, such as the motionless concert audience and reverence for the musical score, as being specifically religious in nature. From this viewpoint based on reception, it is possible to see why there is at least a conceptual problem in considering earlier music (at least from an environment in which it was impossible to question the truths of religion) as instantiating works in the nineteenth-century sense. This is not to say that religion completely disappeared in later centuries; indeed, nineteenth-century religious revivals could themselves be seen as prime examples of 're-enchantment', a compensation for the loss of the interconnected and magical world. Rather, religion became one system among others, to be adopted or contested in various ways.

With disenchantment came the view that the cosmos was not necessarily constructed entirely for mankind's benefit, so that a new form of human initiative was required to render the natural world amenable to human purposes. This is what Hans Blumenberg terms the 'burden of self-assertion'. With the new development of scientific method, it became necessary to adapt man to the impersonal reality uncovered by repeatable experimentation. But this distinction between reality and the human condition also brought with it the contrary tendency: to adapt that reality to the needs and purposes of man.[20] The most positive aspect to arise from this is the potential to see reality as whatever is most actual and immanent rather than as something that must always remain beyond our immediate experience. This might be what gives western society its restless and ongoing energy, a state that I would claim is usefully defined by 'modernity'. On the other hand, this development tends to drive a wedge between the natural world and human civilisation, to suggest that humankind is progressively alienated from the secure and harmonious place in the natural order that our cultural memories always seem to evoke. Hans Robert Jauss usefully relates this line of thinking to a trajectory leading from Rousseau to Adorno, thus suggesting an intellectual epoch that coincides with the latter part of the era of modernity as I am trying to outline it.[21] However, the sense of a growing rift between western humanity and nature did not necessarily prevent the re-invention of the transcendent hidden reality to give human orders support and justification 'from beyond'. It is imperative to make a distinction between 'enchantment' in its earlier (pre-modern) sense and 're-enchantments' of

---

19 Goehr (2007: 157); Erauw (1998).

20 Blumenberg (1983: 137–38, 209).

21 Jauss (1987: 243–68).

various kinds, since the latter are always undertaken in the wake of the breakdown of the former, and against the background of a disenchanted modernity.

As must already be clear, I would argue that Jauss's starting point of Rousseau is really only a later stage in a process begun with the late Renaissance and Reformation. The increased emphasis on subjectivity and individuality in the sixteenth and seventeenth centuries – and by extension, on some notions of workhood – can themselves be seen as a compensation for the increasing uncertainty of the natural order. It is therefore plausible that an increasing sense of individuality in musical composition does indeed parallel a stronger conception of human individuality and subjective presence. Yet this – almost paradoxically – does not necessarily reflect a deeper confidence in the human condition, but more a reaction to a loss of security within the wider order of things. Descartes' famous move was to advocate the total certainty of the thinking – or rather doubting – mind, compensating for the absolute uncertainty of everything else. The whole of nature is swapped for the unshakeable actuality of one's own existence. Reason, no longer at one with surrounding nature, becomes a tool to dissect the world. Charles Taylor links the growing sense of internalisation with the turn against an external, pre-existent order that is 'found' and that determines our station and role in life, towards a form of order that is made with our own minds. This is something made overt in Descartes' work on subjectivity, particularly in the *Discours de la Méthode* (1637).[22]

Hobbes represents the other wing of this turn, by which human order no longer has an unmediated connection with the raw, natural order of the world. From the very outset of *Leviathan*, the 'art' of man consists in constructing artefacts in imitation of nature, which are in essence no different from the given automaton of the human body, as already created by God.[23] The human creation of the state is but a further fabrication of this kind. If such a common power is not constructed, man reverts to a kind of war and famously experiences life as 'solitary, poor, nasty, brutish and short'. It is not so much that there is brutish nature on the one hand and human civilisation on the other, but that humans need to construct order out of the various conflicting natural orders at hand (which, unchecked, represent the condition of 'mere nature' in which all would recklessly pursue absolute liberty). Hobbes's principal departure from the old thinking of mankind as part of a broader chain of being is

22 Taylor (1989: 124).
23 Hobbes (1990: 1).

that the human must take a more active role in ordering nature. The artificial is as necessary as the natural and is indeed part of a more refined aspect of nature. Something of this attitude is evident in the way in which musical instruments rose in importance in the course of the seventeenth century: the fascination with describing and cataloguing instruments may well be part of the wider view of using artifice to improve nature and extend human capabilities.[24]

Another development was noted by Max Weber, namely his linking of the move away from 'natural' tuning towards tempered systems within the broader process of 'rationalisation'.[25] Human capabilities are greatly enhanced by the imposition of an ordered, rational system that patently ignores the 'natural purity' of musical intervals (i.e. that directly derived from the size of the intervals in the spectrum of harmonics, which together constitute the timbre of individual pitched notes) in order to extend the tonal system. Music thus moves out of the natural world into a seemingly richer world of its own. However much humanist reformers at the end of the sixteenth century (together with many music critics of the eighteenth and nineteenth centuries) might have prized music for its supposedly 'natural' qualities, what was becoming increasingly effective were precisely its independent aspects, its deviation and modification of supposed natural principles. With this potential for autonomy came the sense that musical compositions were individuals, following their own implications and potentials, and thus almost of a piece with the individuality of those who created them.

Hobbes's sense of authority also suggests that a circulating process is involved, one by which all authority itself depends on the will of those in an apparently passive position. In the context of art, this would suggest that while the concept of individual authorship is elevated, this is at the same time dependent on the collective will of those who receive the work composed. We might also recall the example of Lully (who produced music drama for the court of Louis XIV) here. He was highly complicit in authorising his monarch's power, but also in creating his own authority within the same hierarchy. A stronger seventeenth-century concept of the musical work thus corresponds to a stronger – but essentially artificial – concept of human subjectivity, which, in turn, coincides with the rise of absolutism (a 'modern' development despite its seemingly retrograde political direction). Discrete musical works also began to adopt a series of internal laws, checks and balances that paralleled Hobbes's artificially

---

24 Austern (2001: 44–45).
25 Weber (1958).

structured state – in other words, something that eschewed the immediate dictates of nature in order to mediate between the competing forms of power and authority.

One exceptionally illuminating theory of the role of art in this period is Lukács's of the novel: to Lukács, Cervantes's *Don Quixote* is the first true novel, in which the old epic practices no longer connect to the surrounding totality. The form of the novel thus compensates for the actual disenchantment of the surrounding world through its very irony. According to Lukács, Cervantes was writing at a time 'when man became lonely and could find meaning and substance only in his own soul, whose home was nowhere; when the world, released from its paradoxical anchorage in a beyond that is truly present, was abandoned to its immanent meaninglessness'.[26] The autonomy of the novel, its formal re-enchantment within its fictional world, its very inessential yet vital place in its culture, thus show the beginnings of crucial traits in a new conception of art, that 'raised the most confused problematic into the radiant sphere of a transcendence which achieved its full flowering as *form*'.[27] This sense of distance from the world, this consciousness of the autonomy of art, clearly resonates with the concept of the musical work as it reached its full flowering in later centuries. However much this type of art resembles aspects of the surrounding world, there is no longer a process of direct imitation, an uncomplicated correspondence between the world pictured and the world from which we read. To Lukács our consciousness of the disintegration and inadequacy of the world is the precondition for the existence of high art and of its becoming conscious and autonomous.

If Lukács is right, then, there *are* actual traces of struggle, irony, distancing, disenchantment and re-enchantment within artefacts that should be described as 'works' in the 'strong' sense (and clearly not just musical ones). The work concept may indeed widely reside in the culture of reception but it also leaves its tell-tale traces in the artefacts concerned. In this somewhat demanding conception, Goehr may well still be correct to doubt the existence of musical works long before 1800. It is clear that earlier music did not generally enjoy that sense of transferability and detachment from its contexts that literature was beginning to experience. One can, of course, point towards developments in compositional practice that do show a sense of abstraction – most significantly an increasing interest in musical form, even in genres, such as opera, where

[26] Lukács (1999: 103–4).

[27] *Ibid.*, p. 130.

the music was assumed to serve other functions. We might even be able to find examples where musico-dramatic works become self-reflexive, directly commentating on their contrivance and necessary detachment from the world. It is perhaps no accident that early operas so frequently concentrate on music as a dramatic theme, specifically in the form of the Orpheus myth. Here, music becomes a topic of re-enchantment, a nostalgia for an ancient age in which music actually had magic power.[28] But such is the complexity of issues of authority, commission, intention and collaboration in early opera, that disenchantment – if there is such – is the net result of these factors and not easily to be attributed to a single composer or librettist. It is precisely the ambiguity as to what music represents or reflects, and by whose authority, that renders the birth of opera so fascinating. As I have tried to argue, Bach's two surviving Passions co-opt the 'modern' technologies of opera in order to serve a traditional religious purpose, thereby creating what is potentially a richer experience and interpretation of the passion story, but one that is also detachable from its original religious context.[29]

There is also the question of pieces that exploit a particular issue of compositional theory (canon, fugue, etc.). It is often these, by composers such as Palestrina, Frescobaldi and Bach, that became so highly esteemed in the nineteenth century, since they are already, to some extent, models of 'absolute music'. Can these pieces really be 'works' if they presuppose a continuity between the fabric of the music and the hidden structure of the world? Indeed, this would seem to suggest that they reflect the survival of a form of musical thought that is yet to be disenchanted, and thus considerably more distant from the 'strong' work concept than might at first seem apparent. We should be very cautious in assuming that pieces approaching musical autonomy (i.e. without a text or specific function) were autonomous in the same way as later works. I am not trying to argue that no music from the earlier centuries can be treated, elevated or 'retrofitted' as a 'work', since the very concepts of work are not inherent just in a musical manifestation in sound or on paper, but in the circulation between these and the wider concepts both held in the period and evolving through reception. It might also be relevant that some Baroque music designed for religious worship transferred particularly easily into nineteenth-century aesthetics, in which music and the formal experience of the concert became a sort of substitute religion. But while it is extremely important to acknowledge that certain aspects of

---

28 Chua (2001: 25–26).
29 Butt (2010: 197–99).

thought and culture developed before the nineteenth century would eventually become crucial in the construction of the stronger work concepts, we should never presume that the earlier period ever had the latter in mind.

Finally, the question arises as to whether the historical foundations of the work concept shed any light on why it suddenly became an issue towards the end of the twentieth century, and was clearly no longer something to be considered self-evident. Much of my argument has been pointing in a particular direction, namely that the development of the type of strong musical work concept, as defined by Goehr, is part of a process that is specific to the West, one that I have identified as 'modernity'. This is not identical with the 'modernism' that characterises much late nineteenth- and early twentieth-century art, but rather something of a piece with what historians have long described as the 'modern age' (modernism is thus a particular intensification, if not exhaustion, of the potentialities of modernity). The exact timelines are not perhaps important, but historians have long used the broad categorisation by which the Ancient World is separated from the Modern World by the Middle Ages. Modernity thus has its beginnings in the era of the Renaissance and Reformation and is fed by the scientific revolution of the sixteenth and seventeenth centuries. Culturally, it surely has some real presence in Montaigne, Shakespeare and Cervantes, the philosophy of Locke, Hobbes, Descartes and Spinoza. It reaches both a peak and a crisis at the time of the Enlightenment and French Revolution and thereafter forges ahead with the industrial revolution and the increasing dominance of capitalism (and thus the period of Goehr's work concept).

The development of modernity shows several parallels with the stronger work concept: the scientific revolution and the notion of empirical experimentation; the development of a stronger sense of subjectivity and individuality; separation and specialisation in different spheres of human endeavour; instrumental reason; and division of labour. It was precisely this same division of labour that facilitated the development of the modern symphony orchestra, where every player has a specific place and a single instrument to perfect to the highest possible level, through methodical practice within an approved pedagogical system. With the foundation of the Paris Conservatoire in the wake of the French Revolution, musicians became trained in very specific tasks that together played a part in a large hierarchical system of orchestras, soloists, conductors and, of course, composers.

Already there might seem to be something rather oppressive about the industrialisation of classical music and its increasing range of re-enchanted texts – those ever more precise scores of musical works.

But perhaps one of the strengths of the classical tradition and its associated work concept lay in the way they sat between the establishment – confirming the status quo in sound, as it were – and simultaneously opposed or subverted it, challenging its secure assumptions. It became an art that took inherited orders as its starting point (thus its reliance on a particularly strong pedagogy of harmony and counterpoint), but through its seeming autonomy and individuality could act as a critique of our own assumptions. It could also develop a feeling of alienation, resistance or even opposition to the surrounding orders. In other words, it worked dialectically in the sense that it could lead to results that could never quite accurately be predicted (at least for the active performer and listener), a real sense of autonomy that distinguished this culture and its emerging work concept from one in which music was always at the service of other arts, religion or politics.

What Goehr's claims may be reacting against, then, seems to be the high modernist mindset that tends to assume that autonomous music's fictional truth is so refined and honest in its own integrity that it virtually outdoes any other kind of truth. It is supremely true because it is so distanced from the messy chaos of the rest of reality. With this in mind, it is easy to see how the later culture of classical music has contributed so much to its own self-regarding sense of exceptionality – as something totally apart from the mundane. The modernist outlook is thus assumed to apply to the whole of this art of modernity. From this point of view, the advent of a 'postmodern' mindset, or at least that part of it that undoes the dichotomy of high and low culture, might have provided a healthy corrective. But, one could ask, might we not also have lost a sort of productive tension between different types of culture? Should we perhaps be lamenting the loss of Goehr's stronger concept of musical works, which was a sort of religious surrogate upheld by its own existential dogma?

If there is some symmetry between the pre-modern and the current situation, one might wonder whether there is a sort of return to the old scholastic prohibition against curiosity in the unknown or unfamiliar, against changing the order at hand and violating our inborn place within that order.[30] The place of the religious order that was previously protected against violation is now reoccupied by that of the global market, often posing as an ideal democratic principle. If this sort of attitude is hardly conducive to the cultivation of 'classical' music, it is surely barely any better for the health of any other kind of music, since it

---

30 Blumenberg (1983), especially pp. 325–29.

tends to efface the resistant or oppositional elements of any music whatsoever.

On the other hand, several new possibilities have arisen for reappropriating the 'museum of musical works'. One particularly rich field is the emergence of performance studies as an area of serious musical enquiry. Among several other directions there is the trend towards trying to move away from works as fixed in scores towards works as events in real time and in which the performer is fully complicit.[31] This involves not just the issues that are not specified in the score (such as absolute tempo and rubato) but also creative deviations. Although this might seem to be a return to the time before the score became dominant, when music could be spontaneously embellished or even composed, it is clear that improvisation has never really disappeared. Rather, it was usually merely devalued and ignored by historians of 'serious' musical works. As Goehr herself states in the preface to the second edition of *The imaginary museum* (2007), the relation of performance to work is rather like that between someone practising law and the law as notated: 'Just as laws are interpreted or even "performed" in their application to specific cases, so works are performed in such a way that we would say that without the performances the authority of works would be of no interest at all.'[32]

One final issue concerning the ontological status of musical works is the fact that the perfection of notation might often have been done for its own sake, and thus not dictating precisely how the music was performed. At least some of the music of Palestrina – so often seen as the epitome of notated perfection – was originally performed with levels of improvised ornamentation that would have wrecked the notated perfection. In other words, the composer may well have thought of ideal 'paper music' and sounding, 'performed music' as two intersecting but not coterminous forms of music ('eye' and 'ear' music). Moreover, rather than thinking that a composer always stood at the beginning of the compositional and notational process, he might well have been imitating what he heard performers doing. For instance, it is highly likely that some of the most spectacular solo numbers by Monteverdi – his 'Possenti spirto' from *L'Orfeo* and Arianna's lament (surviving from the lost opera of that name) – were heavily influenced by the styles of the singers for whom

31 Cook (2013).

32 Goehr (2007: xxxix).

the music was composed; they might even partially be records of what the singer actually did, thus feeding into the composer's compositional process.[33]

In all then, the weakening of the classical work concept has, at the very least, allowed us to consider other factors implicit in the music, particularly to do with performance. New media and methods of communication have also helped to draw attention to different ways of listening to music, something that could be going well beyond the passivity so often assumed for the consumption of musical works. Many scholars and performers relish the ways in which the experience of certain works might come as close to popular or non-western forms as they do to traditional concert-hall practice. It is also clear that there is a pronounced move towards celebrating the human aspects of the classical repertory, the music being no longer so impersonal and heard only as an object in its own right.[34] There are surely many ways in which pieces of music might interact with our ever-changing cultural context to bring forth new meanings, understandings and sensations, but only if we give up the idea of works as fixed and inviolable objects.

But, some might argue, with the exponential growth in the various ways in which musical works can be understood, experienced and enjoyed, might we not have diluted the impact of musical works compared with the time they were actually 'works'? Perhaps, like some of the most unequivocal achievements of western modernity itself (universal justice, equality of rights, freedom of the individual, etc.), classical music is not going to endure – as if it were *the* natural order, one which would survive even if we did not tend it – without some form of positive effort.

BIBLIOGRAPHY

Adorno, Theodor W. and Horkheimer, Max (1997), *Dialectic of enlightenment* (*Dialektic der Aufklärung*, 1944), Cumming, John (trans.), London and New York: Verso.

Austern, Linda P. (2001), '"Tis Nature's Voice": music, natural philosophy and the hidden world in seventeenth-century England', in Clark, Suzannah, and Rehding, Alexander (eds), *Music theory and natural order from the Renaissance to the early twentieth century*, Cambridge: Cambridge University Press, pp. 30–67.

---

[33] For a consideration of several different ways in which notation may have related to performance, see Butt (2002: 96–122).

[34] Goehr (2007: xlvi–xlvii).

Blumenberg, Hans (1983), *The legitimacy of the modern age* (*Die Legitimät der Neuzeit*, 2nd rev. ed., 1976), Wallace, Robert M. (trans.), Cambridge, Massachusetts and London: MIT Press.

Butt, John (2002), *Playing with history: the historical approach to musical performance*, Cambridge: Cambridge University Press.

Butt, John (2005), 'The seventeenth-century musical "work"', in Carter, Tim, and Butt, John (eds), *The Cambridge history of seventeenth-century music*, Cambridge: Cambridge University Press, pp. 27–54.

Butt, John (2010), *Bach's dialogue with modernity: perspectives on the passions*, Cambridge: Cambridge University Press.

Chua, Daniel K.L. (2001), 'Vincenzo Galilei, modernity and the division of nature', in Clark, Suzannah, and Rehding, Alexander (eds), *Music theory and natural order from the Renaissance to the early twentieth century*, Cambridge: Cambridge University Press, pp. 17–29.

Cook, Nicholas (2013), *Beyond the score: music as performance*, Cambridge: Cambridge University Press.

Dahlhaus, Carl (1983), *Grundlagen der Musikgeschichte*, Cologne: Musikverlag Hans Gerig, 1977, trans. J.B. Robinson as *Foundations of music history*, Cambridge: Cambridge University Press.

Erauw, Willem (1998), 'Canon formation: some more reflections on Lydia Goehr's Imaginary Museum of Musical Works', 70 *Acta Musicologica*, 109–15.

Goehr, Lydia (2000), '"On the problems of dating" or "looking backward and forward with Strohm"', in Talbot, Michael (ed.), *The musical work: reality or invention?*, Liverpool: Liverpool University Press, pp. 231–46.

Goehr, Lydia (2007), *The imaginary museum of musical works: an essay in the philosophy of music*, Oxford: Oxford University Press (1992); revised edition, with a new introductory essay by the author and foreword by Richard Taruskin, New York: Oxford University Press.

Hobbes, Thomas (1990), *Leviathan, or, Matter, Form, and Power of a Commonwealth Ecclesiastical and Civil* (1651), Fuller, Nelle (ed.), Chicago; Auckland and London: Encyclopaedia Britannica.

Jauss, Hans Robert (1987), 'Der literarische Prozess des Modernismus von Rousseau bis Adorno', in Herzog, Reinhart, and Koselleck, Reinhart (eds), *Epochenschwelle und Epochenbewusstsein*, Munich: Wilhelm Fink Verlag.

Kerman, Joseph (1985), *Contemplating music: challenges to musicology*, Cambridge, MA: Harvard University Press; published in the UK as *Musicology*, London: Fontana Press.

Latour, Bruno (1999), *Pandora's hope: essays on the reality of science studies*, Cambridge, MA: Harvard University Press.

Lukács, György (1999), *The theory of the novel: a historico-philosophical essay on the forms of great epic literature* (1916), Bostock, Anna (trans.), Cambridge, MA: MIT Press.

Newcomb, Anthony (1980), *The madrigal at Ferrara 1579–97*, 2 vols., Princeton: Princeton University Press.

Nietzsche, Friedrich (1983), 'On the uses and disadvantages of history for life', (1874), in Hollingdale, R.J. (trans.), *Untimely meditations*, Cambridge: Cambridge University Press, pp. 57–123.

Schwörer-Kohl, Gretel (1997), 'Zum Werkbegriff in der Ethnomusikologie und in der historischen Musikwissenschaft', in Mahling, Christoph-Hellmut (ed.), *Ethnomusikologie und historische Musikwissenschaft: Erich Stockmann zum 70. Geburtstag*, Mainzer Studien zur Musikwissenschaft, 36, Tutzing: Hans Schneider, pp. 313–24.

Seidel, Wilhelm (1987), *Werk und Werkbegriff in der Musikgeschichte*, Erträge der Forschung, 246, Darmstadt: Wissenschaftliche Buchgesellschaft.

Strohm, Reinhard (1993), *The rise of European music 1380–1500*, Cambridge: Cambridge University Press.

Strohm, Reinhard (2000), 'Looking back at ourselves: the problem with the musical work-concept', in Talbot, Michael (ed.), *The musical work: reality or invention?*, Liverpool: Liverpool University Press, pp. 128–52.

Taylor, Charles (1989), *Sources of the self: the making of the modern identity*, Cambridge: Cambridge University Press.

von Loesch, Heinz (2001), *Der Werkbegriff in der protestantischen Musiktheorie des 16. Und 17. Jahrhunderts: Ein Mißverständnis*, Hildesheim: Olms Verlag.

Weber, Max (1958), *Die rationalen und sozialen Grundlagen der Music*, appendix to *Wirtschaft und Gesellschaft* (written 1911, published 1921), trans. as *The rational and social foundations of music*, Martindale, Don, Riedel, Johannes, and Neuwirth, Gertrude (trans. and ed.), Carbondale: Southern Illinois University Press.

Wiora, Walter (1983), *Das musikalische Kunstwerk*, Schneider: Tutzing (1988), 'Das musikalische Kunstwerk der Neuzeit und das musikalische Kunstwerk der Antike', in Danuser, Hermann et al. (eds), *Festschrift Carl Dahlhaus zum 60. Geburtstag*, Laaber: Laaber Verlag, pp. 3–10.

2. Music performed: what is beyond the score?

Charlotte Waelde

In 2009, and as part of a Beyond Text network project funded by the Arts & Humanities Research Council (AHRC), I, along with Philip Schlesinger, Professor of Cultural Policy at Glasgow, carried out a series of interviews with musicians, singers, record producers and performers, all engaged in the music industry.[1] The purpose was to probe deeply around the question: in music, what is beyond copyright?[2] We wanted to find out what if anything in music was not captured by the law of copyright, and if not captured, what the policy response was. We found that while copyright focuses on the work – or the product of creative efforts – what was really important to participants tended to be the process of creation. However, and as this is also fleeting and intangible, it makes policy intervention challenging. Rather than asking what is beyond copyright in music, building on the previous piece ('What is a musical work?'), this chapter will ask what, in terms of copyright, is beyond the music score? It will discuss the findings alongside current trends in copyright law and cultural policymaking, asking whether some of the recent changes to the law in areas such as originality will have any impact on the work of the musicians and other stakeholders, and what the current policy environment might hold for the industry participants.

INTRODUCTION

In 2009 the AHRC funded our research network, Music and Dance: Beyond Copyright Text? This two-year grant comprised the following

[1] Music and Dance: Beyond Copyright Text? AHRC grant number AH/G000565/1.

[2] We were also investigating what in dance was beyond protection by copyright.

participants: Charlotte Waelde, then Edinburgh now Exeter; Philip Schlesinger, Glasgow; Fiona Macmillan, Birkbeck; Helen Thomas, University of the Arts London; Michael Alcorn, Queen's University Belfast; and Gillian Doyle, Glasgow. In terms of discipline we were cultural policy; intellectual property; dance; music composition; and cultural economics. What we sought to discover in that research was whether experimental, experiential forms of music and dance were beyond copyright text.[3] The purpose of this chapter, and drawing on the fieldwork already done, is to delve a little deeper into the findings and to ask: when music is performed, what is beyond the score?

What we found in our original research was that much artistic work in the experimental, experiential music genre escapes institutionalisation, making policy intervention difficult. What tends to be important to participants is the process of making a work.[4] In other words, what comes before copyright as, in the UK at least, copyright only arises once a work is fixed in some material form.[5] Policy focuses on what can be captured – the product. We did find that there are aspects of the experiential, experimental forms of music that defy fixation and thus copyright protection. How much of this in law is not clear will be discussed later in this chapter, and with the developing case law from the Court of Justice in Europe (CoJ), most particularly on the criteria of originality for copyright protection, these edges are becoming increasingly fuzzy. It was also striking from our interviews that fairness among participants when sharing revenue was very important. Interestingly, and given the developing case law, this sharing may be more in line with how the law would allocate authorship than are the mechanisms thought to be used by industry.

---

[3] C Waelde and P Schlesinger, 'Music and Dance: Beyond Copyright Text?' (2011) 8:3 *SCRIPTed* 257, http://script-ed.org/?p=83; P Schlesinger and C Waelde, 'Copyright and cultural work: An exploration' (2012) Innovation 25(1), 11–28; P Schlesinger and C Waelde, 'Performers on the edge' (2011) Audiovisual Thinking 3.

[4] This finding is echoed in a piece of work commissioned by the AHRC: C Waelde, S Kheria and N Levin, 'Copyright and Publicly-Funded Arts and Humanities Research: Identifying and Developing Sustainable Exploitation Models in the Digital Economy', February 2015.

[5] Copyright, Designs and Patents Act 1988 (CDPA) s 3(2).

SO WHAT IS BEYOND THE SCORE?

Case law has dealt with a series of scenarios concerning the composition (the score), the arrangement, and the performance of music. Broadly speaking, while the composition has generally been considered the musical work, the legislation provides, and case law suggests, that the arrangement of the composition is also protected by copyright. The challenge however has been where the arrangement results from performance in the interpretation of the composition and from performance when there is no underlying composition: to what extent could that performance result in copyright in the arrangement and to what extent can copyright subsist in music resulting from performance? It had not been previously thought that performance had the qualities to result in a work capable of protection, but in respect of which the law may now have changed. There remain, however, questions around elements of interpretation of the music that are not directly linked to the music, but which arise from the individual interpretation of it: elements such as vocal expression, pitch and contour. The first question however is what is the work – the composition, the arrangement and the performance – for the purposes of copyright? What level of originality is required for copyright to subsist in a musical work, particularly in the light of emerging jurisprudence from the CoJ? And who is or who are the author(s) of the work?

While the Copyright, Designs and Patents Act 1988 (CDPA) is superficially quite clear on copyright in a musical work and provides that a musical work is one consisting of music exclusive of any words or action intended to be sung, spoken or performed with the music,[6] that definition does not actually capture the essence of music, which turns out to be a much more slippery concept. Words have their own literary copyright and are not considered a musical work. Case law has made clear that music goes well beyond the score: it is not mere noise[7] but should be something intended to produce effects of some kind on the listener's emotions and intellect. It includes melodies, harmonies, the figuring of the bass, ornamentation and performance directions.[8]

In addition, and also beyond the score, copyright can exist in the arrangement of a composition, and in the performance of a composition or arrangement. The CDPA provides that an adaptation in relation to a

---

6 CDPA 1988 s 3(1).

7 *Sawkins v Hyperion Records* [2005] RPC 32 (CA).

8 ibid.

musical work 'means an arrangement or transcription of the work'.[9] As we shall see, in the case law focus has been on the required level of originality needed to create something new – in other words, something beyond the score. In terms of the arrangement, while it has been suggested by commentators that little is needed on the part of the arranger '*by way of changes to an antecedent musical work*' to enable a new copyright to exist[10] the courts have had more difficulty with the concept. Where copyright does reside in the arrangement, it will generally still subsist in the composition, and any exploitation of the arrangement will depend on consent of the owner of the copyright in the composition. That is, unless the arrangement ends up in an entirely new work – although it may be challenging to determine when that occurs. In *Bauman v Fussell*[11] a photograph of two cocks fighting was used as the basis of a painting. While the composition was followed closely, the painter used different colours to dramatise the effect of the painting. The court held that it was appropriate to consider the different effects on the viewer of the works in assessing whether there had been an infringement of copyright, which in this case there had not. So that was the effect on the eye of the viewer. Presumably for music what would be important would be the effect on the ear of the listener, and on their emotions and intellect.

Also beyond the score is the performance of the score. While a performer will get performers' rights in the interpretation of the score or the arrangement,[12] more recently it has been held that a performer may also be granted copyright in the music where he or she contributes the right sort of 'original' input.[13] But it would seem that some elements that have historically remained beyond the score, those more directly associated with the attributes of the performer than to the music, might remain so. But even here it may be that the contours of the law are changing as CoJ jurisprudence relevant to this area develops.

---

9 CDPA s 21(3)(b).

10 (Mr Justice) R Arnold, 'Reflections on "The Triumph of Music": copyrights and performers rights in music' [2010] IPQ 153 at 158.

11 [1978] RPC 485.

12 CDPA Part II Rights in Performances.

13 *Fisher v Brooker* [2006] EWHC 3239; *Fisher v Brooker* [2008] EWCA Civ 287; *Fisher v Brooker* [2009] UKHL 41.

CASE LAW

A series of cases in England over the years has sought to determine in particular who has put the right sort of creative effort (skill, labour and effort) into the arrangement of the music to be considered an author in law Relatedly, the questions have focused on whether the conditions for joint authorship have been met: often the process of music making is such that more than one individual will contribute to an interpretation of the composition, so the question becomes who has expended the correct creative effort, and has that resulted in a new work, or in joint authorship of a single work? These cases were decided before the recent CoJ case law relevant to this area, but are important for giving a flavour of the processes involved in the layered creation of music, why and over what disputes between musicians have arisen, and how the courts have applied the law to those disputes. In this next part a number of cases that have been decided by the courts since the 1980s will be described. The purpose is to highlight the challenges that the courts have faced in applying the law to authorship in and ownership of music focusing mainly on questions of originality and joint authorship: what level of originality is needed for joint authorship; and whether performance is capable of resulting in copyright authorship.

Godfrey v Lees 1995:[14] Originality for Joint Authorship

Godfrey was associated with the band Barclay James Harvest between 1969 and 1971. During this time the band collaborated on a number of musical works which were subsequently recorded on albums called 'Barclay James Harvest' and 'Once Again' and released in 1970 and 1971 respectively. Godfrey claimed to be joint author of six of the works. The focus of the court was on the type of originality required for joint authorship. The court said that what a claimant to joint authorship of a work must establish is that he has made a significant and original contribution to the creation of the work, and that he has done so pursuant to a common design.[15] However, relatively little originality was required of a person's contribution to a piece of work in order to attract copyright in the work which resulted. It was not necessary that the collaborators' contribution to the work was equal in terms of quantity, quality or

---

[14] (1995) EMLR 307 Ch D; P Groves, 'Better than it sounds: originality of musical works' (2005) Ent. LR 16(1), 20–23.

[15] *Stuart v Barrett* [1994] EMLR 448.

originality. Nor did it matter in the case of a song that the contribution was to the orchestral arrangement of the song rather than to the song itself. While the court did find that Godfrey was a joint author of the works, it was a borderline case as his 'accompaniment [was] of a straightforward and largely repetitive nature'.

This is an early case in the development of court jurisprudence in relation to authorship in music (and songs) and raises some questions. While the degree of originality is in line with the skill, labour and effort standard that existed at the time, and the law that something must be 'not copied',[16] the need for a *significant* contribution from each joint author sits uneasily with this low threshold, although 'significant' seems to mean something other than contributing to originality as little originality was needed in respect of the resulting work. It is also the case now that the common design intention has been abandoned:[17] a joint copyright work can arise even if the contributors have no intention of creating a joint work. Instead, there needs to be collaboration in creation of the work and a 'significant and original' contribution from each joint author that must not be separate. The abandonment of the common design requirement would seem to sit more easily with the actual working practices of musicians where works emerge through creative contribution and where they may well not set out with the intention of creating a work of joint authorship.

Redwood Music v Chappell 1982:[18] Whether the Input of an Arranger was Original

Godfrey v Lees cited the earlier 1982 case of *Redwood Music v Chappell*[19] in support of the originality requirement. *Redwood* was not about joint authorship, but was about copyright in a number of adaptations and arrangements made by Chappell of an original song. For an arranger to claim copyright, it was accepted that the degree of originality is such that

> it can be seen to have originated from the arranger rather than having been copied from the original but that … an arrangement could attract copyright

---

[16] *University of London Press v University Tutorial Press* [1916] 2 Ch 601 at 608.

[17] *Beckingham v Hodgens* [2003] EMLR 18.

[18] [1982] RPC 109.

[19] ibid.

> notwithstanding that it is no more than a straightforward arrangement of a well known song employing for the purpose well known musical devices and clichés.

As was said in *Godfrey*, this case demonstrated, at the time, how little originality was required of a person's contribution to a piece of music in order to attract copyright in the resulting work.

Hadley v Kemp 1999:[20] Whether Contributions to a Song were Original to Qualify for Copyright

In *Hadley v Kemp*, the court held that there was a distinction between the composition or creation of a musical work, and its interpretation or performance. Only the composition or creation resulted in authorship of the work because performance – including in this case saxophone improvisations – was just that, performance. The court found that copyright in a number of songs belonged to Gary Kemp, who was Spandau Ballet's main songwriter and guitarist. Other members of the band, Tony Hadley, John Keeble and Steve Norman, contributed vocals, drum and saxophone – but their contributions were found to be insufficiently significant and original to result in joint authorship.

> … the musical works in this case – the Spandau Ballet songs – are totally original, and, in my judgment if contributions to them by the members of the group other than Gary Kemp are going to be sufficient to make the other members joint authors, the contributions need to possess significant creative originality.[21]

It has been argued that the effect of this was that 'the higher the quality of the contribution of the main songwriter the higher the quality of the contributions of other musicians would have to be if they were to be considered joint authors'.[22] A distinction was also drawn between performing music and composing it – holding that the members of the band had done no more than interpret the music through performance. This was a questionable finding as Kemp had composed the chords of the song, but nothing that either Keeble or Norman could have interpreted through their 'performance'.

---

[20] [1999] EMLR 589.

[21] ibid, p 642.

[22] D Free, 'Beckingham v. Hodgens: the session musician's claim to music copyright' (2002) Ent. LR 1(3), 93–98, at 96.

The facts of this case are difficult to distinguish from the earlier case of *Stuart v Barrett*.[23] Stuart was the drummer in the band Keep it Dark, and claimed joint authorship in the music of the band's songs after he had been expelled. The music resulted from jamming sessions during which one band member would start with an opening phrase or series of notes, which the group then played together, improvising and composing by ear. The judge held that the music was the result of joint authorship:

> I also have no doubt that in principle a drummer may claim copyright in a piece of music if, as here, he had collaborated with the other members of the group to produce an original piece of music … . The work is given shape and drive by the drummer and a good drummer, as I accept the plaintiff is, can significantly influence the whole composition.[24]

Beckingham v Hodgens 2003:[25] Originality and Joint Authorship

Beckingham (professionally known as Bobby Valentino) maintained that he had composed the violin part of the song 'Young at Heart', which was recorded by the Bluebells in 1984 when it was a hit, and revived again in 1993 when used for a VW advertisement. The court found that Beckingham had indeed composed the part, holding that in line with the requirements of joint authorship: there must be a collaboration in the creation of a new musical work; there must be a significant and original contribution from each other; and the contributions of each other must not be separate.[26] Different to the rather high standard of originality suggested in *Hadley*, where the higher the originality of the original author the higher the originality needed for joint authors, in *Beckingham*, the court concluded after listening to the piece that the violin part was significant and original, and Beckingham was thus entitled to joint authorship.

Fisher v Brooker:[27] 2006 High Court; 2008 Court of Appeal; 2009 House of Lords: Whether a Contribution through Performance to a Song was Original

Fisher v Brooker concerned the iconic organ solo in the song 'A Whiter Shade of Pale'. Thirty-eight years after the song was released, Fisher

---

23 [1994] EMLR 448.
24 ibid, p 460.
25 [2003] EWCA Civ 143.
26 CDPA s 10(1).
27 [2006] EWHC 3239; [2008] EWCA Civ 287; [2009] UKHL 41.

claimed joint credit for the composition for his contribution to the organ solo. While it was a complex case that was appealed up to the House of Lords, most particularly because of the delay in bringing the case, throughout it was found that Fisher was indeed entitled to be considered a joint author of the work, his share of which was quantified at 40 per cent. It was found that the organ solo was original in the copyright sense:

> Mr Fisher's instrumental introduction (i.e. the organ solo … as repeated) is sufficiently different from what Mr Brooker had composed on the piano to qualify in law, and by quite a wide margin, as an original contribution to the work.[28]

On the originality requirement, the High Court had this to say:

> Provided the contribution of the individual band member to the overall work is both significant (in the sense of more than merely trivial) and original (in the sense that it is the product of skill and labour in its creation) and the resulting work is recorded … that band member is entitled to copyright in the work as one of its joint authors and to any composing royalties that follow.[29]

As has been noted by McDonagh, this was a complex case and it is not ultimately clear as to what Fisher was entitled to authorship in.[30] The piece was created during performance; so it was not an arrangement of a composition, but the creation of a new work through performance. What however is odd when considering joint authorship is the acceptance by the court that the organ solo was quite different to other parts of the work composed by Mr Brooker. Normally one would expect contributions to be indistinguishable for joint authorship. An analogy would be with an edited collection: here the authors of the individual chapters retain authorship in their contributions – they are not merged into joint authorship. If the organ solo was so different, why did Mr Fisher not have sole authorship of those parts? In terms of the standard of originality, by contrast, this does seem to be more in line with the generally understood level existing at the time of the case. However, and given authorship was attributed on the basis of music contributed through performance, the case did push boundaries, and led Arnold to opine that:

---

28 [2006] EWHC 3239 (Ch D), para 42.

29 ibid, para 46.

30 L McDonagh, 'Rearranging the roles of the performer and the composer in the music industry: the potential significance of Fisher v Brooker' [2012] IPQ 64.

> it will often be the case that a recorded piece of music created through performance is sufficiently original over any antecedent musical work to attract copyright and that piece of music will often be a work of joint authorship between some or all of the musicians.[31]

Sawkins v Hyperion 2005:[32] Performing Editions and Copyright

The key question in *Sawkins v Hyperion* was whether copyright subsisted in modern performing editions of the music of Michel-Richard de Lalande, the court composer at the courts of Louis XIV and Louis XV. Sawkins had spent many hours researching and creating new performing editions of the works. Hyperion produced a CD featuring performances of the works. Hyperion paid Sawkins a hire fee for providing the scores, but refused copyright royalties on the grounds that an editor should not obtain copyright for works that were out of copyright. Sawkins brought an action for infringement of copyright. The Court of Appeal held that the 'effort, skill and time' that had gone into 'performing indications, tempo and performance practice' was sufficient for the subsistence of copyright.

By contrast with the cases discussed above on copyright arising from performance, here the focus was very much on the score, what Sawkins had added to the score and how that might be protected by copyright. Sawkins's contribution was not 'beyond' the score, but was part of the score. In terms of originality, once again the focus was on the effort and skill in making the performing editions available, with the court also noting the time that it took for Sawkins to carry out the research and add the necessary performing indications.[33]

Coffey v Warner/Chappell Music Ltd 2005:[34] The Work for the Purposes of Copyright

The question in *Coffey* was as to what amounted to the musical work. Coffey claimed that Madonna had infringed copyright in parts of the song 'Forever After', in particular the vocal expression, pitch, contour

---

31 Arnold, 'Reflections', at 163.

32 [2005] EWCA Civ 565.

33 Note also *Brown v Mcasso Music* [2005] FSR 40, where Brown amended lyrics to give greater authenticity as a rap song and was held to be a joint author of the song.

34 [2005] EWHC 449. See also *Tate v Thomas* [1921] 1 Ch 503, where the individual who supplied ideas and some lines of a play 'Lads of the Village' was not an author of the copyright.

and syncopation surrounding the words 'does it really matter', which were repeated throughout the song. The claim was that the recording of the song 'Forever After' '*includes* an original musical work *comprising* the combination of vocal expression, pitch contour and syncopation of or around the words "does it really matter"' (emphasis added). So the claim here differed from other cases in that what was being claimed were elements arising from the way in which the song was performed, rather than the song itself, or of an arrangement of the song. In an attempt to pin down what was being claimed, the court noted:

> By 'voice expression' is meant, in effect, 'timbre' (illustrated by a comparison between the 'gravelly' vocal expression of one well known performer and the 'twangy' vocal expression of another). By 'pitch contour' is meant 'the general shape of the pitches to which the words "does it really matter" [in 'Forever After'] are sung' rather than, as I understood it, the notes themselves. By 'syncopation of or around the words "does it really matter"' is meant the 'unnatural metrical stress' given to the syllables of those four words in terms of their placement within the two bars [in which they are sung] and the unusual rhythmic and durational stress in terms of their elongated durations.[35]

This, the court said, went to the interpretation or performance 'characteristics' rather than to composition. As such these were not the legitimate subject of copyright protection in a musical work.

SUMMARY

As the cases above show, the courts have grappled with what is protected by copyright in music and for whom; what music is; what is original in music; and who the author is. One underlying concern, notably around those cases where finding an original contribution would result in multiple authorship, seems to have been just that: if copyright were found to exist in arrangements and arise from performance, then multiple authors would be entitled to the proceeds of exploitation of a musical work making management complex. But complexity in management is not a reason for denying copyright. As will be explored below, musicians and performers seem to have no difficulty in coping with multiple interests in a work.

---

35 *Coffey v Warner/Chappell Music Ltd*, para 5.

A EUROPEAN STANDARD OF ORIGINALITY

For the cases that have turned on what amounts to the work, and which raise questions of originality, the law has now changed. Developing CoJ case law has modified the originality criteria in a way that appears to conflate the concept of the work with the requirement of originality.[36] The CoJ has stressed that the European scheme of protection for copyright protects works where the subject matter is original in the sense of being the author's own intellectual creation.[37] What the work is called, in other words for our purposes whether it is a musical work, is irrelevant, although it seems that a work would need to fall under the Berne Convention categories of a literary or artistic work.[38] The standard of originality for all types of work is the same: it is one of the author's own intellectual creation.[39] To reach this level the author should express her creative ability in an original manner by making free and creative choices;[40] she should stamp her 'personal touch' on the work.[41] Where

---

[36] Case C-5/08 *Infopaq International A/S v Danske Dagblades Forening* (*Infopaq*); Case C-393/09 *Bezpečnostní softwarová asociac*e (*BSA*); Case C-406/10 *SAS Institute Inc. v World Programming Ltd* (*SAS*); Case C-145/10 *Painer v Standard VerlagsGmbH et al.* (*Painer*). M van Eechoud, 'Along the road to uniformity – diverse readings of the Court of Justice Judgments on copyright work' (2012) JIPITEC 3(1), para 60; C Handig, 'The "sweat of the brow" is not enough! – more than a blueprint of the European copyright term "work"' (2013) EIPR 1; A Rahmatian, 'Originality in UK copyright law: the old "skill and labour" doctrine under pressure' (2013) IIC 3; E Rosati, 'Towards an EU-wide copyright? (Judicial) pride and (legislative) prejudice' [2013] IPQ 46; J Pila, 'An intentional view of the copyright work' (2008) MLR 71; C Handig, '*Infopaq International A/S v Danske Dagblades Forening* (C-5/08): is the term "work" in the CDPA 1988 in line with the European Directives?' (2010) EIPR 32(2), 53; E Rosati, *Originality in EU Copyright: Full Harmonization through Case Law*, Edward Elgar: Cheltenham, UK and Northampton, MA, USA, 2013.

[37] *Infopaq*, paras 33–38; *BSA*, para 45, what is not protected is expression which is limited by its technical function. *Painer*, para 38.

[38] Berne Convention Article 2(1). *SAS Institute Inc. v World Programming Limited* [2013] EWHC 69 (Ch), para 27.

[39] *Infopaq*; *BSA*, para 45; Joined Cases C-403/08 and C-429/08 *Football Association Premier League and Others* (*FAPL*); E Rosati, 'Originality in a work, or a work of originality: the effects of the *Infopaq* decision' (2011) EIPR 33(12), 746. E Derclaye, 'Wonderful or worrisome? The impact of the ECJ ruling in Infopaq on UK copyright law' (2010) EIPR 32(5), 248.

[40] *Infopaq*, para 45; *BSA*, para 50; *Painer*, para 89; Case C-604/10 *Football Dataco Ltd v Yahoo! UK Ltd* (*Football Dataco*), para 38.

[41] *Painer*, para 92; *Football Dataco*, para 38.

choices are dictated by technical considerations, rules or constraints that leave no room for creative freedom, then these criteria are not met.[42]

The CoJ has developed this jurisprudence through a series of cases dealing with a sequence of 11 words;[43] the graphical interface on a computer program;[44] football fixtures;[45] database copyright;[46] functionality of a computer program;[47] and a portrait photograph.[48] While the standard of 'the author's own intellectual creation' applied to photographs and to computer programs by virtue of the Term Directive[49] and the Software Programs Directive[50] respectively, through these cases the Court has extended the test to all copyright works which would include musical works. At the same time the CoJ seems also to have conflated the requirement of originality with the requirement (in the UK at least) that the subject matter fall into one of the specified categories of work in the CDPA.

What this emerging case law means in the UK is not entirely clear as yet.[51] In *SAS* the Court of Appeal concluded its discussion on originality in English law in the light of the CoJ case law by saying:

> If the Information Society Directive has changed the traditional domestic test, it seems to me that it has raised rather than lowered the hurdle to obtaining copyright protection.[52]

So it is not entirely clear whether the English courts fully embrace the standard of originality. As regards the conflation of originality with the

---

42 *BSA*, paras 48 and 49; *FAPL*, para 98; *Football Dataco*, para 39. See also the articles at n 36.

43 *Infopaq*.

44 *BSA*.

45 *FAPL*.

46 *Football Dataco*.

47 *SAS*.

48 *Painer*.

49 Directive 2006/116/EC of the European Parliament and of the Council of 12 December 2006 on the term of protection of copyright and certain related rights (Codified version).

50 Directive 2009/24/EC of the European Parliament and of the Council of 23 April 2009 on the legal protection of computer programs (Codified version).

51 *Newspaper Licensing Agency Ltd and others v Meltwater Holding BV and others* [2011] EWCA Civ 890; *Lucasfilm Limited and others v Ainsworth and another* [2011] UKSC 39; *Temple Island Collections Ltd v New English Teas Ltd and another* [2012] EWPCC 1.

52 *SAS Institute Inc v World Programming Limited* [2013] EWCA Civ 1482, para 37.

concept of a 'work', it is only Mr Justice Arnold in the High Court in *SAS* who has suggested that the categories of works as they exist in the CDPA may not be compatible with the developing CoJ case law.

> In the light of a number of recent judgments of the CJEU, it may be arguable that it is not a fatal objection to a claim that copyright subsists in a particular work that the work is not one of the kinds of work listed in section 1(1)(a) of the Copyright, Designs and Patents 1988 and defined elsewhere in that Act.[53]

Arnold did suggest that the categories of works in the Berne Convention would remain a requirement, so something would have to be either classed as literary or artistic. So what would this mean for our cases if they were decided under the new threshold? There are diverse views. On the threshold of originality, some argue that it would mean that those works at the very bottom of the 'creativity threshold' that would once have been protected under English law no longer would be – the photograph taken by accident perhaps, or the 'accidental' few notes played on an organ.[54] In terms of categorisation, some have argued that despite what Arnold has said, categories are still relevant, while others argue that more types of subject matter will now be protected, as there is no need for it to be corralled into one of the categories of work. So the scope of works protected expands (fewer fall between categories) but some fall below protection because the depth of protection (slightly) reduces.[55]

What might this mean in practice for the works that we have been considering through the case law? There could be room for hitherto unprotected elements, or combinations of elements, of music to be protected by copyright given the (possible) doing away with the need to place a work within a particular category. It will be remembered that in *Coffey* the elements of voice expression, pitch contour and syncopation were found to be not '*the legitimate subject of copyright protection in the case of a **musical work***' [emphasis added]. If the requirement now is that something needs to be classed only as literary or artistic, and that the category of musical work is not relevant, then the performance elements might be included as part of copyright (not performers' right) protection, so long as they were the author's own intellectual creation. But it might

---

53 *SAS Institute Inc. v World Programming Limited* [2013] EWHC 69 (Ch), para 27.

54 See in general the references at n 36.

55 See in general the references at n 36. For proposals for a scaled originality test for music see E Steel, 'Original sin: reconciling originality in copyright with music as an evolutionary art form' (2015) EIPR 37(2), 66–80.

mean that some arrangements do not meet the 'higher' test of author's own intellectual creation. In *Redwood* it will be recalled that the court held that an arrangement could attract copyright 'notwithstanding that it is no more than a straightforward arrangement … employing for the purpose well known musical devices and clichés.'[56] Could such input really be described as exhibiting free and creative choice? It seems that we could see a repetition of references to 'significant and original' contributions to a work that would need in some way to be distinguished from 'relatively little originality' when the courts seek to apply this test in the cases that will inevitably arise over time. There may also be some works that have historically been protected but may no longer receive copyright status because they are limited by their technical function. An example might be where musical scores are updated to re-create the music of the original composer: that input may be considered to be dictated by technical requirements and therefore not capable of protection by copyright.[57]

So what does this mean for some of the works that our interviewees told us about during our interviews?

WHAT IS THE SCORE (OR COMPOSITION)?

Our case studies offered some fine examples of contemporary musical practices, raising key questions around the score, the arrangement and performance for the purposes of copyright authorship.

Michael Alcorn, Professor of Composition, explained one of his recent works to us.

> So an example – a new piece which I have been working on which is being performed next week. There is … the score is presented to the performers and the audience on the screen, on a massive big screen, so everybody can see what is going on. And I have written a computer program that controls all the objects on the screen. Quite often they behave in a random way. Sometimes they collide with one and other – there are things that I have no control over. I am sure it will be recorded – I have asked for it to be recorded. But still that is not the piece, the piece is probably the code.[58]

56 See above n 18.

57 *Sawkins v Hyperion Records Ltd* [2005] EWCA 565. See the slightly different interpretation of *Sawkins* by Andreas Rahmatian in Chapter 4.

58 A picture of this can be seen at C Waelde and P Schlesinger, 'Music and Dance: Beyond Copyright Text?' (2011) 8:3 *SCRIPTed* 257 http://script-ed.org/?p=83.

So here, Michael has identified as the score the computer program that controls the objects on the screen. When these are seen on the screen they move in a random way. The musicians watch this ever-changing kaleidoscope and play what they see, as Michael says, 'seemingly in an ad hoc way'. So for the purposes of copyright, what is the score? It is certainly not a conventional piece of sheet music. The computer program controls the objects on the screen, but Michael has identified the score as being presented to the performers on the screen. So are the ever-moving objects on the screen the score? The law might have a problem with this if it follows the rationale of the Australian case of *Komesaroff v Mickle*.[59] In this case Komesaroff developed and marketed a product named 'moving sand pictures', which were made by enclosing a mixture of liquid, coloured sands, and a layer of air bubbles inside glass panels. Miniature sand landscapes were created when the sands trickled through the bubbles – a process that could be repeated by shaking the product. Mickle copied and commenced marketing an identical product. It was held that Komesaroff's product was not a work of artistic craftsmanship because her input did not directly bring about the sand landscape that resulted from shaking the product. While it is not the suggestion here that the moving objects should be classed as works of artistic craftsmanship, it is being suggested that the finding that Komesaroff's input did not directly bring about the sand landscape might be relevant: by analogy, Michael's input did not directly bring about the moving objects on the screen. But this in turn may be called into question if we follow Arnold's view that the work only has to be literary or artistic, which might suggest that objects on a screen could be protected (assuming the correct level of originality).

Another way of looking at it might be to argue that authorship may not reside in the moving objects, but rather in the computer program that controls them. So the score might be the computer program. In terms of our current legislation this would have a copyright in its own right, as a computer program.[60] Could the moving objects on the screen be an arrangement of the computer program? But they are produced by the running of the program, rather than as arrangement of it. Furthermore, in our legislation, something that is computer generated is granted copyright protection – the author being the person by whom the arrangements necessary for its creation are undertaken.[61] It would seem that the moving

---

59 [1988] RPC 204 (Sup Ct of Victoria).
60 CDPA s 3(1)(b).
61 CDPA s 9(3).

objects are computer generated, in which case Michael, as the person who undertook the arrangements necessary for their creation, would be classed as the author. But this, it would seem, would run into difficulties with the European notion of originality. Undertaking arrangements is not the same as author's own intellectual creation. Further, the Advocate General in *Painer* said that in her view it is only human creations that are protected:

> According to the first sentence of Article 6 of Directive 93/98 and of Directive 2006/116, only human creations are therefore protected, which can also include those for which the person employs a technical aid, such as a camera.[62]

Is a computer-generated object the same as a photograph for these purposes? Or a computer program the same as a camera? This could bring into question the compatibility of the provision in our legislation on authorship of computer-generated works.

During conversation Michael sought to articulate what for him, as a composer, was important and what he wanted to be protected:

> Well the whole history of music is built on sampling other people's music, from the very beginning. But obviously it has become, … so much easier and so much … but also so much more difficult to trace. I guess I would feel pretty miffed if … I wouldn't worry so much a … actually this is interesting – I wouldn't worry so much, say if somebody took part of an orchestral or chamber music piece of mine and decided to sample it, because that really isn't the work – for me the work is something else, it is the piece itself. But if I'd been in the studio working on a sort of electronic piece where you come up with a sound that really has its own special identity, that is the creative thing – I would be pretty put out about that, because those are, … creating those sorts of sounds is extremely hard work, so I would feel pretty miffed about that.

Would a sound created by Michael come under the umbrella of a literary or artistic work? Would it be a computer program? Or a computer-generated work? Or something else? When recorded, copyright could subsist in the sound recording, but that is not protecting the sound and brings into play a whole different regime of protection in the CDPA.[63] Protecting an electronic sound by copyright would seem to be as, if not

---

62 Opinion of Advocate General Trstenjak delivered on 12 April 2011 Case C-145/10 *Eva-Maria Painer v Standard VerlagsGmbH*, para 121.

63 CDPA s 5A.

more, challenging than protecting moving objects on a screen. Yet it is this that Michael considers would be a truly creative part of his work.

What then, in these forms of contemporary works, is beyond the score: what is the arrangement?

MUSIC PERFORMED: WHAT IS BEYOND THE SCORE?

What is the Arrangement?

For a musical work, an adaptation is defined as an arrangement or transcription of the work[64] and must be a conscious act.[65] Remaining with the example of Michael's work described above, if we look at the case law on copyright in arrangements, it would seem that the interpretation by the musicians of the score (the moving objects) would be an arrangement in which they had their own copyright. But, if there is no longer a category of musical work in our law, can there be an arrangement of a literary or artistic work? As noted, the CDPA is very specific on what is meant by arrangement in relation to a musical work. No mention is made of artistic works in connection with the adaptation right. In relation to literary works the CDPA has this to say, none of which seems germane for an arrangement of a musical work.

> In this Part 'adaptation' –
>
> (a) in relation to a literary work, other than a computer program or a database, or in relation to a dramatic work, means –
> (i) a translation of the work;
> (ii) a version of a dramatic work in which it is converted into a non-dramatic work or, as the case may be, of a non-dramatic work in which it is converted into a dramatic work;
> (iii) a version of the work in which the story or action is conveyed wholly or mainly by means of pictures in a form suitable for reproduction in a book, or in a newspaper, magazine or similar periodical.[66]

Certainly there can be derivative works – a work that is derived from an original where sufficient new originality is put into the derived work. Here there will be copyright in the original work and in the derivation.[67]

---

64 CDPA s 21(3)(b).
65 *Francis Day & Hunter v Bron* [1963] 1 Ch 587, 611.
66 CDPA s 21(3)(a).
67 *ZYX Music GmbH v King* [1995] 3 All ER 1.

As noted above, in other circumstances, a wholly new work may be created from a work where little or nothing of the first remains. To qualify as a derivative work the English courts have said that there must be more than skill, labour and judgement; in addition the works must have 'some quality or character which the raw material did not possess and which differentiates the product from the raw material'.[68] *Macmillan v Cooper* was decided long before the CoJ's judgments on originality, but as none of these has concerned originality in derivative works, it remains to be seen how they will be treated. Will there need to be something more than creative input? Did the musicians interpreting Michael's 'score' create a derivative work through performance? But given that it is questionable as to what the score actually is, is it possible to create a derivative work if there is no score? That seems implausible as, by definition, a derivative work derives from one already in existence. Perhaps then the musicians have created a wholly new work from their performance – which in terms of musical classification is the composition.

Moving beyond Michael's examples, Steve Beresford also had some interesting illustrations for us.

> I interviewed a prospective student who played a CD of hers which she said was her song – so we said, okay, 'so who is playing the piano?', and she said 'no, no, I downloaded the beats'. But what she meant by 'beats' was in fact the entire backing track – not just the drums, but also the baseline and the chords and the structure. So actually she had downloaded everything except the top line which she did write herself. But clearly there is a confusion about what you call sections of entirely conventional music, because she thought of the whole structure as just being beats, which is funny.

Has the student produced an original arrangement – so what she has done would be beyond the score but not beyond copyright? It seems if we look at case law including *Godfrey, Redwood* and *Fisher*, then the level of originality would be sufficient to have created a new element to the work under that standard. More pertinently, while we have not heard the 'top-line' that the student wrote, there is no reason to suspect that it would not meet the European level of originality. It would seem, however, and despite the confusion that arose in *Fisher*, that the work would not be one of joint authorship as the contribution by the student seems, from Steve's description, distinguishable from the original 'beats'. This may also be arguable if what has been produced is an arrangement

---

[68] *Macmillan v Cooper* (1924) 40 TLR 186, 188.

of the original work, as it seems that the original work was not re-worked: rather new work has been added 'on top of' the original, so therefore a reproduction rather than an arrangement with a new work on top? – which may foreclose some of the difficult discussions around musical works and adaptations rehearsed above.

What is the Performance?

Our final question for our interviewees was: what is both beyond the score and beyond the arrangement? What, in other words, is the performance?

When we asked Steve Beresford what is beyond capture, he turned the question around in a thought-provoking way.

> … that is a very interesting question. I mean I always remember Misha Mengelberg, the great Dutch composer and piano player, who said that they do things specifically for a recording. And in fact Misha and Hans, his friend who plays the drums, would listen, in the break between sets, they would listen to the first set, which seems completely bonkers to me. I definitely couldn't do that. So I think people do do things that are specifically for a recording, even if it is a live performance.

Here it seems Steve is describing how Misha and Hans add to a recording of the music that they perform with the intention perhaps of re-working what they are doing if they do not like what they hear. It would seem that these activities would fall under the 'classical' definition of an arrangement of the score, most particularly now as *Fisher* seems to suggest that there is no bar to performers being authors for copyright albeit that the European standard of originality would need to be applied.

Tamara Schlesinger and Daniel Deavin explained that they did more for a live performance.

> Yes, I think enthusiasm … we always try and interact with the crowd and … make the recording as enjoyable and energetic live as possible … I think that is the bigger difference …
>
> I think when you have got people in front of you, you are going to react differently than in the studio, and you probably get a bit more raucous, a bit more uplifting … And we change some of the arrangements sometimes, to make them a little bit more, you know, crowd friendly, so we can allow some singing from the crowd, interaction, that sort of thing. And it works really well – we always get great responses.

What of Tamara and Daniel's example? It would seem indisputable that changes to the arrangement would be protected by copyright (subject to the discussion noted above on whether the CDPA category of arrangement in relation to a musical work remains valid). What about the more performative elements? If we consider the arguments made in *Coffey v Warner* against certain elements of performance being included, but read these now in the light of *Fisher v Brooker* which seems to accept that music composed through performance would now be protected, and then consider both the new standard of originality and the question as to whether we still have categories of protected works, then it seems not implausible that the elements of interpretation by Tamara and Daniel of the music in front of the live audience that go beyond the arrangement of the original music could be protected by copyright. Why not? It will be remembered that in *Coffey v Warner* the court thought that the interpretation or performance 'characteristics' were not the legitimate subject of copyright protection in a *musical work*. However, if we no longer have the category of musical work, and what is required in terms of originality for the subsistence of copyright is that the author makes free and creative choices, and stamps her personal touch on the work, then Tamara and Daniel's interpretation of their work seems quintessentially the stuff of copyright. It is not '*petite monnaie*' (the accidental click of the camera button); it is creative energy expended in the creation of the work.

But how then does all of this play out when allocating the money?

Allocating the Money

The music industry is supported by an exceptionally complex web of organisations representing different interests. Broadly, the industry relies on three types of property in composition, recordings and media. The songwriter or composer may assign or license the composition rights to a publishing company. The publishing company (or collecting society) collects publishing royalties when the composition is played. Royalties are distributed in accordance with contractual arrangements between the parties. Recording companies make and own recordings and pay mechanical royalties to the recording artist from the sale of recordings. In addition, royalties are collected for performers arising from live performance. Both because copyright developed before performers' rights and the music industry has been in existence for a long time, copyright owners are favoured over the performer in exploitation of rights and size of income.[69] The industry convention is that the songwriter(s) who compose the chords of a song and its main vocal melody are considered the authors and entitled to the music copyright. Members who contribute other musical parts are not considered to be joint authors and neither is any session musician. When a group composes a song together in a jam session, then group members, but not session musicians, are considered joint authors and owners.[70] As Bently notes, the share of the royalties payable to the composer and songwriter can be quite large and as a result 'a songwriter in a successful band can end up significantly more wealthy than the non-songwriting members.'[71] While these comments were made before the judgment in *Fisher v Brooker* by the House of Lords was handed down, and before the CoJ started to rule on the originality requirements, it is hard to obtain data to see whether the law has changed practice as regards allocation of royalties within the music industry. In terms of what our interviewees said about sharing income, what was notable was their reliance on PRS, mentioned several times by Tamara Schlesinger, 'well, we have got a deal – I own it – I am down on PRS as owning it …', and by Steve Beresford,

> It's an instant composition. It's a composition – we put a PRS form in and it is written by whoever played it. The only problem is if there are 40 people playing it, you have got to get all those names on the sheet.

Noting ownership on PRS forms is clearly important and can lead to unexpected revenue as evidenced by an exchange between Michael and Steve:

> Sometimes strange things happen. I mean my last PRS statement arrived and something of mine had obviously appeared in a keep-fit video. – Wow.

But how the money was allocated differed from industry norms and was heavily reliant on notions of equity. As Tamara noted:[72]

> well, we have got a deal between us … whereby he [Daniel] gets a cut of the copyright of the songs. And then it is kind of tiered by how long people have

---

69 L Bently, 'Authorship of Popular Music in UK Copyright Law' (2009) Information, Communication & Society 12(2), 179–204, at 187; A Parker, 'A raw deal for performers: Part 1 – term of copyright' (2006) Ent. LR 17(6), 161–66.

70 *Stuart v Barrett* [1994] EMLR 448. D Free, 'Beckingham v Hodgens: the session musician's claim to music copyright' (2002) Ent. LR 1(3), 93–97, at 93.

71 Bently n 69 at 189.

72 Tamara Schlesinger.

been in the band and how much input they have had. I don't think it's fair that I take all the income from that … as Dan and I have worked together, the rhythm is so important to our songs, then it is right that … is a percentage of the song-writing really, and that is what people are hearing … So it is not through arguments or anything, I mean it is something we had to decide on and it is ongoing … it is a weekly thing.

CONCLUSION

Between 1995 and 2009 the English courts grappled with matters of authorship and originality in musical works although never really achieved much clarity. With the changes to the law emanating from the CoJ, it would seem that there may be significant challenges in applying our current domestic copyright legislation to the music industry. No longer, it seems, do we have a musical work, a modification that impacts on the notion of a musical arrangement in the CDPA. Combine that with the 'new' standard of originality, and it seems that our current Act may need significant revisions if it is to reflect the emerging European law.

The new law may have difficulty in protecting or being applied to contemporary forms of music making. Michael Alcorn's project is an example of this: how to protect what Michael considered was the most creative element of his work? What can be said is that it is notable that the ways in which our interviewees shared income arising from their projects did seem to reflect the law as it is being shaped by Europe – where all manner of creative input is recognised and which, it would seem, would preclude neither performance nor performers. It is argued that industry practices are changing especially with the advent of digitisation and experimentation with new business models,[73] but how this affects royalty flows is not clear.

Our conclusion in 2011 was that our interviewees engaged in musical practices that were both before and beyond copyright. 'Before' in the sense that much of what really engaged our collaborators and was important to them was the process of creation. This was an iterative and collaborative process. Then, 'beyond copyright' were the performative elements of a work. While we stand by our first finding, we think that now, with the changes in the law on originality and the work classification, the scope of copyright is broader, and elements of the music making

[73] See PWC publication: 'Making sense of a complex world: Accounting for royalty arrangements – issues for media companies' 2012 available at http://www.pwc.nl/nl_NL/nl/assets/documents/pwc-accounting-for-royalty.pdf.

and performing process that were once before copyright are now captured by the law. Granted this may make allocation of ownership challenging, but, and despite some case law that may suggest otherwise, that is not a reason to deny authorship where it properly falls due.

We noted that, as much within this sphere of the music sector is before copyright, this makes policy intervention challenging: policy prefers to focus on things rather than processes. We stand by this finding, but would argue that we are starting to detect small shifts in the complex policy environment. A stream of initiatives is currently taking place that seeks to put a value on the arts. Much of this is in response to the 'age of austerity' and to the cuts in public funding. In 2010–2011 public grant-in-aid funding to the Arts Council stood at £450 million.[74] In 2011–2012 it was reduced by 14 per cent to £388 million; in 2012–2013 by 7.5 per cent to £359 million; in 2013–2014 by 3 per cent to £348 million and in 2014–2015 it will be reduced to £343 million.[75] There is pressure to show the value that the arts contributes to society – which often means a focus on economic value, and economic value often focuses on things, and not intrinsic value or processes.[76] Not all policy has economic value at heart. The very different approaches taken to the funding of the arts in different jurisdictions within the UK were demonstrated by the speeches of then UK Culture Secretary Maria Miller and Scottish Culture Minister Fiona Hyslop in 2013, illustrating a sharp divergence between economic and intrinsic values as the starting point for investment. Maria Miller's approach focused on the economic value

---

[74] https://www.gov.uk/government/policies/supporting-vibrant-and-sustainable-arts-and-culture.

[75] This is not the only source of funding for the Arts Council. The national lottery gives a significant amount of money via the Arts Council to support the arts. Total funding including lottery funding in 2010–2011 was £601 million. In 2014–2015 it is expected to be £605 million.

[76] Although it is notable that, in the arts and humanities at least, the value of process is starting to be recognised. S Upton, P Vallance and J Goddard, 'From outcomes to process: evidence for a new approach to research impact assessment' (2014) Research Evaluation 23(4), 352–65. This conclusion is supported by the AHRC 2013 guidance on planning and demonstrating effective policy engagement. See also C Waelde and P Schlesinger, 'Music and Dance: Beyond Copyright Text?' (2011) 8:3 *SCRIPTed* 257. In a piece of research commissioned by the AHRC, using a case study approach we highlighted the value that the participants placed on collaboration and the research process. See 'Copyright and Publicly-Funded Arts and Humanities Research: Identifying and Developing Sustainable Exploitation Models in the Digital Economy', n 4.

of the arts. Her speech was peppered with references to 'the potential economic impact of culture', to public funding distributed by the Arts Council being 'seed funding', the need for 'venture capital', and to exploit 'commercial opportunities' within the creative sector. Put bluntly, 'when times are tough and money is tight, our focus must be on culture's economic impact.'[77]

Hyslop, whose focus was more on the intrinsic value of the arts, said of Miller's approach:

> If there was ever a way to suck the vitality out of a sector of society that should energise, invigorate, inspire and move – it is to make a perfunctory nod to generic social benefits and then, in the next breath, reduce it to nothing more than a commodity.[78]

There are a number of current initiatives that seek to deepen our understanding of the value of the arts beyond the purely economic. These include the Arts Council report on the value of culture to people and society;[79] the AHRC cultural value project;[80] and the Warwick Commission on the Future of Cultural Value.[81] These all form part of an ongoing dialogue through which we are starting to learn more about the value of the arts, and what it is that we value in the arts. The work is also starting to recognise the value of process as well as of the product, with new methodologies being sought for ways in which we might capture and measure non-economic value.

One other strand worth noting within this cultural milieu is the availability – or otherwise – of finance for those working in the creative industries. Maria Miller laid great stress on philanthropic giving acting as

---

77 Culture Secretary Maria Miller, 'Testing times: fighting culture's corner in an age of austerity', 24 April 2013, British Museum available at https://www.gov.uk/government/speeches/testing-times-fighting-cultures-corner-in-an-age-of-austerity.

78 http://www.thestage.co.uk/news/2013/06/scotland-culture-minister-brands-maria-millers-arts-policy-reductive/ 5 June 2013, David Talbot Rice Memorial Lecture.

79 http://www.artscouncil.org.uk/media/uploads/pdf/The-value-of-arts-and-culture-to-people-and-society-An-evidence-review-Mar-2014.pdf.

80 http://www.ahrc.ac.uk/Funded-Research/Funded-themes-and-programmes/Cultural-Value-Project/Pages/default.aspx.

81 See also DCMS *Classifying and measuring the creative industries* consultation https://www.gov.uk/government/consultations/classifying-and-measuring-the-creative-industries-consultation-on-proposed-changes. CMS Select Committee Inquiry: Support for the Creative Industries; Culture, Media and Sport Committee – Third Report Supporting the creative economy.

a complement to, if not a substitute for, public funding. While this may have some success in cultural capitals, anecdotal evidence suggests that beyond these geographical boundaries raising this form of finance is highly challenging. Indeed, this was the point made by Alison Wenham of the Association of Independent Music when giving evidence to the CMS Select Committee Inquiry: Support for the Creative Industries:

> Appropriate forms of finance are much more difficult to come by, particularly when you look at the caricature of the independent entrepreneurial nature of music businesses being somewhat countercultural to traditional finance mechanisms, institutions and language.[82]

Work is being done in this regard by the Intellectual Property Office (IPO). Through a series of initiatives aimed at implementing proposals made in a commissioned research paper called 'Banking on IP?',[83] the IPO is seeking to raise awareness of and avenues through which IP in general could be used as an asset against which to borrow money from banks. But there are also other forms of raising finance and social media has opened up many possibilities. Kickstarter is one example, describing itself as a funding platform for creative projects. Backers, those who like the projects on offer, pledge money in return for 'rewards', which might include a copy of what is being produced (a CD), or an experience unique to the project. At the time of writing there were 912 music projects on Kickstarter.[84] Another example is PledgeMusic, a site that describes itself as 'a direct-to-fan music platform, which brings artists and fans together to share in the experience of music as it happens' and through which the fans can 'become part of the music making experience itself'.[85] Much of what is sold is product, including such things as personalised CDs, artwork, and T-shirts, but, as with Kickstarter, also on sale are experiences including guitar lessons, tickets to gigs, and the opportunity to spend a day in the studio with the musicians.

If we return at this point to the question that we started with: music performed: what is beyond the score? The answer is, 'a great deal' – not

---

[82] Session 2013–14 Culture, Media and Sport Committee – Minutes of Evidence HC 674m Oral Evidence Taken before the Culture, Media and Sport Committee on 4 December 2012.

[83] M Brassell and K King, 'Banking on IP?: The role of intellectual property and intangible assets in facilitating business finance' 2013/34 Intellectual Property Office 2013 https://www.gov.uk/government/publications/banking-on-ip.

[84] February 2015.

[85] See for instance Tamara Schlesinger at http://www.pledgemusic.com/projects/malka.

just beyond the score, but also before the score and surrounding the score. Questions abound around originality, of the fitness of purpose of our domestic legislation, of the value of the arts, and of the state of play of cultural policy making.

Despite this state of flux, many argue that the UK is a great place for musicians to ply their trade. As such it is fitting to end with two statements made by senior executives in the music industry:

> The one thing we do in this country better than anyone else is we have the raw creative talent. We are the country that gave Iron Maiden to the people and the Sex Pistols and the Clash and David Bowie and the Beatles. It goes on and on.[86] (Jo Dipple, CEO UK Music)

> It is worth mentioning that in four of the last five years the world's biggest selling album has come from a British artist. There is an enormous appetite for British artists and music around the world.[87] (Alison Wenham, CEO The Association of Independent Music)

---

[86] Session 2013–14 Culture, Media and Sport Committee – Minutes of Evidence HC 674 Oral Evidence 4 December 2012.

[87] ibid.

3. Creativity and possessive interests

Martin Parker Dixon

We can readily agree with Andreas Rahmatian that 'the development of the notion of the "Romantic author" is a mishmash, with contradicting developments which have always run parallel and which do not allow a meaningful and decisive conclusion in one way or another. The "Romantic Author" construct the critics offer is an oversimplifying exaggeration.'[1] This being the case, it follows that supporters of such a notion of authorship are either being naive or rather devious in their presentations. It also follows that any concerted attack on Romantic authorship as an ideology will inevitably succumb to a little 'strawmanism': the critic can extract any number of *imagos* of the creative artist from this historical-cultural *mishmash* (the artist as individualistic, dominating, inspired, virile, divinely endowed, vehicle for world spirit) and there will be reason enough to find fault in them. And by the same token, more prosaic accounts (artists as humble craftsmen, working with the sweat of their brow) fare no better. It can always be insisted – or suspected – that the 'real' picture of human creativity is more complicated, for many are diligent in their craft but few ever make it into the Pantheon. Talk of creativity by artists, journalists, philosophers – or lawyers for that matter – can easily appear parodic.

When artists themselves have stepped into the breach, the results can be similarly unsatisfactory. Take the following example. A *bon mot* attributed to Pablo Picasso runs 'The bad artists imitate, the great artists steal'. In a work by the English graffiti artist Banksy, the same phrase is taken and carved into a fragment of marble in Roman face, whereupon the phrase takes on a certain classical solidity and stature. However, Picasso's name is crudely scratched out (though it is still visible, it is 'under erasure') and Banksy clumsily inscribes his own name beneath it. Admittedly, the joke is old and thin: in this childish vandalism so typical of the avant-garde since Duchamp, the great artistic thief (Picasso) has an

1 Rahmatian (2011: 166).

idea stolen from him by the subversive pickpocket Banksy, and he thus re-enacts Picasso's advice, seemingly at the painter's expense. Circulating here is a rather staged play on superior versus inferior, and on who-owns-what. What is unsatisfactory is that Banksy honours Picasso's words in a phoney classical inscription, and attempts to bury them in one gesture. There is no harm done because the material object which is defaced has no prior historical or cultural interest or value, and it certainly has nothing to do with Picasso. Neither can Banksy effectively prise the words or their propositional content away from Picasso simply by virtue of this hasty defacement of the ennobled inscription, because Picasso's name is still visible, and Banksy's nominal presence is impertinent, parasitical. In short, there is no theft, there is no crime. Picasso's insight into the nature of art (or his arrogant self-appointment as great) is still resplendent, and it remains absolutely Picasso's: Picasso said it, Picasso is the origin, and it is *his* voice and authority that we hear and care about. What is doubly disappointing is that Banksy has genuine credentials as a fashionable criminal because his art defaces public spaces (and it is often removed because of this) and his usual wit and ingenuity is not apparent here.

Regardless of the merits of this particular work, it, and the aphorism it lampoons, disclose a certain truth that it is the business of this chapter to explore: artistic making is liable to be troubled by the *affections* of possession and ownership. What I have learned from Andreas Rahmatian's work is that the legal concept of the author follows from the concept of property: there are authors because there are properties. Writing here from the perspective of a composer, what this foray into legal theory has helped me understand is that obsessing about the nature of creativity (and this obsessing can be highly speculative) can ignore a simple teleology: given that it is the business of art (and craft) to make *something*, theories and claims relating to creativity could with every good reason start with reflection on the nature of the *thing* being made. Claims relating to authorship are organised around the fact that there is a thing (it could also be a property), and it might be that we reverse engineer our explanations of the coming-into-being of work-things from our suppositions about the role those things play in the world. If musical works are supposed to arouse emotion and feelings in us, then talk of the emotional lives of those that make and perform them has utility and pertinence: it closes the empathetic circle and dignifies what we undergo in the course of listening. If we suppose, in formalistic mode, musical works to be beautiful structures then our talk – or more precisely our language game – will benefit from the use of active verbs supporting the view that the composer intended to construct this music in such and such a manner. Furthermore, and leaping ahead to a position I set out later in this chapter, it is characteristic of a *thing* that someone can take possession of it. For Jean-Paul Sartre, it might be that fundamentally the artist makes *in order to possess*; to have not only a thing but also to *have* the work they 'put into' it (constructive work, emotional work, spiritual work, etc). What is noteworthy is this exchange: we can suspend talking about creativity and talk instead about possession, asking, *what is it that is possessed*? and *what are the claims being made to substantiate that possession*? Then, talk of creative process amounts to a special manner of making persuasive or compelling possessive claims with regard to a directly or indirectly defined artwork-thing.

Not every claim about the creative process (even – or especially! – those made by artists themselves with respect to their own work) is persuasive or compelling. A rule of proportionality applies: a trite little poem is just 'dashed off' without thought; this we can accept. *Paradise Lost*, dictated late in life when Milton was already blind, and taking many years to complete, seems to us like a labour of Herculean proportions. The earnest young song writer who pens the lines *Roses are red, violets are blue / I wrote this song, because I love you*, and also insists that he 'poured his soul' into them, and thereby 'expressed his deepest feelings', seems, by contrast, to be severely misguided: the work done and the quality of the thing do not agree; the intention, however sincere, has miscarried and the song writer does not have what he thinks he has. Our description of what was done must include an assessment of the outcome of the deed. In this last case, some kind of delusion was at work in the midst of all the rending of heart strings; this is the actual genetic narrative of the work.

In many ways, this issue need not trouble the copyright lawyers – for the song writer is responsible for his song, however weak and uninteresting – but it greatly exercises compositional pedagogy, for the amateur's problem is the absence of a moment of reflection on the concrete value of the object itself. The teacher has to break the bad news that whatever the young composer thought they were putting 'into' the music, the results are dreadful and the mismatch an embarrassment. The prudence of the artist is to know as much as they can about the objects they are trying to make, and not to recover significance and value merely from how it *feels* to make something. Of course, no effort at all will produce no results (so the 'Just Do It' faith in sheer endeavour has some truth), but what I am insisting on here is that in an aesthetic context, the object – the thing – matters enormously; it might be all that matters.

When, below, I consider 'moral rights', because I am not a lawyer, I do not involve myself with the legal complications or the application of legal principles. What I recognise in these principles is that the ideas of paternity and integrity have a strong resonance with the possessive interest of the artist. There are two affective logics that interest me: (*a*) I made (created) X and this fact entitles me to insist that I am in a privileged and unique position with respect to X, this is how X's 'being-mine' is experienced. And (*b*) because X is mine, I don't want it interfered with by someone else. This status of 'being-mine' is alienable: if X is tampered with by someone else, its organic, declared or demonstrable link back to me is lost. It ceases to be mine, and someone else can derive benefit from work which I began and I believe I should retain. I want the object to be judged as having value, and I want to be the one responsible for it.[2] These are indeed very simple observations but they are, in nascent form at least, genuine affective dimensions – the anxieties if you will – of the creative process.

What I want to show in the remainder of this chapter, however, is that under certain conditions the fundamental claim – or aspiration – 'X is mine' becomes equivocal. Indeed, it might be said that a certain trajectory of artistic development results with the lessening of possessive interest. Arguably, when the concern for the aesthetic object as such attains full maturity, every creative decision is essentially anonymous: everything is done for the sake of the object, and it scarcely matters who it is that acts.

Accordingly, the arguments in this chapter explore two basic theses:

(A) The *auteur* thesis presents a model of the author[3] as the singular and pre-eminent – the necessary and sufficient – origin of the work of art.[4]

(B) The *artisanal* thesis understands the author to be (at best) co-responsible for the formation of a work of art.[5]

---

[2] As Andreas Rahmatian showed, any discussion of creativity can easily stray into deep theological waters. Creativity is the province of God, not man. But if God is only an idealised projection of human interests, it is worth pointing out that in addition to being creative, God was deeply jealous. (See Rahmatian 2011: 160–64.)

[3] In line with the language of the copyright statutes I refer to an 'author' as a covering term for all writers, directors, artists and composers.

[4] This singularity is often presented as part of the model of Romantic authorship.

[5] This thesis goes beyond a collaborative model of multiple (singular) authors.

I use these two theses to construct contrasting interpretations of the value claims of the rights of paternity and integrity. We will see that when considered in the light of (a), the concepts of paternity and integrity arise easily and uncontroversially. In the light of (b), however, paternity and integrity cannot take hold in our thinking or practice. My contentions with respect to these theses are as follows:

1. The concept of an auteur meshes successfully with the development of property concepts and with the establishment of the exchange value of the work of art. Paternity and integrity suit the workings of the cultural market where the artwork is a kind of *exchangeable thing*.
2. Opponents of moral rights dispute the plausibility of the genetic model implied by (a). But in this they fall prey to the strawmanism mentioned above.
3. The notions of integrity and paternity can be defended inasmuch as they respond to a compelling human interest in the appropriation of properties.
4. The artisan model of artistic production does not prove amenable for the generation of property, and the concepts of paternity and integrity are much harder to substantiate.
5. (a) is a restricted presentation of (b).

My interest in these questions is analytical. This is to say, I am interested in bringing to light certain embedded interests, structures and entailments that inhere in the practices and ideologies surrounding 'creativity'. I will now proceed to elaborate upon and defend each of these contentions.

1. THE AUTEUR, PROPERTY AND QUALITY

The term auteur is used in the cinema (especially the French cinema) to capture a new role and responsibility for the director whereby he or she has such an overriding influence on the film's qualities and attributes – and creative control of the overall product – that this individual henceforth deserves the designation 'author' as opposed to director. An *authored* film implies that we can look to *one individual* as being answerable for that film's qualities, and to that same individual as deserving praise for the film's merits, or blame for its weaknesses.

The concept of the auteur is supported by an axiological prejudice which might run something like this: the artistic vision of an individual will (or is more likely to) yield a distinctive, consistent, high-quality product. This is in contradistinction to the watering-down and confusion that – it might be supposed – result when many individuals attempt to make a contribution to a project, or when certain aspects of the film are 'compromised' because, for example, of worries concerning the reception of the film by the intended audience. The auteur principle represents a change in the relations of production in the film industry. The cultural values of a film are inextricably bound to the activity of the auteur (whatever the financial arrangements of film production might be). Furthermore, the adoption of the auteur model was pivotal for the acceptance of studio film production as 'art'. Thereby film production can adopt the same genetic model as (say) novel writing or symphonic composition and, therefore, is subject to the same expectations and treatment.

The concept of an auteur allows for a particular language game: we can refer synecdochically to a film via the name of its writer-director. We can say 'let's go see the latest *Woody Allen*', or 'I'd really like to watch a *Fellini*'. The name features in the formation of a contract between a distributor and consumer: the name tells us something helpful or even decisive regarding the quality and nature of the experience we wish to purchase.

The notion of 'purchasing an experience' deserves a little more attention. I am assuming that in contemporary consumer society, most will choose to dispose of their limited leisure time in ways that suit their interests. Many listen to music to 'relax', watch 'trashy' TV to 'zone-out', see a movie to experience the stimulation of thrilling special effects and so forth. Much of this can be understood as a way of contending with the debilitating effects of wage labour. Cultural products are also categorised by genre according to the kinds of experiences one is likely to enjoy when engaging with them. For every thriller, horror, comedy, romance, whodunnit, or documentary we can assign a corresponding reaction, outcome or mode of engagement on the part of a consumer. That said, no outlay of time and capital in the cultural sphere is absolutely guaranteed to yield the expected return: the comedy might be clichéd and slow, the horror film might be gory and implausible, the documentary uninformative. Investment in a 'classic' (i.e., *Citizen Kane*, *La Bohème*, *Pickwick Papers*, *Hamlet*) – because they are tried and tested, have critical acclaim and market durability – can be seen as a safe bet and, furthermore, adds to personal cultural capital. 'Serious' works of art also afford peculiar modes of engagement and experiences: we can, for example, expect to have our tastes 'challenged' by new music, or be given access to deep and profound emotions by great masterpieces. It is not necessary to make any distinctions regarding the inherent value of these particular experiences; nothing will be added to the argument by insisting that serious art is inherently superior to light entertainment.

I am suggesting here that from the consumer's perspective, the auteurial model – in which the author's name acts as something like a brand – has the virtue of simplicity and efficiency. Assuming that the author has control over the qualities of the work, and/or has direct contact with the material that forms the work, the author's name advertises the inherent qualities of the cultural object that is placed on the market. Informed consumers know (or think they know) what to expect from a Birtwistle opera just as they know what to expect from an iPhone.

We can propose that: *When an author's name is materially relevant to a purchasing or 'investment' decision, then that name needs to be advertised and the relationship between author and work needs to be secure.*

The validity of the consumer perspective can be demonstrated in the following example. In commercial popular music, consumer preference on the whole follows the performing artist and not the song writer, arranger or lyricist. (Accepting that in some circumstances these roles are covered by one individual.) The consumer knows (and cares about) the identity of the performer, but not the composer of the song being performed. When the role of the producer began to be acknowledged, it became desirable to publicise music via the name of the producer as this information delivers something pertinent regarding the nature of the music. In the sphere of classical music, the performer can on occasion be preferred to the composer as the marketable commodity; i.e., the 'Three Tenors', or, at the height of his fame, Nigel Kennedy.

Such is one reason to respect the rights of attribution and integrity. The consumer desires a piece by Beethoven, and the consumer expects to engage with the music that Beethoven actually wrote. These rights reflect the need for an orderly and transparent working of the market for culture. If I ask for Mozart I don't expect to get Salieri.

This seems straightforward enough, but it is worth considering the following objection: should not the rights in question be decided from the perspective of the author and not the consumer? There is, after all, a very complex debate regarding whose interests copyright actually serves or hinders. For example, Paul Goldstein writes that:

> Copyright, in a word, is about authorship. Copyright is about sustaining the conditions of creativity that enable an individual to craft out of thin air, and intense, devouring labor, an *Appalachian Spring*, a *Sun Also Rises*, a *Citizen Kane*. Copyright is as much about the pages of deleted text, the scenes that lie

> on the cutting room floor, as it is about the refined work, the final cut, that ultimately reaches the author's public. (Goldstein 1992: 80)

Copyright theory in general seems to have formed a view regarding the difficult and tortuous labours of the author and it is these labours that are protected – and honoured – in law, and it is for these labours that remuneration is due. However, Goldstein also goes on to write: 'By "authorship" I mean authors communicating as directly as circumstance allows with their intended audiences. Copyright sustains the very heart and essence of authorship by enabling this communication, this connection. It is copyright that makes it possible for audiences – markets – to form for an author's work, and it is copyright that makes it possible for publishers to bring these works to market.' (ibid.)

The point to draw out here is that whatever Goldstein supposes takes place during artistic labour (the 'crafting out of thin air'), what is at stake in copyright is the maintenance of a relationship, an honest contract between author and audience. The auteurial model seems to favour a contract which amounts to the intimate communication between the two interested parties.[6] The communication has a possessive tone also: the author can refer (with or without hyperbole) to 'my public!'. Indeed, Goldstein uses the phrase 'author's public' without comment. It seems to me that accepting the communicative paradigm, one could just as easily refer to the *public's author*.

The interest generated when it is alleged that a prominent author is not quite who we think she is, is a case in point. Consider Professor Kathryn Sutherland's suggestion that Jane Austen's punctuation was polished up to be the immaculate exemplar of English it is now taken to be by a studious editor, a certain William Gifford.[7] In a sense, *Emma* as we read it today is the product of the work of two people, Austen and Gifford, and our initial – and as it turns out, groundless and ill-informed – image of the author of *Emma* must adapt accordingly. But whatever is the case, 'Austen' is, in both the pre- and post-revelatory phases of our encounter with 'her', an imagined entity, a kind of fiction. If Austen was once supposed to be *x*, and today she is *y*, and tomorrow she is *z*, it is a mistake to suppose that the movement from *x*, to *y*, to *z*, reveals

---

[6] One of Dickens's greatest characters, Sam Weller, appears for the first time only in the tenth instalment of *Pickwick Papers*. Circulation for *Pickwick* was not strong to begin with and Weller was introduced to address this. The public's liking for Weller was enormous. He was in a sense created by communicative market testing.

[7] See Kennedy (2010: 7).

asymptotic progress towards a definitive presentation of the real Austen. Arguably, in each case 'Austen' is functioning as a predicate for a set of imagined characteristics, characteristics that are subject to revision. There is no encounter or communication with 'her' as such. There is nothing realistic about reducing real people (living or dead) to a series of characteristic adjectives. The introduction of new facts about Austen's biography, her working methods, motives, and the contributions of editors in fact brings us no closer (nor moves us further away from) the 'real' Austen for there is no such entity. After all, a living individual has no means of answering the question 'who is the real you?' either.[8] Authors, especially historical authors of significance, are to some extent imagined entities based on a substructure of market relations and personal desire.[9]

My response to the objection is that there is no particular requirement to deal with the author's interests as distinct from the consumer's. In this sense we rediscover what Amy Adler calls 'the pivotal assumption in moral rights law that an artist's interests and the public's interest in a work of art will be aligned.' (Adler 2009: 265) With regard to Goldstein's paradigm of two-way communication, the notions of an *author communicating with 'her' public* and a *public communicating with 'their' author* are commutative and operate according to the same principles whereby the rights of paternity and integrity provide a kind of assurance that this contract is sound. At this stage in the argument, it is not important to question what this communication might be thought to 'contain' or amount to, but only that there exists a tone of possession in the language. We must speak of 'having': the author *has* 'something to say' and thereby give to her public, while retaining control of what it is that is given through the right of integrity. The consumer wants to take possession of that particular work – and that which the work offers –

---

8 This, at any rate, is the anti-essentialist position. The belief that a created work of art must be an extension of the essential person is, therefore, at least one presumption too far. As Barthes would say, the person of the author does not precede the act of writing: writing makes the writer. The writer does not stand behind the work.

9 In Sartre's analysis, we construct a hypothesis regarding the nature of agency based on what we suppose others seem to do and are apparently capable of: 'My self becomes the origin of its acts as the other of his.' (Sartre, *Being and Nothingness*, 1986: 42). So, popular representations of artistic activity as being driven by great forces and attaining singular and worthy accomplishments might just be a fantasy we would like to entertain regarding ourselves.

through ownership, or appreciative or emotional engagement. Now to my second contention.

2. OPPONENTS OF MORAL RIGHTS WILL DISPUTE THE PLAUSIBILITY OF THE GENETIC MODEL IMPLIED BY THE AUTEUR THESIS

I will now consider two critical attacks on the rights of integrity and paternity: these are Amy Adler's essay 'Against Moral Rights' and Roland Barthes's famous diatribe 'Death of the Author'. Though Adler's essay is focussed on what she thinks of as the negative effects of legislation, and Barthes is more interested in cultural ideology, both in their own way ridicule the notion of an intimate and exclusive link between a single author and a particular work, and also of the cultures that depend on this supposed relationship: the cultural marketplace, and, for Barthes, that includes the scholarly attention paid to the author as a figure whose biography necessarily 'nourishes' the work. I will treat these accounts as providing objections to auteurialism.

Moral rights, Adler argues, enshrine in law a model of artistic production that cannot be applied impartially in the contemporary art world.[10] The old model – which Adler characterises as 'Romantic' – encapsulates the following belief: that there are in society those peculiar individuals who are endowed with 'creative genius' and who are, by virtue of unusual levels of skill, spiritual insight, drive and so forth, capable of producing works that have enormous complexity, emotional depth, or otherwise reveal aspects of the human condition with such truth that these objects – along with their authors – are to be revered and therefore protected. These beliefs feed easily into the concept of the pantheon, a guarded, holy and unchanging space which houses in perpetuity the worthiest and most excellent of human achievements and endeavours.

This model admits very readily a further and highly dubious hypothesis, that of an unbreakable spiritual–genetic link between artist and artwork:

---

[10] For the sake of simplicity, I will concur with Arthur C. Danto and suppose that the contemporary art scene (which extends far beyond the visual arts) begins in 1964 with the exhibition of Andy Warhol's *Brillo Boxes*. (See Danto 1997.) It was also the year that The Beatles appeared on the Ed Sullivan show in the USA. At this juncture, patterns of disruption to the artworld perpetrated by the avant-garde become the norm.

> Embedded in moral rights law are two basic assumptions about visual art. First is that a work of art is an extension of the artist himself … Scholars invoke the metaphor of paternity to explain the artist's profound connection with his work: he cares so deeply about the fate of his art because it is somehow his child and not just another object. Thus the artist feels personal anguish when someone else modifies his artwork/child. This is so even though the child has grown up and left home, and even though the artist/father has sold his child … The work of art is not just another product he has sold, but rather an 'expression of his innermost being.' As the Second Circuit observed, moral rights 'spring from a belief that an artist in the process of creation injects his spirit into the work.' (Adler 2009: 269)

What are we to make of these assertions? We might tolerate, in everyday conversation, the insistence that *X* put her 'heart and soul' into that performance, that poem, that composition and so forth, and, presumably, something cogent and meaningful is meant by these locutions. But to have these sentiments reproduced in legal interpretation seems like quite another matter. How could one empirically establish that spirit had been successfully injected into a work? We can object at once, without reflection, that there is no spirit to inject, there is no substance capable of receiving an injection, there is no injecting.[11] Why is it then that we can still so readily care that we are listening to the music *of* a certain composer, rather than just *some* music? It is, perhaps, because the genetic link between author and work arises so easily, but is so difficult to substantiate, that *non-substantial* words like 'spirit' and 'soul' enter the language game.[12] If an author insists 'I put my soul into that music' one could object that this must be indefensible nonsense since, even allowing

[11] The metaphors here can also be read as if not dead then as a coy invocation of a ridiculous analogy with the male contribution to procreation and conception.

[12] David Hume is particularly lucid here. Writing in the *Treatise of Human Nature*, he isolates three ways of engaging with the apparent manifestation of cause and effect. The first – and lowest approach – is the 'vulgar', habituated consciousness: 'It is natural for men, in their common and careless way of thinking, to imagine they perceive a connection betwixt such objects as they have constantly found united together; and because custom has rendered it difficult to separate the ideas, they are apt to fancy such a separation to be in itself impossible and absurd.' (Hume 1962: 273). What Hume calls 'false philosophy' goes looking for deeper, substantive grounds for these connections, and thus misses the arbitrariness of these conjunctions. Their endless frustration in failing to abstract fundamental mechanisms and causes is 'consoled' by formulating an absurd conclusion: 'They need only say, that any phenomenon which puzzles them arises from a faculty or an occult quality, and there is an end of all dispute and inquiry on the matter.' (ibid., 274–75).

that one has a soul, how can it be put *into* anything and remain there? However, dealing with this assertion charitably will incline us to seek the sense in it. I am suggesting here that such an assertion does indeed carry a meaning that is not cancelled out by the failure to evidence a physical connection between author and work: the assertion follows from the need to 'make-mine', to take possession of objects in and through making.

In a sense, moral rights bestow something of this dignified ideal upon all creative undertakings. Adler explains: '[a]s a prominent French legal decision explained, moral rights protect "the superior interests of human genius." We must preserve a work as the artist intended it so that his genius can be "conveyed to posterity without damage."' (270) In principle and in practice, *anything* the authentic genius laid a hand upon will contain a 'trace' of their genius and have some interest or value in that it affords a remarkable form 'contact' with that individual and their world. There is, of course, something unexceptionable in the notion that historical objects and documents, regardless of their intrinsic monetary or historical worth, should not be interfered with in ways which falsify their material substance or qualities. Yet this notion disguises any number of values. If the varnish applied to an old painting is removed to reveal the vivid colours of the original, are we not thereby cutting off 'contact' with those cultures that valued the ageing effects of varnish since the patina established, in their mind at least, a link back to the old masters? Why is the 'original' condition of an object (insofar as this can be established) to be preferred to an object which bears the traces of interference by subsequent cultures? Suffice it to say here, Adler objects to the foreclosure of these questions by the proprietorial dominance of the figure of the creative artist (auteur). The situation whereby artistic evaluations are always necessarily to be decided on the basis of the presumed interests of the artist is actually anathema to the real workings of artistic culture today.

Of course, if we allow for the existence of the genius, we are bound to accept that they ought to have the last say on how work is to be made, presented and understood, such is their prerogative. If the concept of the genius has any legitimacy (Kant for one was able to identify a peculiar function in art for such individuals) then it is quite proper to expect the genius to provide the last word on the interpretation of their work.

Adler protests that this Romantic model has been superseded. What is evidenced most forcibly by contemporary practice is an indifference to the permanence of artworks, even a relishing of destruction and vandalism. To take one of Adler's examples, in 2003 the Chapman brothers exhibited *Insult to Injury*, which consisted of a series of etchings (*The Disasters of War*) by Goya upon which they had drawn figures and faces taken from their own repertory of the monstrous and grotesque. The pristine Goya prints were themselves of enormous rarity and value, and they were bought by the Chapmans in 2001. After two years of pondering they resolved to 'rectify' them by systematically substituting the faces of the victims of war with the faces of clowns and puppies. Setting aside the merits of the exercise, Adler cites this work as but one amongst many instances of artists showing disregard for the supposed *sanctity* of the work of art. Works of art are not to be uncritically and slavishly respected: an artist can intervene in, deface, remake or destroy a work and in the same gesture violate the ideology of art's hallowed status. Indeed, these kinds of gestures are common to every avant-garde movement since Marcel Duchamp.[13]

If the avant-garde has un-exalted the work of art, equally they have de-emphasised the manual skill of the artist. Indeed, part of the aesthetic effect of *Insult to Injury* is the combination of Goya's technically brilliant etching with the Chapmans' crude cartooning. Furthermore, works can be completed by assistants, or plans sent to a foundry or an engineer for execution. It would be quite wrong, therefore, to expect anything remarkable in the physical connection between producer and product. Artists do though have 'ideas' or produce methods or types that can be readily executed by others. In such cases, while the artwork offers no interest in terms of workmanship, the conceptual content can still be esteemed.

I do not accept, however, that Adler's emphasis on the destructive tendencies of the avant-garde do much more than temporarily obscure the ordinarily asserted value claims made with respect to artworks, those that produce them, and that take an interest in them. Arguably, however disenchanted one might be with the posturing and celebrity status of 'Young British Artists', it can be accepted, for example, that the idea behind *Insult to Injury* is very striking. It can be recognised that Adler and any commentator who references *Insult to Injury* will inevitably speak of what the Chapman brothers themselves achieved in making this work, an achievement for which they are unambiguously responsible. The work is the product of some rare and peculiar judgement, built up through many years of working, that treads a fine line between black humour, bad taste, pornography, shock and visceral disgust. They also exhibited certain virtues, say, courage and determination, in producing this work (I do not underestimate how difficult it must have been to

---

13 In 1919 Duchamp famously drew a moustache and beard on a postcard reproduction of the Mona Lisa and entitled it *L.H.O.O.Q.*

scrawl cartoons over an acknowledged masterpiece). Despite the palimpsestic presence of Goya's work, *Insult to Injury* is very much the *Chapmans'*. And if one was fortunate enough to be in a position to purchase the original vandalised etchings – and many hundreds of thousands of pounds would be required – one would be comfortable in knowing that one was investing in an entirely genuine Chapman brothers' artwork. It can also be admitted that in a wholly traditional sense, the aesthetic effect – that is to say the sheer emotional response on a viewer – is the decisive aspect of encountering these pictures. In this sense, the way we *see* these pictures is in no way unusual and they would constitute a perfectly normal gallery work. As a genuine artistic achievement, many would be inclined to preserve *Insult to Injury* as the Chapmans intended it. Equally, there is in all likelihood an artist who would, given the opportunity, have a point to make by perpetrating a second level of vandalism to *Insult to Injury*, but in the meantime, the concepts of paternity and integrity can be applied unproblematically to the Chapmans' work.

What I am suggesting here is that it is a straightforward matter to situate avant-garde work in the normal workings of the artworld whereby very valuable and interesting objects are exhibited in galleries, are bought and sold by dealers and wealthy collectors, and are made by individuals (or groups[14]) with seemingly special abilities.[15] It follows then that Adler is quite inaccurate when she writes 'Moral rights law thus purports to protect art, but does so by enshrining a vision of art that is directly at odds with contemporary artistic practice. It protects and reifies a notion of art that is dead.' (Adler 2009: 265) The conventional arrangements of art (creative genius producing unique and highly valued objects) are far from 'dead', they apply adequately in a vast number of cases, and in such cases moral rights principles can be entertained without too much difficulty. Furthermore, there is nothing in moral rights legislation that would have actually prevented the Chapman brothers making the work they did. Arguably, all that has happened is that certain connotations of the Romantic model of genius have fallen away, or, more accurately, have become secularised: namely, we do not think of artists as 'divinely

[14] It is worth pointing out that the fact that some avant-garde work is the product of more than one person (and is not the output of the lonely genius) does not in practice disturb the workings of the artworld or the market.

[15] Adler admits that one of the special abilities that artists have developed since Warhol is an acute market awareness: 'Of course, Warhol's spirit reigns over this merger of retail and art. It was Warhol who wrote that "being good in business is the most fascinating kind of art."'(Adler 2009: 297–98).

inspired' or their works as being 'sacrosanct', and consequently the taboos regarding the interference with the work of artists can be challenged with a certain alacrity by those with sufficient courage and acumen. (It would be going too far to say that the taboos have vanished altogether since the iconoclasm of the avant-garde, and the public interest in their actions, is still feeding off the effrontery they cause.) The genius of the contemporary artist is not unlike the genius of the entrepreneur: there is a fortune to be made in spotting market opportunities, developing a brand, and drawing the attentions of the super-wealthy. By the same token, the age of the 'great work' is probably over.[16] Admittedly, given that this is the case, some of the rhetoric in the interpretation of moral rights can sound rather quaint, but this is not enough in itself to render moral rights empty, regressive or contradictory.

I will now turn to Roland Barthes and ask in a more pointed fashion: is it possible to disenchant the supposed bond between work and author, and does this weaken the credibility of the moral right of paternity?

As I indicated above, it would seem that even in extreme and unusual cases, a minimal sense of responsibility can be attributed to artists, enough to satisfy the proposition *without the specific activity of the artist X there would be no artwork Y*. The work of the artist might entail nothing more than the giving of an instruction, having an idea, signing her name, or giving approval, and yet, nevertheless, such actions have a seemingly remarkable power to institute the coming into being of a peculiar class of objects called artworks. It is hard, therefore, to conceive of an authorless or unintended work of art.

The crucial issue in Barthes's *Death of the Author* is the extent to which we defer to the figure of the author in determining and controlling the meaning of a text. While we can accept that a certain person, at a certain point in their life, put certain words in a certain order, and accept that they might have wished to communicate a meaning by what they wrote, should we – *can we* – posit the author as the final signified of a

---

[16] Morris Weitz's theory of the 'open concept' in art is helpful here. In his famous 1956 paper he proposes that it is impossible to provide a stable, unexceptionable definition of art: art has no transhistorical essence, it has no 'nature', there are no necessary and sufficient conditions that will yield the judgement 'that is art'. Consequently there can be no possibility of insisting that art must be made in a certain way by a specially endowed class of persons, or that artworks must be held in a certain kind of esteem. Such might be the case, but this is not necessarily the case. What is at stake is the decision to extend whatever concept of art we might have at any given moment to new kinds of objects or phenomena. (See Weitz 1956.)

text? To repeat the hackneyed sentiments mentioned above, if the author pours their 'innermost soul' into their work, surely the goal of engaging with a work – of grasping its meaning – is to establish a connection to that 'soul'? If the notion of a 'soul' sounds too supernatural to take literally, let us treat the word to imply a kind of existential investment in a project: we assume that an author 'suffers for their art', makes sacrifices, faces moral challenges, withstands criticism and setbacks, and the spectre of self-doubt, all for the sake of the artwork. Creation entails not merely (if at all) physical labour, but intellectual, emotional and imaginative exertion. This inclines one to suppose that the work is (somehow) inseparable from these exertions, and that understanding what the author endured in the process of writing will bring us into a proximal relation to the meaning of the text. As Barthes put it: '[T]he Author is thought to *nourish* the book, which is to say that he exists before it, thinks, suffers, lives for it, is in the same relation of antecedence to his work as a father to his child.' (Barthes 1977: 145) The temporality latent in this picture – the order of events – is decisive: if we suppose that the author has found within themselves 'something to say' and, in their studio or at their desk, is labouring night and day to say it, and that the work is therefore the realisation of that conception, the spiritual–genetic link is both apparent and has interpretative utility: understanding the intention (which precedes the work) is vital in understanding the work itself.

Instead Barthes continues: 'In complete contrast, the modern scriptor is born simultaneously with the text, is in no way equipped with a being preceding or exceeding the writing, is not the subject with the book as predicate; there is no other time than that of the enunciation and every text is eternally written *here and now*.' In this description what becomes impossible to admit is the notion that the artist – or her 'soul' – can be usefully treated as the origin of the work, its very cause, and that a text relates back to that cause. The modern view of language that Barthes exploits does not treat language as a medium for the imprinting and communication of spiritual entities (ideas and emotions), but insists that words relate only to other words in a vast, originless and de-centred field of language which necessarily precedes any expressive intention. To enunciate and to write is to quote from that field: 'We know now that a text is not a line of words releasing a single 'theological' meaning (the message of the Author-God) but a multi-dimensional space in which a variety of writings, none of them original, blend and clash.' (Barthes 1977: 146) However appealing it might be to suppose that a text is delivering a message that issues from the mind of an author, the fact is that *language speaks*, not authors.

Does this represent a challenge to the principle of paternity? What Barthes presents is, like Adler's celebration of the destructive instincts of the contemporary avant-garde, a transformation in the model of what it means to 'create'. Barthes cannot tolerate fanciful notions such as producing work 'out of thin air' because all works are made in concrete acts using pre-given materials: words, genres, idioms, forms and so forth are rarely the invention of the author, but are instead quoted, combined and recombined into texts.[17]

Shall we insist that the name of the author is now superfluous? Or that all texts are essentially anonymous? Indeed not: Barthes remains minimally yet securely the author of his text. All that is being claimed is that the meaning of the text is subsequent to its being written. Barthes does not control the meaning of his essay *Death of the Author*, and the meaning of that essay is not rooted in either the intentions of the author or its historical context: what is happening is that a writer working in 2014 is quoting passages from an English version of Barthes's text in another text, and you, the reader, is making sense of these sentences and arguments as part of a process of reading. There is no possibility of either a Roland Barthes or a Martin Parker Dixon forcing readers to assent to any proposition without interested cooperation and involvement on their part. Barthes closes his essay with the injunction that the 'birth of the reader must be at the cost of the death of the Author.' (Barthes 1977: 148). Barthes seems to quote a pattern of Christological sacrificial exchange whereby the death of one party yields the birth of another. The good news of post-modern readership is that it is empowered to enjoy the text *qua* text and the debt to the author is eliminated.[18] Neither is the post-modern reader obliged to 'decipher' a text and seek its secret: the text is entirely flat, everything is 'in the open'. It is also clear that a text is a very different kind of thing to the *work*, and the *book*. The movement from work to text entails new ways of writing and reading.

In this section, what I have attempted to show is that the principles of paternity and integrity are not bound to a Romantic model of artistic production and its attendant metaphysical suppositions. It is sheer hubris to believe that, just because authors work collaboratively or that artists are interested in destruction or appropriation of another's work, preserving the integrity of a work of art and nominating its author(s) in our current culture suddenly becomes absurd and irrelevant. What can be

---

[17] Cf. Mallarmé's dictum: We do not write poems with ideas, but with words.

[18] It is worth pointing out that the additions made by the Chapman brothers to the Goya prints could be interpreted as a 'scriptorial' activity.

noted is that, however useful it might be in organising a consumer or scholarly culture, auteurialism can easily lapse into a Romantic interpretation, with the author assuming a domineering and controlling influence over the work and which posits the author (or, rhetorically, the Author-God) at the origin and therefore at the interpretative and evaluative epicentre of the work. I would be inclined to uphold the criticism of Barthes in this regard.

3. THE NOTIONS OF INTEGRITY AND PATERNITY CAN BE DEFENDED INASMUCH AS THEY RESPOND TO A COMPELLING HUMAN INTEREST IN THE APPROPRIATION OF PROPERTIES

In this section I will be arguing that the controversy regarding the *values* of integrity and paternity with regard to works of art is contextualised by a deeper human concern with property. To address this point we must invoke the philosophical concept of existence and to that end I will touch upon the phenomenology of Jean-Paul Sartre.

To return to Adler for a moment, at the outset of her essay, we notice at once the problematising of property:

> Normally when you buy something you can do what you want with it. If you buy a chair, or a dress, or a car, you can alter it, embellish it, neglect it, abuse it, destroy it, or throw it away. But if you buy a work of art, your freedom to do what you want with that object – your own property – is severely curtailed. This is because artists have powerful special rights, called 'moral rights,' unlike the creators of other objects. Moral rights allow an artist to control what you do with his work of art even after he has sold it and even if you are not in privity of contract with him. (Adler 2009: 263)

Phrased this way, the artist retains what appears to be an unwarranted and uncontracted controlling interest in his work and its use, even though it has been handed over to a consumer. But this is mere hubris: the comparison between the work of art and the mass-produced, replaceable consumer goods and private properties that Adler lists (chairs, dresses, cars) is gratuitous and inapt: artworks are rare and remarkable objects which have, *de facto*, an enormous and distinct value in and to our society in a way that chairs (chairs that exist outside design museums, that is) do not. That is why they currently enjoy special arrangements and privileges and why many feel disinclined to tamper with the substance of them. In some philosophical frameworks artworks are also 'beyond use', they are not materially worn out by being placed in the service of some operation, role or task. Legitimate external interference with works of art would extend only to expertly administered restoration and preservation. In short, artworks enjoy a radically different mode of *existence* in comparison to the 'equipment' of the ordinary lifeworld: they *persist*.

The temporal and practical transcendence of art may well be something to be celebrated. But equally a certain deadliness can be suspected to lurk in the museum mentality as unchanging, canonical masterpieces exert a repressive force on the ludic, irreverent and vital moments in aesthetic activity.[19] As much as we might wish to preserve what is worthy in the past, this process is not without psychological consequences or ideological abuses. I will interpret this structure in one of its aspects and suggest that an abyss separates ageless art objects from the harsh existential facts relating to the transience and vulnerability of human life as such. One need look no further than one of the most famous (and enduring) English poems for corroboration of this tension between the incorruptibility of art and the fragility of human life in its most vivid manifestation, youth and beauty: Shakespeare's Sonnet 18 concludes by asserting to the addressee of the poem she will not, in one sense at least, lose the beauty that she currently possesses because it is memorialised and is re-bestowed by the poem itself. The artwork's persistence compensates for human mortality:

> (…)
> But thy eternal summer shall not fade,
> Nor lose possession of that fair thou ow'st,
> Nor shall death brag thou wand'rest in his shade,
> When in eternal lines to Time thou grow'st.
> So long as men can breathe, or eyes can see,
> So long lives this, and this gives life to thee.

---

[19] The metaphor of the deadly is borrowed from the director Peter Brook's characterisation of the Deadly Theatre presented in his manifesto *The Empty Space*. Brook writes, for example: 'Grand opera, of course, is the Deadly Theatre carried to absurdity. Opera is a nightmare of vast feuds over tiny details; of surrealist anecdotes that all turn round the same assertion: nothing needs to change. Everything in opera must change, but in opera change is blocked.' (Brook 1996: 17). And: 'Deadliness always brings us back to repetition: the deadly director uses old formulae, old methods, old jokes, old effects, stock beginnings to scenes, stock ends; and this applies equally to his partners, the designers and composers, if they do not start each time afresh from the void, the desert and the true question – why clothes at all, why music, what for?' (ibid., 45–46).

This interpretation could rightly yield a deep ambivalence, even resentment: is this poem really a compensation? Is there not a lack of compassion here, a certain conceit – in all senses of that word – when an artist boasts that their art need not fear death?[20]

Let us reiterate and take forward the notion that artworks potentially manifest a privileged mode of existence through stability and persistence. I will not defend this impression by engaging with complex ontological descriptions; instead, I will take up simpler *existential* interpretations taken from Jean-Paul Sartre's analysis of the human being in *Being and Nothingness*. He describes two structures of human behaviour which are directly relevant to my analysis of moral rights: at the heart of these structures is the desire to possess and appropriate goods, knowledge and experiences which, he argues, arises from an essential lack in the human, a *nothingness*. I will summarise them as follows:

(i) The desire to possess is always-already immanent in making.
(ii) The relation of the maker to the made is double: the object that I make is 'of' me (my ideas, my labour) but it is also encountered as an external thing-in-itself.

Proposition (i) relates to the following observation from Sartre:

> If I create a picture, a drama, a melody, it is in order that I may be at the origin of a concrete existence. This existence interests me only to the degree that the bond of creation which I establish between it and me gives to me a particular right of ownership over it. It is not enough that a certain picture which I have in mind should exist; it is necessary as well that it exist *through* me. (Sartre 1986: 576)

Sartre is insisting that in the most general sense, humans make and fashion objects because they are interested in *having and possessing*. Bringing an object into being is a creative act that yields not only an object but a concrete opportunity to assert ownership. So the seemingly banal illocutionary act 'I made that' is at the same moment a covert

---

20 To concede to works of art qualities that humans lack is, in Freudian terms, to transform them, by means of projection, into *totems*. One could also surmise that should this be the case a certain ambivalence is due when creating totems out of works of art and the hagiographic transformation of artists into semi-human 'geniuses' who are touched by the divine and through whom history passes: these objects and persons have an esteem and a longevity that we can never experience. Lauding the masterpieces of the past is also a rather painful experience.

assertion of ownership – 'that is mine' – because it is 'of me'. The rather strained rhetoric surrounding paternity, the feeling that works of art are (or are analogous to) biological offspring, can be accounted for by this principle; except to say that the artist's being responsible for the coming into existence of a work does not occasion a genuine 'genetic' relationship between artist and work but is prefigured rather by a possessive claim, a 'genitive'. From this, Sartre completes the necessary step to the legal codification of this possessive claim: 'although society confers in fact the right to possess according to certain rules, it does not follow that it creates the relation of appropriation. At the very most it makes it legal.' (Sartre 1986: 586)

Regarding point (ii), Sartre continues: 'But in another sense it [the object] must be radically distinct from myself – in order that it may be *mine* but not *me*. … hence it must of necessity exist also in itself, must perpetually renew its existence *by itself*.' (Sartre 1986: 576) So the work, while it 'carries indefinitely my "mark"; that is, it is for an indefinite period "my" thought', it must also be 'out there' in the environment so that it can be added to my life world. Thus 'people who like to surround themselves with everyday objects which they themselves have made, are enjoying subtleties of appropriation.' (ibid., 577).

The implication of Sartre's insight here is that the rights of paternity and integrity are not subsequent on there having been a 'creative act' (whatever that might be) which of itself effects a (mysterious) bond between author and work; rather, the 'mystery' of creativity and the metaphysical notion of artists 'injecting their spirit' into their work is explained by the *desire* for a lasting appropriative bond with a yet-to-be-made object being coextensive with the actual making. It is a mistake to suppose that this bond is actually, materially, established by virtue of a specific deed on the part of an artist; it is instead merely an instance of a human struggle to be-in-the-world through appropriation. Furthermore, there seem to be enormous benefits in establishing a relationship with an object which might enjoy extraordinary privileges and longevity.

The double relation mentioned in proposition (ii) complicates matters because as an object in-itself, others are able to lay claim to it and make it *theirs* (as the Chapmans managed with the Goya prints). But this desired possessive relation can only be *effected* through use, through making or re-making. The music of J.S. Bach is Bach's; until, that is, someone of the stature of Glenn Gould begins to play it, at which point Bach becomes *Gould's* Bach. For it would be hard to argue that faithfully executing the instructions in a score amounts to really making music. Authoritative interpretation might entail an appropriative seizure of the composer's music by the performers. Without such a move the music might never stop being the property of the composer; it is not, to coin a hackneyed journalistic metaphor, lifted 'off the page'.

Contra Adler, the mass-produced consumer object is the anomaly here, not the true measure of what it means to possess: for mass-produced objects are presented anonymously, there is no authorial-possessive claim to break or interfere with, and certainly there is no kind of claim that cannot be broken by a simple monetary exchange. The consumer, in order to effect possession, *does nothing* but part with their money. However, to *enjoy* possession in its fullest, the consumer can occupy themselves with maintenance via auxiliary activities: cleaning, tuning, upgrading, personalising, recharging, etc. One could establish possessive relationships with old vinyl records – along with the music they mediated – because they needed to be cleaned, managed and kept scratch free. The same obviously cannot be said of music stored in digital formats.

4. THE ARTISANAL THESIS

We have reached a point in the argument when we can say with confidence that the rights of integrity and paternity are the legal expressions of what are very deeply held desires: the constancy of the thing-in-itself, maximised in the durability of the artwork, is experienced and valued – albeit ambivalently – in contradistinction to human finitude. Auteurs begin a creative process with the desire to possess, to create for themselves the position of *having-made* an object and therefore have a unique right to claim it for themselves (and, to an extent, *as* themselves). From the consumerist-contractual perspective developed in section 1, it would be uncontroversial for the cultural consumer to uphold the auteur model and moral right because they too want to possess: the art collector wants to possess not just a picture but a *Damien Hirst*; the music lover loves the music of *Wagner*, and in loving will manifest all the ruses of appropriation.[21]

It would seem difficult, if not impossible, to undermine the auteur model since this would require reorganising the entirety of consumer culture, not to mention the transformation of this apparently fundamental structure of human existence. But such is not the case, for a subtle shift to the *plural* changes everything: for it is possible, in the manner of a language game, to substitute *mine* for *ours*, and *responsibility* for *co-responsibility*, and what transpires is a model of artistic production in

---

[21] Oaths of love are also hymns to the logic of permanence and possession: 'I am yours forever!'

which the artist is not and cannot be the *sole cause of the work*. And if the artist is not the sole cause of the work, then the property claim is significantly weakened. It becomes impossible at this point to assert the artist as the singular origin of the work.[22]

To show this I will reread one of Sartre's examples of makerly appropriation. He writes simply: 'I cut a cane from a branch of a tree (I *do*[23] a cane out of a branch) in order to *have* this cane.' (Sartre 1986: 576). This seems an acceptable picture of how canes are 'authored' and why their authors come to possess them. But Sartre has *radically underestimated* – even misrepresented – what is entailed in the making of this simple object. To fashion a genuinely serviceable cane from a natural resource, a huge number of factors come into play. One can ask: from whose tree is Sartre cutting this branch? Who planted it? Who tended it? Who owns the land where the tree is growing? What did he use to cut the tree? A saw? Then who invented the saw? Who made the saw? Who sharpened it? Who cut and fashioned the wood to make the handle of the saw? When did Sartre learn to cut wood so accurately? How and when did Sartre develop the art of identifying suitable branches to cut for canes? What does he know about suitable types of wood? Will the wood be dried? Will it be straightened? How will this be done? Will he need to fit a ferrule and a handle? Will it be sanded and polished? What tools will he use? What design will he follow? What kinds of use will it be put to? Will it have aesthetic qualities: rusticity, robustness, elegance? To call oneself a maker of walking canes is have acquired these skills, to have this knowledge, to have access to tools and techniques. A skilled maker, an artisan, is in the *debt* of all those agencies that are behind the making of tools, to the models and techniques derived from the great stick makers of the past, to the opportunities he was granted to learn his trade, to the needs and tastes of his market, and so forth.

This intuitive picture can be formalised. Martin Heidegger, drawing on Aristotle – or rather the Scholastics' appropriation of Aristotle – refers to the 'four causes': the *causa materialis* (the material from which objects are made); the *causa formalis* (the forms and patterns which objects assume or are modelled upon); the *causa finalis* (the manner in which an object will be deployed, the reason that it was made); and the *causa efficiens* (the forces that bring about the making of the object, generally speaking, the artist). (See Heidegger 1993: 313–14.) So the maker of a

---

22 Barthes's conjunction 'Author-God' is as much about depicting the author's singularity as her power.

23 Note that in French the verb *faire* means both to do and to make.

cane is, according to the classical model, only one amongst three other 'causes'. In this context, the maker can assert 'that cane is mine', but will also have to admit that the wood from which the cane is made wasn't of his making, the basic design was common property, and the use to which it will be put (to aid walking) was not his idea, his 'intellectual property'. And, given that every tool (saw, sandpaper) that the maker takes up and uses will itself also have 'four causes', the artisan's art is caught up in a vast network of other dependent causes.

The property claim can still be made, however, because the singular, effective, contribution of the artisan appears decisive: it is only by his will and energy, and his *métier*, that the object comes into being. In Heidegger's view, this is because the Latin understanding of the verb to cause as a 'bringing about and effecting' (Heidegger 1993: 314) skews our thinking and interpretation and, conveniently, allows it to harmonise with modern mechanistic thinking. But in a typical move, Heidegger attempts to recover a far more nuanced understanding of the original Greek word *aition* that the Latin *causa* translates. *Aition* carries the additional senses of indebtedness and responsibility: and debt and responsibility imply a reciprocal structure, a bi-directionality. An example will help here. According to one logic, the pianist, by striking the keys, will cause the hammers to strike the strings and produce sound. The pianist intends the sound, performs the technical work, and appears to be at the causal origin of the sound. Perhaps a cause resides deeper still in the pianist, in her feelings, her soul? In any case, the pianist seems to be the author of the sound. But according to the second Heideggerian interpretation, the pianist is at the same moment in the debt of the instrument, the instrument maker, the piano tuner, the acoustics of the room, the historical development of equal temperament, the institution of the concert recital, and so forth, for these factors are also in part responsible for what we are hearing. The pianist is *grateful* to all these causes. 'Cause', if we still wish to use this word, passes in more one than one direction: for it is possible to insist, for example, that the existence of pianos and piano music causes people to want to practise and perform, it causes institutions to be founded to train people to play this music to a high standard, it causes new professions and modes of life to come into being, new legal arrangements, new economies. Likewise, a significant cause of a new composition is not the composer but the commission; it makes perfect sense, therefore, if one wanted to understand at least part of the 'meaning' of a new composition, to seek an explanation in the practice of commissioning and the interests of the commissioning body. Composers clearly need commissions, and commissioning needs composers: together they are co-responsible and indebted to each other for the existence of new music. The individualism of the Romantic model that affronts so many cannot be sustained. As Henry Staten put it: 'the *techne*[24] that empowers the individual is itself a socially accumulated and instituted knowledge.' (Staten 2012: 54).

It is interesting to note that T.W. Adorno, whose aesthetic theories are self-declared as radically opposed to Heidegger's, also develops a picture of aesthetic production which limits the role played by the artist. Adorno's materialist aesthetics valorises, as it were, the *causa materialis* over the *causa efficiens*:

> The act carried out by the artist is minimal, that of mediating between the problem that confronts him and is already determined, and the solution, which is itself similarly lodged in the material as a potential. If the tool has been called the extension of an arm, the artist could be called the extension of a tool, a tool for the transition from potentiality to actuality. (Adorno 1997: 166).

He suggests that musical materials and the task of forming them into works throws up inherent 'problems' – albeit problems which are less definite than those of, say, mathematics – and it is the minimal task of composers to actualise the solution that is latent in the material that confronts them.[25] According to this theory, composed music is *caused* by the identification and resolution of problems in the forms and materials bequeathed by history and by the ensemble of means and methods (*techne*) at the composer's disposal, and decisively *not* by composers pouring out their souls and expressing feeling through the compliant medium of music. To my fifth and last point:

5. THE AUTEUR IS A RESTRICTED FORMULATION OF ARTISANSHIP

To complete the differentiation between the auteur and the artisan, it will be necessary to show that the artisan does not intend to form possessive relationships with made objects in the way that the auteur might. In fact,

---

[24] The Greek word *techne* is the origin of the English word technique and technology, but in Greek it also means art. It is often left untranslated to preserve its polysemy.

[25] It is indeed uncomfortable and risky for a confirmed Adornoian like myself to even dream of subsuming Adorno's complicated, progressive, dialectical thinking into ancient scholastic categories. That said, the concepts of actuality and potentiality are scholastic through and through.

the multiple indebtedness inherent in the Heideggerian model will not tolerate a jealous relationship to be set up between artisan and object. In that sense, possessiveness with respect to an object cannot begin. Additionally, it might be the case that for the artisan what takes priority is the development of their own skill, and the enhancing of their own productive power. The artisan enjoys the feeling of *possessing an ability*, of being able to say 'I can', or 'I have that ability', not just 'that thing is mine'. And the making of an object is the testing of that ability. Perhaps the object is satisfactory, perhaps not, but there must be more work, another attempt can be made, even at the same basic form, because without that continued exertion in the same direction, there is little chance of reasonably assessing the state and direction of development. What then is the status of the artisan's product? They are points on a continuum, samples of what can currently be done, not totems of perfection.[26] And if one more skilled should intervene and say, 'No, not like that, like *this*', and make a change which improves the object in some way, then who is to complain about the loss of integrity when the object has been made more itself?

It is possible to conclude that: *to behave proprietorially is an act of bad faith* since it would entail denying the contributions made to one's work by others: by materials and traditions, by expert teachers, and including, not least, one's good fortune.[27] This is enough to indict some behaviours associated with auteurialism. For instance, the striving for an 'individual voice' in one's art, which, in the terms of my analysis, amounts to an attempt to reconstruct for oneself an opportunity to assert a property claim such as that which seems to be established by *other artists* over *their* work, will repress the social-historical origins and co-dependencies of materials and techniques, and results in an impoverishment of artistic opportunity: so much will seem out of consideration because it cannot now be done.[28] Anxiety over individuality inclines us to

---

26 In high-modernism there is a certain mortification of resolve regarding the notion of steady practice, of artisanal application in the 'plane of the feasible', because both the rewards and the ambition seem too small. Samuel Beckett wrote: 'Yet I speak of an art turning from [the plane of the feasible] in disgust, weary of puny exploits, weary of pretending to be able, of being able, of doing a little better the same old thing, of going a little further along a dreary road.' (Beckett 1965: 103)

27 For a detailed analysis of how luck is an ineliminable component of moral choice (and artistic vocation), see Williams (1981: 20–39).

28 The anxiety over ownership penetrates the object itself and leads to an anxiety about intervention, borrowing and transformation of material. Sartre

deny the usefulness of following in practice the good example of others, and in making free and constructive use of the abundance of material that is actually available to us. By contrast, a bearing of *gratitude*, an active and reciprocal appreciation for what is given to us and what we give back, is entirely compatible with artisanship. Artisanship, which is grounded in concrete relationships and demonstrable abilities, also avoids the metaphysical intrigues of Romantic creation, which, I have argued, are disguised forms of appropriation. As Staten writes:

> The moving principle of *poiesis* is always in its *origin* that of the associated *techne*. Anyone afflicted with mysterianism about art is likely to feel that accounts of art as a historical growth and as a social practice are superficial, external to the essence of art, a flattening of the depth and richness of art into 'tradition,' 'convention,' 'mere rules,' or 'mere technique.' But there is nothing shallow or flat about *techne*; the shallowness is in our perception of it, a perception that has not grasped it in a social and historical perspective, as a millennial growth, and also as a phenomenon that is not essentially walled off, either conceptually or concretely, from the entire ensemble of *technai* that constitutes its culture of origin.' (Staten 2012: 61)

When a culture is apprehended in terms of its 'ensemble of *technai*' and not via the stockpile of its most valued objects, everything changes: we could value and preserve concrete human capabilities a little more, and the mystique of property considerably less.

BIBLIOGRAPHY

Adler, Amy M. (2009), 'Against Moral Rights', *California Law Review*, vol. 97, no. 1, pp. 263–300.

Adorno, Theodor W. (1997), *Aesthetic Theory* (ed. Gretel Adorno, Rolf Tiedemann, trans. Robert Hullot-Kentor), London: Athlone.

Barthes, Roland (1977), *Image, Music, Text* (ed. Stephen Heath), London: Fontana.

Beckett, Samuel and Duthuit, Georges (1965), *Proust. Three Dialogues*, London: John Calder.

Brook, Peter (1996), *The Empty Space*, New York: Simon & Schuster.

Danto, Arthur C. (1997), *After the End of Art: Contemporary Art and the Pale of History*, Princeton, NJ: Princeton UP.

---

writes: 'If I consider the object which I possess, I see that the quality of being possessed does not indicate a purely external denomination marking the object's external relation to me; on the contrary, this quality affects its very depths; it appears to me and it appears to others as marking a part of the object's being.' (Sartre 1986: 587).

Goldstein, Paul (1992), 'Copyright', *Law and Contemporary Problems*, vol. 55, no. 2, pp. 79–91.
Heidegger, Martin (1993), *Basic Writings* (ed. David Farrell Krell), London: Routledge.
Hume, David (1962), *A Treatise of Human Nature: Book 1*, London: Collins.
Kennedy, Maev (2010), 'Pride, Prejudice and Poor Punctuation', *The Guardian* (London, 23 October 2010) 7.
Rahmatian, Andreas (2011), *Copyright and Creativity*, Cheltenham, UK and Northampton, MA, USA: Edward Elgar.
Sartre, Jean-Paul (1986), *Being and Nothingness. An Essay on Phenomenological Ontology* (trans. and introduction by Hazel E. Barnes), London: Methuen & Co.
Staten, Henry (2012), 'The Origin of the Work of Art in Material Practice', *New Literary History*, vol. 43, no. 1, pp. 43–64.
Weitz, Morris (1956), 'The Role of Theory in Aesthetics', *The Journal of Aesthetics and Art Criticism*, vol. 15, no. 1, pp. 27–35.
Williams, Bernard (1981), *Moral Luck: Philosophical Papers, 1973–1980*, Cambridge: Cambridge UP.

4. The elements of music relevant for copyright protection

Andreas Rahmatian

1. MUSIC AS A LIVING ART: PERFORMANCE AND TEXT

The protection of music by copyright is a fascinating conglomerate of simplifying reconceptualisations, approximations and auxiliary measures that remodel the phenomenon of music in a way that renders it intelligible to the concepts of law. In truth, copyright law has no genuine understanding of the nature of music as an art form;[1] it attaches to certain aspects of music which it declares as normatively relevant and thus ascertains the building blocks of the legal protection system. Generally this method works satisfactorily, mainly because lawyers (and court decisions) frequently disregard the artistic phenomenon of music itself as a starting point for protection. They presuppose 'music' as a 'black box' and concentrate on, say, the score as a normatively relevant aspect for protection purposes. In most cases, however, their focus is on assignment and licensing rights in relation to specific musical works. In this way music is considered as an object of legal transactions, especially as an object of transferable property. This is a result of the translation process of music into legal categories. Here we look at the elements and stages of this process. We therefore have to start with some attempts at the definition and description of the phenomenon of music.

[1] See also Craig and Laroche (2014: 44–45).

1.1 Music and Time

Music is embellished time.[2] I maintain this aphoristic definition[3] and for present purposes I consider its inherent imprecisions as a virtue. One may render this definition more neutrally as 'music is fashioned time', but it is in the nature of music that this fashioning is *always* an enhancement (at least an intended one) of the time experience.[4] Music has no clearly discernable aim beyond that, and the idea of 'enhancement' is deliberately diffuse. Time, supplemented by music, obtains an aesthetic quality: it is 'aesthetic time'.[5] It is not directed at the existence and quality of a specific object or at a possible purpose.[6] For the present conceptual discussion it is irrelevant whether a given individual does or does not like a specific piece of music. There is no need either to go into aesthetic discussions in the tradition of the eighteenth and nineteenth centuries as to what 'beautiful' really means,[7] particularly with regard to music.[8] We will see later that aesthetic or artistic qualities are also irrelevant from a legal perspective. Both definitions assume, however, that the most fundamental constituent of music is *time*. This means that time is not just presupposed, but the art form of music must deal with the problem of time actively as part of making the art.[9] Music can be seen as a *temporal structure*, not as a structure in time: the structure unfolds in time; this is its very nature. Time is not the framework for what happens in it (structure in time). Music is rather intrinsically a time-bound process

---

2 Even where the element of 'embellishment' is deliberately removed, as in experiments with time frame by John Cage (for example his 4'33"), it still refers to that idea as a negation of it, and it is an inevitable emphasis of the element of time as the central constitutive factor.

3 First in Rahmatian (2005: 272).

4 From the perspective of a utilitarian or economist one could say: music is value-added time, but I refuse to accept this terminology. On the 'aesthetic experience' of music, see Coker (1972: 24–28).

5 Stambaugh (1964: 274). Whether this aesthetic quality is the primary aim (or an aim at all) of music in a given situation depends on the function of the specific piece of music (for dancing, worshipping, for example).

6 This argument is influenced by Kant's discussion on the arts in general in his *Critique of Judgment (Kritik der Urteilskraft)*, book 1 (Kant 1974: 129–34) [A24–32/B24–32].

7 Kristeller (1952: 17).

8 Scruton (1997: 369–79); Hanslick, *Vom Musikalisch Schönen* (1902: 72–83).

9 Adorno, *Über einige Relationen zwischen Musik und Malerei* (2003a: 628).

(temporal structure).[10] So music is a *process* as an aspect of time (dynamic), not an object or *product* within the framework of time (static), like a statue or an architectural work. Such objects are obviously also subjected to the influence of time (ageing etc.), but time here is framework, not constituting element. If we could stop time, there would be no music, but a statue would still be here, and even one image of a movement in a dance, although we would obviously not be able to perceive it and register the perception in our mind, as this would also require the flow of time.

Husserl's transcendental phenomenology[11] sees music as an example of the inner awareness of time. The event of a sound is superseded by the mental retention (memory) of the sound event that has just passed. So the present is extended beyond the physical event (the specific sound) by retention of the event in the immediate past and by pro-tention of the immediately expected event (the difference being that the retention corresponds to a fading of real experience, while the pro-tension relates to expectations that may or may not be fulfilled, and so does not directly correspond to real experience). According to Husserl perception operates in a fourfold sense: (a) the perception of, for instance, the whistle of a pipe; (b) the actual sound of the whistle as to its contents, especially duration and sound colour; (c) the present of the tone and the perception of the correlation of the tone with the tones of the immediate past; (d) the perception of the awareness of time in the present, for example the whistle tone appearing in the now. The immediate past is shadowed by the occurrence of the event in the present.[12] Although one can never listen to a piece of music as a whole at the same time as one can look at a painting as a whole,[13] one nevertheless perceives the whole piece of music as a complete entity because one recognises the sounds of a

---

[10] Stambaugh (1964: 266–67). See also Barron (2006: 39–40) quoting Herder and Humboldt on music as an art form that works 'in the sequence of time'.

[11] See Husserl, *Ideen zu einer reinen Phänomenologie* (2009: 6), for the definition of transcendental phenomenology as 'eidetic' science.

[12] Husserl, *Phänomenologie des inneren Zeitbewußtseins* (2000: 25–27, 63, 99, 101). On the reproduction of music heard at an earlier point in time, see Husserl (2000: 42–43).

[13] Because in case of a painting everything is at the same time, see Adorno, *Über einige Relationen zwischen Musik und Malerei* (2003a: 631). Even if one looks at a section of a musical score which comes closest to a depiction by an image a painting gives, the difference remains that a score reflects a visualised flow of time, while a (figurative) painting reflects a frozen visual scene, unless one considers the score as a graphic image, detached from its musical purpose.

melody in a correlation to one another. Only when the last sound fades away is the piece perceived as being in the past.[14]

1.2 Music and Space

The central role of time in music is obvious. However, there are spatial qualities, in that, first of all, music sounds in a space.[15] The sound expands in the air of a room, is subjected to acoustical refractions; there is a reverberation, an echo – all of which is central to the location of sounds and the musical experience of the listener and the musician alike. It appears here already that music means interaction between the sound and a listener,[16] being the musician himself or the member of an audience. But apart from the acoustical phenomena in the physical space there is also a psychological space.[17] The perception of movement requires listening in a space (physical) but sound itself almost always appears as being in motion (psychological) – as it really is physically (air waves). The frequency and the sound colour or timbre of a tone are also perceived in a notional 'space': high and bright tones higher up, low and dull tones lower down.[18] But that is culturally dependent. African peoples would refer to low sounds as 'big' sounds and call high sounds 'small' sounds.[19] This is nevertheless familiar to Western cultures: for example, in Prokofiev's *Peter and the Wolf* (1936) nobody would expect the big wolf being represented by the flute and the small bird by the lower registers of the French horn.

1.3 Music and Music Notation

The terms 'lower octaves' or 'higher octaves' also connote a certain spatiality, and in Western musical notation lower notes appear on the lower ledger lines of the stave. There is a notional (psychological) horizontal–spatial dimension in music, reinforced by the musical 'text', the characteristic pictorial music notation of Western music, as we know

---

14 Husserl, *Phänomenologie des inneren Zeitbewußtseins* (2000: 32).

15 Not according to Schopenhauer, *Die Welt als Wille und Vorstellung*, book 3, § 52 (2008: 352), for whom music is 'perceived solely and entirely in and through time, to the complete exclusion of the space.'

16 Cook (1992: 10).

17 Wellek (1963: 296–99).

18 Hornbostel (1986: 317).

19 Kubik (1988: 100). The example here is from Southwest Africa, but applies to numerous peoples in many parts of Africa.

it from the usual music scores. This has prompted some musicologists to claim that there is a musical space in its own right and without it our familiar musical notation would not be possible.[20] Be this as it may, but the converse does not apply: non-Western classical and popular music can and does exist perfectly well without a too complex notation system,[21] or indeed without any notation at all:[22] traditional African music, for example, passes on its musical traditions through 'oral notation', a form of phonetic patterns and symbols which the musicians associate with syllables, words and meanings in the respective languages.[23] Even Western classical music can perfectly well be taught through oral tradition, and in historically informed performance practices aspects of 'authentic' interpretation of early music, for example ornamentation, are indeed handed down orally to a significant extent, though fortified by academic research[24] (and imitation/'*imitatio*' is an important factor in that 'oral' tradition at least). Music notation is not constitutive of music or music performance. It may, however, be constitutive of the *composition* of certain types of music in Western classical music in certain epochs, such as polyphonic music,[25] especially in the Late Medieval, Renaissance and Baroque periods, where the notation was also part of musical expression beyond the performative component. One can hardly imagine the development of the motet and other polyphonic music without notation.[26] Classical teaching of musical composition requires the student to imagine the music to be composed without the aid of an instrument, so to develop the ability to compose music as an abstract idea first.[27] In copyright law the score has a significant importance irrespective of the style and type of music.

---

[20] Wellek (1963: 309).

[21] Such as in (Northern) Indian classical music, see Daniélou (1949: 49–57, 82–98).

[22] Nettl (1983: 65).

[23] Kubik (1988: 87–88).

[24] See, for example, Donington (1992: 236–66) on the trill and the mordent.

[25] Adorno, *Über einige Relationen zwischen Musik und Malerei* (2003a: 632).

[26] On the simultaneous nature of layers of the visual and aural texts of late-Medieval motes, see, for example, Bent (1997: 82–84).

[27] Impressively, A.B. Marx in his textbook on composition, *Die Lehre von der musikalischen Komposition*, vol. 1 (1868: 17). This presupposes the notion of an 'inner ear' that can 'hear' everything the notation shows.

1.4 Performance and 'Text'

Music is a living, performative art. It exists in, and through, performance. The score, if there is any, is not the music. We will see that copyright law also recognises that. Musical pieces are not only the work of their composers; it is the performance and the opportunity to listen to the performance that renders the piece into a musical work.[28] There is the presupposition that someone will hear the music (whether or not that happens in reality).[29] However, there are also other views: what the author has created is already the work of music.[30] In any case, the text of the score reflects the intention of the composer, but not conclusively, and 'intention' is a vague idea anyway.[31] This touches upon the equally vague notion of the 'musical work' and the question of the limits of an 'appropriate' or 'authentic' performance of the musical work.[32] With the beginning of the early Romantic period, the role of the performer of music was formulated, especially by the great novelist E.T.A. Hoffmann (1776–1822), who was also a notable composer: for Hoffmann the real performer lives in the work of the composer, which he has comprehended in the composer's spirit and which he seeks to perform in this way, thereby restraining his own personality.[33] In classical music that is still the prevalent opinion.[34] Different types of performances are still performances of the same work, presentations of the same edifice from different viewpoints, as it were.[35] However, the particularly detailed and precise notation of modern scores of certain types of contemporary music

---

[28] Gadamer (2003: 110); Kivy (1995: 147): 'A performance (product) of a work simply *is* the work, or (if you are a Platonist in these matters) an instance of the work.' (emphasis original).

[29] Butt (2010: 6).

[30] Wiora (2000: 24).

[31] Dahlhaus, *Musiktheorie* (1988: 100); Kivy (1995: 146). Besides this 'intention' by the composer there is some kind of 'intentionality' in the production of the score and in the very symbols of the notation.

[32] Goehr (1989: 55–58); Kivy (2007: 93, 115). See also Chapter 1 by John Butt, and briefly below under section 3.

[33] Hoffmann, review of *Two Trios for Pianoforte by Beethoven op. 70* (1988: 147).

[34] For example Brendel (2001: 367–68), on the idea of 'Werktreue' and reading music, ibid. (2001: 30, 32). See also Goehr (1989: 55).

[35] Gadamer (2003: 118). A separate, but related, point is where a 'performance' departs so significantly from a 'right' representation that the new work is derivative, or a variation of the pre-existing work, but artistically sufficiently independent. See below under section 4.

(for example 'total serialism', in which every parameter of pitch, duration and expression is prescribed) can restrict the scope of interpretation extremely, so that the text or notation itself can be regarded as coming close to the realisation of the work.[36] The problem of the division between composition and its performance is also relevant to copyright law, since the musical work and its interpretation attach to two separate sets of rights.

The text of the score is certainly the starting point for any performance. But the score can only be seen as an incomplete and imperfect representation of the music, a building instruction for the performance.[37] Normative as the score is as the expression of the composer's intention, the symbols are only a limited aid to the reconstitution of the intended musical sound. During the reading the symbols have to be synthesised to an interpretation that translates the signs into sounds in the course of an inner hearing.[38] This is very dependent on the familiarity of the reader with the type of music, and its historical and cultural context.[39] So even a composer may not be able to read (silently) another composer's score if that other music is based on a completely different and unfamiliar conceptual structure.[40] The same applies to music in several parts or voices, even where the style is well known, because the players in the orchestra or a string quartet must synthesise the different parts to a musical whole in an intelligent interpretation process which involves much mutual listening of the players.[41] The listener is also part of the interpretation process, at least where she is the musician herself who reacts to the immediate auditory feedback.[42] Music always happens between produced sound and listening ear or mind, that is, psychologically and sociologically, between player and listener. One can distinguish three different types of listeners (and music catering for these three

36 Or, pointedly, it *is* the realisation already, according to Adorno, *Musik und Technik* (2003a: 233). Another example would be the fixation of 'tape music' in the late 1950s, which is fixed without even needing a score.

37 Rahmatian (2005: 273).

38 This is a process of understanding, both in the case of silent reading and of listening to performed music, see Gadamer (2003: 91).

39 Cook (1992: 122–28).

40 That was apparently the case with Gustav Mahler trying to make sense of Arnold Schoenberg's first string quartet which Schoenberg showed Mahler, see Cook (1992: 129), note 7.

41 This has already been remarked by Hoffmann, review of *Coriolan Ouverture by Beethoven op. 62* (1988: 102).

42 Cook (1992: 10–11, 127); Gadamer (2003: 110) with the example of chamber music.

types), the 'hearers', the 'intentional listeners', and the 'implied listeners', who create a specific self over the duration of the listening experience and map consciously the music in time.[43]

1.5 The Philosophers' Problem with the Temporary, Ineffable Nature of Music

Philosophers generally had problems with the intangible, fleeting, ephemeral quality of music. Several philosophers have developed ideas about music, few really competently (particularly Rousseau[44] and Adorno), and only in very few cases was music a central part of their philosophical system. The most prominent example of the last category was Schopenhauer. While for Schopenhauer the other arts objectify man's will (and in this way depict the appearances of the world in the form of ideas), music depicts man's will directly (not via the ideas): it is the immediate expression of man's will as a general language without concepts. Since music depicts the will, but not ideas, then it does not display a shadow, but the will itself in its very being. Hence the effect of music is infinitely stronger compared to the other arts.[45] From here it is not a great step to the interpretation of music as the most 'Romantic' art, something the Romantic writers had maintained slightly earlier, in particular Hoffmann, again, for whom music 'is the most romantic of all the arts – one almost wants to say: alone *purely* romantic. … Music opens up to man an unknown realm; a world which has nothing in common with the outer world of the senses …'.[46] Although Hoffmann's emphasis is different from Schopenhauer (who rejected the Romantic philosophers but was of course familiar with the Romantic theory of art), the consequence is similar. For Wackenroder, being full of romantic enthusiasm, no art except music is so full of heavenly spirit. But the musical material is at the same time organised and structured, a feature which unfortunately encourages educated men to doing arid and uninspiring analyses.[47] Hegel also emphasised the realisation of the Romantic

---

43 Butt (2010: 8–9).

44 Gülke (1989: 332, 344–5, 346, 360, 374) *et passim*.

45 Schopenhauer, *Die Welt als Wille und Vorstellung*, book 3, § 52 (2008: 339–41). See also Hamilton (2007: 76–78).

46 Hoffmann, review of *the Fifth Symphony by Beethoven op. 67* (1988: 23) (my translation from the German).

47 Wackenroder, *Das eigentümliche innere Wesen der Tonkunst* (2011: 124–25). Similar metaphysical romantic approach to music by Robert Schumann, *Schwärmbriefe* (1982: 61–65).

through music. By being more subjective than painting, music is the idealisation of the senses through the complete removal of anything spatial, so that the visual is made abstract and transformed to the aural and detached from the material.[48]

Wackenroder's and Hegel's struggle with music as the most romantic, non-visual, non-spatial and ineffable art, the epitome of the senses on the one hand, and on the other hand music as a most abstract and very disciplined, precise and organised systematic art, shows a common and characteristic tension in reflections about music. Leonardo Da Vinci disposed of the unsettling qualities of music as a non-spatial, non-visual, ephemeral time-bound art simply by postulating that 'painting excels and is superior in rank to music, because it does not perish immediately after its creation, as happens with unfortunate music'.[49] Others decided to say little about the nature of music, but concentrated on the craft of music composition, music making and the anthropological development of music. One of these was Rousseau, who was, as is little known outside the circle of music scholars, a theoretician of music and minor composer, besides his work as a political philosopher and *homme de lettres*. Rousseau also worked as a copyist of music scores throughout most of his life to supplement his income, perhaps the only real profession he had.[50] In his *Dictionnaire de musique* (1768) he discusses mainly the craft, science and terminology of music, and says next to nothing about the qualities of music as such. Only in his *Essay sur les origines des langues* (1781) does Rousseau go more into the elements of music, melody, harmony (and his aesthetic criticism of complex harmonies in the then modern music[51]), but he really concentrates on the evolution of music from sounds and human utterances. Music has a common origin with language and verse: '... cadence and sounds are born together with syllables ... verse, song, speech have a common origin.'[52]

The eighteenth century, in its fondness of the nascent natural sciences, would have found it attractive to remove the ineffable (later: 'Romantic') element by scientific examination of music and its rational foundation (something Rousseau doubted), but that proved difficult. Diderot spoke of musical sounds as being abstract words, so that every listener can make of them what corresponds to his sentiment in a given point in time.[53] The

---

48 Hegel, *Vorlesungen über die Ästhetik, Einteilung* (1986: 121).
49 Da Vinci (2001: 35).
50 Gülke (1989: 370).
51 Rousseau, *Essay on the Origin of Languages* (1997: 286).
52 Rousseau, *Essay on the Origin of Languages* (1997: 282).
53 Gülke (1989: 433).

aesthetic thinking of the Scottish Enlightenment had little to contribute to the understanding of music,[54] as too had Kant.[55] One may be tempted to think that this avoidance of a discussion of the essence of music is typical of the early modern period. But the nineteenth-century music theorist Adolf Bernhard Marx, author of a widely used textbook on the composition of music in the nineteenth century and influenced by the aesthetic thinking of Hoffmann and Hegel, also says at the beginning of his four-volume treatise that the student must not succumb to the arbitrary choices of a dilettante and to fashionable tastes but has to study thoroughly the works of the great masters, no matter whether they are currently modern or not; only that will educate him in the art and its aesthetics.[56] The emphasis on study and craftsmanship, instead of philosophical speculation, is noticeable. In short: whatever music is, let us do it well according to the rules of the craft, *lege artis*, then it will speak for itself and speak to us.

Music can be seen as a kind of language.[57] That much we can certainly say if we follow Walter Benjamin, who regarded every expression of human intellectual life as a kind of language; music is only one example.[58] But once we want to understand what the language of music tells us, we are quickly thrown back to the philosophical-aesthetic speculations outlined before.[59] Musicologists have nevertheless attempted to detect and develop a consistent musical equivalent of a vocabulary as in a language, so that music can be defined as a language of expression similar to words, and is not just to be understood metaphorically.[60] But even eminent composers were sceptical about that.[61] While music is a

---

54 See especially, Lord Kames (Henry Home), *Elements of Criticism, vol. 1* (1970: 166–70). Reference is made here to the facsimile edition of the first edition of 1762. Like Rousseau, Kames favoured melody over harmony. Kames's friend, Benjamin Franklin, criticised precisely the terseness of the discussion on music in Kames's *Elements*, see Franklin's letter to Lord Kames, London, 2 June 1765, Franklin, *Papers*, Vol. 12 (1968: 162).

55 Kant, *Kritik der Urteilskraft*, book 2, § 53 (Kant 1974: 269, 272–73) [A218–19, 222–23/B221, 225–26]. See Hamilton (2007: 70–72).

56 A.B. Marx, *Die Lehre von der musikalischen Komposition*, vol. 1 (1868: 13); Dahlhaus (1983: 34–35).

57 Craig and Laroche (2014: 47).

58 Benjamin, *Über Sprache überhaupt* (2007: 95).

59 Jankélévitch (2003: 11); Kivy (1991: 93); Coker (1972: 144–45).

60 That is what is argued particularly by Cooke (1973: 10–11) *et passim*.

61 Cooke (1973: 11, 15) on Stravinsky and Hindemith, although Cooke disagrees with them. Critical about music as a language in the usual sense is Hanslick, *Vom Musikalisch Schönen* (1902: 111–16).

language, it does not translate into ordinary language to reveal its meaning. That never stood up against drawing parallels between music and poetry and rhetoric in particular, also in regard to the teaching of the proper craft, especially during the time of the Baroque.[62]

1.6 The Lawyers' Problem with Time and Music

While some philosophical theories are able to incorporate time as a central and foundational element of their system, law finds it extremely difficult to recognise the phenomenon of time. Anyone who now retorts that there are limitation of action rules, regulations on perpetuities in trust law, term of protection provisions for intellectual property rights and the like, has not understood the problem. In such rules the law refers to time as an extraneous structure which a legal institution or relationship is subjected to: after a certain period of time an action to enforce a right can no longer be brought, or copyright expires and the work passes into the public domain. However, the object as it is created/recognised by the law is itself conceptualised as static, immutable. Such an 'object' is particularly property, which is the most relevant legal institution in the present context of music and its protection by copyright. For the law, time acts on the object, but is not part of its making. The object is like a statue that gradually decays over the years and will need restoration at some point. This is directly in conflict with the art form of music – music is above all time, as has been said before. Property law, and copyright law in particular, creates notional structures in time, but it cannot deal with a temporal structure, such as music. The way in which the law seeks to incorporate the purely time-bound phenomenon of music in a notionally timeless structure is to freeze specific aspects of music by declaring them as legally relevant elements of protection. In this way the law turns the flow of music into certain static X-ray-like shadows of the breathing musical body to which the protection system of the law is able to attach.[63]

This abstract discussion benefits from a concrete example as an illustration. When a piece of music is performed, one perceives a flow of sounds, one superseded by the other, but in correlation to one another in the listener's mind, and incessantly sustained by the notion of a living force which is, together with the sounds themselves, an instance of the

---

[62] For example Mattheson, *Der vollkommene Capellmeister*, §§ 8–11 (2011: 79). See also Knaus and Scholz (1988: 22–25) for the use of terms of rhetoric in the description of elements of musical compositions (motif, theme, melody etc.).

[63] See also Rahmatian (2005: 273, 281, 285).

inner awareness of time.[64] In contrast, copyright law splits apart performance and composition of the music. In relation to the composition the law freezes the compositional flow, itself a time-bound phenomenon, which runs through many stages and drafts, into one final version. In order to be a final version recognised by the law, this version must be recorded or fixed as a 'musical work' (being a technical term of copyright law) with boundaries separating the discrete work from the material of musical inventiveness (or 'intellectual commons'[65]) available to any composer. The requirement of recording or fixation, a characteristic feature of copyright law systems,[66] emphasises the removal of the variability of the piece under the influence of time:[67] notionally, time is taken out and the music is fixed as an immutable and precisely determinable musical object, the 'musical work'.[68] The performance of the musical composition is a separate act (and separately protected in law) which animates the musical work, but does not make it in law the object of copyright protection: the object of protection is already the written piece recorded in a score or recorded on a sound recording as a past musical event: time and the necessary volatility and imprecision which time entails have been removed. By way of this reconceptualisation of the law, the music can become a static 'musical work' and 'propertisation' (i.e. the turning of the music into an object of property[69]), or, from a socio-economic

64 See above the discussion of Husserl's concept of the phenomenology of the inner awareness of time, Husserl, *Phänomenologie des inneren Zeitbewußtseins* (2000: 25–27, 63, 99, 101).

65 See Rahmatian (2011: 111–13) for the specific meaning of the term 'intellectual commons' here: it denotes the reservoir of intellectual material and contribution of collective human creations (for the purpose of the law these are *ex nihilo* creations, because the term intellectual commons is as much a normative creation as its counterpart, intellectual property). I call 'intellectual commons' all intellectual material, whether protected by copyright or not, and 'public domain' intellectual material that is no longer, or has never been, in copyright. So 'public domain' is a subset of 'intellectual commons'.

66 For the UK, see Copyright, Designs and Patents Act 1988 (CDPA 1988), s. 3(2).

67 Similarly also Adorno, *Vers une musique informelle* (2003a: 516–17): 'The graphical-spatial system of signs locks the successive into simultaneity, into the static.'

68 In the UK, CDPA 1988, s. 3(1), partial definition of 'musical work'. See also Rahmatian (2009: 566–69) for the meaning of 'musical work' in law, and below under section 3.

69 A detailed discussion of the 'propertisation' process by copyright law is in Rahmatian (2011: 35–43). The word 'propertisation' is unappealing but is a useful shorthand reference for this conceptual process. Incidentally, the verb 'to

perspective, commodification can become possible.[70] The music, a temporal structure, is depicted, and at the same time replaced, by a 'musical work' in law, which is recognised as an object of property (musical copyright). That is not a temporal structure, but a structure in time: for example, copyright in the musical work in question expires seventy years after the end of the year of the composer's death[71] – being subject(ed) to time, but not an intrinsic part of it, unlike the living art of music in reality.

During the time period of protection the musical work is a static entity in the eyes of the law. It is interesting to note that microeconomic market analysis, which is the basis for the widespread law-and-economics approach to law, also eliminates the element of time and turns the continuum of market forces into artificially frozen and timeless event-points,[72] for example where supply and demand are supposed to meet in a market equilibrium[73] with no consideration of the time-related processes before and after. The omnipresent obsession in business with risk management (for example through the derivatives trade) in the structuring of financial investments[74] is, besides a certain narcissistic disposition of man,[75] ultimately the symptom of an inability to acknowledge the reality of time and the unpredictability of the future which the time-process necessitates. In this context, music appears as an unintentionally subversive art form.

---

property', though with the different meaning 'to appropriate', existed in the English language until the early seventeenth century, see the relevant entry in the Oxford English Dictionary.

[70] On the criticism of art as a commodity by Adorno (and Marx) in Hamilton (2007: 166–67).

[71] In the EU provided by the Term Directive, Directive 2005/116/EC (amended by Directive 2011/77/EU), Art 1(1), referring to Art 2(1) of the Berne Convention which includes musical works in the definition of 'literary and artistic works'.

[72] Hence for any Law-and-Economics analysis the Classical School of economics with its emphasis on long-term analysis (i.e. time) would be a better starting point than the Neo-classical School of economics which effectively eliminates the time factor, see Rahmatian (2013a: 225–26).

[73] For example Mankiw (2012: 77).

[74] See for example Hudson (2013: 24–27, 1175–76).

[75] This comprises especially the belief in the immortality of the *Ego* and the fear of death as not only a likely but a certain event, and, by extension, the fear of risk and the fear of loss of property/money as a narcissistic object-love; see the starting point of this analysis, Freud's article *On Narcissism* of 1914: Freud (1957: 91) *et passim*.

Where the composer produces several drafts during the composition process until she declares one of the versions as final, copyright law follows the time-bound creative process and postulates each draft as a copyright-protected musical work in its own right.[76] Thus the law creates (potentially infinite[77]) notional stills of a 'film', similar to the way in which mathematicians conceptualise motion through calculus.[78] So time and temporal structures, such as music, act in an 'analogous', continuous way, while the law, assuming discrete points, has a 'digital' approach of essentially durationless instants. This is reminiscent of the philosophical paradox in antiquity when the Presocratic philosopher Zeno claimed that a flying arrow is in fact at rest because (at least in Aristotle's controversial interpretation of Zeno's paradox[79]) a time period is the sum of indivisible moments with no temporal magnitude. The argument behind this is that, since anything that is occupying a space equal to its own size is at rest, the arrow is at rest in each single moment of flight.[80]

2. THE ARCHITECTURE AND BUILDING BLOCKS OF MUSIC

Ephemeral, ineffable and enigmatic as music may be, it nevertheless rests on the firm physical foundation of acoustics, and, in connection, mathematical principles of proportion.[81] The correlation between mathematical proportion and music – 'How sour sweet music is, when time is broke, and no proportion kept!'[82] – has a long history. The connection between music and proportion has existed at least since the Pythagorean School.[83] This *harmonia* (i.e. coherent or harmonious relationship) as a

---

76 *Sweeney v. Macmillan Publishers Ltd.* [2002] R.P.C. 651 at 666. See also Rahmatian (2005: 283).

77 *Potentially* infinite, because the normative border between one 'still' and the next one is determined by copyright-originality, also a normative term, see below, under section 4. To separate one 'still' from another, the new one must be sufficiently 'original' in the copyright sense, and thereby distinguishable.

78 Devlin (2000: 96, 100–101).

79 See Lear (1981: 93–98), discussing the probably erroneous interpretation of Zeno's argument by Aristotle.

80 Aristotle regards this premise as false, see Aristotle, *Physics*, book 6, ch. 8, at 239b.

81 See also Kant, *Kritik der Urteilskraft*, book 2, § 51 (Kant 1974: 263) [A210/B212–213].

82 Shakespeare, *Richard II*, Act 5, Scene 4.

83 Hamilton (2007: 19–24).

principle of order was also considered to be the basis of the movement of the heavenly bodies in a music of the spheres.[84] Two thousand years later, Kepler had the same Pythagorean conviction that the planets from the centre of their orbits follow a 'harmonious' mathematical law, which he sought to ascertain in his research:[85] in this context he discovered what is now called Kepler's third law of planetary motion.[86] Proportion is also the link between music and architecture,[87] and between music and painting.[88] The importance of mathematical proportion in music often leads to the inadequate characterisation that music and mathematics are necessarily connected or music is 'applied mathematics'. Not only musicians, but also mathematicians reject this popular belief,[89] but it is nevertheless true that proportion and patterns (and the recognition of these) are the elements which draw music and mathematics together.[90]

Acoustically the matter is straightforward: a plucked string will oscillate with its fundamental frequency and then gradually the wave nodes of the vibrating string develop: 1, 1/2, 1/3, 1/4 and so on (that is, the proportions of parts of the string of 1:2, 2:3, 3:4, 4:5 etc.), creating the harmonics in intervals of the octave, fifth, fourth, major third, major second and so on. So the major scale is literally 'natural',[91] since it is based on natural intervals (but the construction of the scale as such with their order and selection is obviously a cultural phenomenon). However, from then on everything is the product of craft, ingenuity and cultural tradition. We concentrate on Western classical music[92] when we ascertain the elements of music now.

---

84 Toulmin and Goodfield (1968: 79–81).

85 Kepler, *Harmonies of the World*, book 5 (2002: 652) *et seq*.

86 Kepler's third law of planetary motion means that the cubes of mean distances of the planets from the sun are proportional to the squares of their periods of revolution.

87 Padovan (1999: 215), with reference to Leonardo Da Vinci, and Padovan (1999: 267) in relation to early eighteenth-century architectural theory.

88 Da Vinci (2001: 37): '[M]usic, in its harmonic intervals, makes its suave melodies, which are composed from varied notes … the harmonic proportionality of painting is composed simultaneously from various components …'.

89 Gowers (2002: 130); Hanslick, *Vom Musikalisch Schönen* (1902: 107–10).

90 Root-Bernstein (2001: 63, 65); Vaughn (2000: 149).

91 Roederer (2008: 115–16) on the standing wave modes in a vibrating string. For wind instruments, see Roederer (2008: 135–37).

92 For the purpose of further discussion of copyright protection of music that will also give sufficient insight into Western jazz and pop music. The following discussion is, however, of limited relevance to non-Western music.

The elements of music are particularly: *tone* (pitch and timbre), *volume*, *rhythm*, *melody*, *harmony*, *counterpoint* and *form*. The latter five components depend on the specific type of the composition and the historical period of the music and do not necessarily appear in any one musical piece. What is called here 'elements' or 'components' is the subject-matter of music theory – here understood in the broad sense as the teaching of the appropriate craftsmanship of composition as well as the philosophical and scientific examination of music as an abstract structure. Modern music theory is usually defined more narrowly as dealing with the fashioning principles within musical realisation and comprehension.[93] However, the physical foundations of music, such as tone and timbre, and their perception are commonly examined separately in physics and psychology (acoustics and psychoacoustics).

Pitch and *timbre* are acoustical phenomena, pitch being the frequency of a sound (for example 440 Hertz, which is the tone A in today's standard), timbre (sound-colour) being the result of the specific mixture of harmonic components in a (complex) tone. This mixture of harmonics is different for the recorder when compared to the piano, the human voice or the violin, and these specific mixtures give each instrument its characteristic timbre. A computer spectrograph will depict a typical image of the spectrum of partials for each instrument. Or, within different ranges of a single instrument, diverse mixtures of harmonics may appear which are responsible for a different timbre in each range. A good example is the clarinet: the near-absence of the even harmonics (2, 4, 6 etc.) in the low register gives a hollow sound, while the presence of all harmonics in the upper register leads to a sharp sound.

What is called '*volume*' in music (indicated as '*piano*, *forte*' etc.) is a combination of acoustics (amplitude of the vibration), and the perception by the ear and processed by the brain (psychoacoustic phenomenon: intensity and loudness).[94]

---

[93] Music theory has been understood as being the philosophical examination of an abstract structure in Antiquity, the Middle Ages and the Renaissance (being *musica theorica* as opposed to the *musica practica*: composition manuals dealing with the craft of composing and music making), especially with regard to the connection between mathematical and musical proportion. As from the early nineteenth century, the theoretical-scientific or philosophical approach to music experienced a new upturn. See Dahlhaus, *Musiktheorie* (1988: 95–98).

[94] Roederer (2008: 93–99), and the curves of equal loudness according to Fletcher and Munson, at 98. See also the 'spatial' definition of volume by Coker (1972: 45): 'The *volume* of a chord refers not to its loudness … but rather to the measure of the chord's bulk or the musical space occupied by the pitches.'

Rhythm can be defined as the temporal relation of each note to another as against the background of an arrangement of strong and weak beats (metre) in the flow of measured time. Its constituting elements are measured time and tensions between accented or strong and non-accented or weak beats: this makes the rhythmic accents as projected against the metre, syncopation (a special form of rhythmic accent whereby the accent is shifted from a strong to a weak beat) and so on.[95] Rhythm is an organisational principle of sounds.[96] Some methods of musical analysis stress the nature of rhythm as a pattern.[97]

Melody is extraordinarily difficult to define. For present purposes it should suffice to say that melody is an organised sequence of sounds that are perceived as intrinsically connected. The smallest unit of a melody is (often) the motif.[98] In the melody, in particular, music reveals itself as a temporal structure and as a phenomenon of the inner awareness of fashioned time.[99]

In Western ('art') music the most complex building blocks or elements within music are often harmony and counterpoint (this is obviously entirely dependent on the musical culture, type of music and epoch). In this area, the difficult and sophisticated aspects of the craft of music had to be learned by generations of composers to fulfil the standards of the art of their time, and this tradition continues to give these topics a particular weight in music education and musical analysis. The '*musica practica*', the practical craft of music composition, has here strongly shaped the '*musica theoretica*'.[100] *Harmony* deals with the composition

---

95 In fact the matter is more complex, and a generally agreed definition of rhythm probably does not exist. See Hamilton (2007: 127–36) with definitions based on the history of philosophical thought. See further, for example, Cooke (1973: 36); Rahmatian (2005: 269) with a musical example and further references.

96 Scruton (1997: 22–23) with examples.

97 Cook (1994: 76–77) on Leonard Meyer's musical analysis method.

98 On the construction of melodies out of motifs or without motifs from a musical analyst's and composer's perspective, see for example De la Motte (1993: 29–44). A not very clear definition of 'melody', but influential, by A.B. Marx, *Die Lehre von der musikalischen Komposition*, vol. 1 (1868: 26, 28): 'a tonally and rhythmically organised line/series of sounds'. Overview of definitions of 'melody', 'motif', 'theme' etc. in the eighteenth and nineteenth centuries in Knaus and Scholz (1988: 17–19).

99 See also Scruton (1997: 41) with reference to Husserl, and discussion above under section 1.

100 Or *musica theorica*. For these terms and their meaning in the early 1500s, see also Nicolas Listenius (1549), quoted in Goehr (1992: 116).

of chords and their relation to one another, that is, the accepted or acoustically and aesthetically desirable progression of chords. These chords are at least triads; the typical musical examples in harmony are however in four parts (soprano/alto/tenor/bass) which correspond to the mixed chorus (as they developed in the seventeenth century). In harmony there are two viewpoints, that of a composer – how to compose in an artistically acceptable way – and that of an analyst or music theorist – how a given piece of music is harmonically structured. In practical reality, harmony consists largely of rules that guide us in which way one may achieve a musically satisfying harmonic progression, modulation (key change) and harmonisation of a melody. For instance, in 'classical' harmony octaves, parallel fifths and false relations[101] must normally be avoided.[102] Another more complex rule that is a typical example of the 'academic' treatment of harmony is the following one: if the bass part consists of a scale movement of 1–2–3 (for example c–d–e), it is to be harmonised with Ib–Vc–I (with a passing 6/4, the second inversion chord), or especially in a chorale in the style of Bach, with I–viib–Ib.[103] If Vc is used, the bass (being the 5th of the second inversion chord) must be doubled. Traditional harmony textbooks are full with such rules. It is not possible, and not necessary, to go into more detail in this context.[104]

While harmony regards music vertically, being the simultaneous combination of sounds, counterpoint looks at music horizontally as the separate parts in their melodic development. *Counterpoint* is the art of

---

[101] On parallel octaves and fifths, see for example De la Motte (2009: 23) with a critical discussion of the usual justifications. See also nineteenth-century discussion by A.B. Marx (1868: 84, 86, 530, 534–35). A false relation is especially the situation that, for example, d appears in the bass part and d sharp in the alto part at the same time (or for some time at the same time), and so creates an augmented prime (so-called chromatic false relation). Such rules depend very much on the musical era one looks at. False relations have always been used as an expressive device. A good overview of false relations ('*Querstand*') is found in A.B. Marx (1868: 499–506).

[102] One sees in such examples the cultural context of these rules, which are often also (rather arbitrarily) extracted from a particular epoch in Western history of music, for example the era of J.S. Bach. In modern popular music, for example, this rule has little relevance.

[103] I = tonic (first degree of the scale), root position of the chord (for example c–e–g), Ib = tonic, first inversion (e–g–c), Ic = tonic, second inversion (g–c–e), V = dominant (g–b–d) (fifth). I = major chord, i = minor chord, etc.

[104] Slightly more discussion in Rahmatian (2005: 269–70). Books on harmony cannot be replaced by single examples and superficial paraphrasing in any case. For a concise description of harmony also for the non-musician, see for example Karolyi (1987: 60–84).

setting one or more melodically and rhythmically independent parts (counterpoints) to a given melody (subject), whereby (in classical music) the rules of harmony have to be observed at the same time. Hence progressions of chords in harmony already have an intrinsic movement of the parts: two or more parts move (1) in the same direction (similar motion, *motus rectus*); (2) in different directions (contrary motion, *motus contrarius*); (3) one part moves up or down and the other does neither but stays (oblique motion, *motus obliquus*). In counterpoint, emphasis is on the line of each part, its horizontal melodic aspect and the melodic and rhythmical independence of the different parts, not on the harmonic combination of the sounds, which is (from this perspective) incidental.[105] Fugues are a prominent example of this technique. Different musical epochs had different rules of counterpoint,[106] but generally the most influential exposition of the rules of counterpoint is by the Austrian Baroque composer Johann Joseph Fux (1660–1741) who distinguished five prototypes ('species') of counterpoint: (1) note against note; (2) two notes against one; (3) four notes against one; (4) two half notes/minims against a whole note/semibreve in form of a ligature (tie) or syncopation; (5) a combination of all species (*contrapunctus floridus*).[107] Historically, the relevance of Fux's counterpoint textbook *Gradus ad Parnassum* is beyond doubt; indeed Haydn and Beethoven learned counterpoint with it. Whether it is pedagogically still satisfactory today is less clear.[108] Composition in technical counterpoint ceased before the end of the eighteenth century, except in church music, where it lasted much longer. However, modern classical composers are very familiar with this technique and use or allude to it.[109] Pop music is more conservative in the use of harmony and counterpoint: whenever a harmonisation of a melody uses a contrary motion (and it typically does), that is a vestige of the old counterpoint. Again, this little outline must suffice here.[110]

---

[105] The harmonic aspect of the counterpoint becomes, however, particularly important in the Bach era, see De la Motte (2010: 221–22).

[106] De la Motte (2010: 8).

[107] Fux (1971: 27, 41, 50, 55, 64). Fux's textbook was intended to teach the craft of musical composition, not analytical music theory, see Cook (1994: 25).

[108] De la Motte (2010: 11).

[109] For example Whittall (2003: 133–34) (on Hans Werner Henze's *Requiem*). See also Adorno, *Die Funktion des Kontrapunkts in der neuen Musik* (2003a: 145).

[110] Slightly more discussion of counterpoint (for copyright analysis) with an example in Rahmatian (2005: 270–71). Harmony and counterpoint can be the basis of large-scale analysis of whole musical pieces in some analytical techniques, such as the Schenkerian analysis method, see Cook (1994: 36). In

What is 'acceptable' and what are established rules of harmony and counterpoint are aesthetic questions, by no means answered concordantly in various textbooks, and in any case dependent on the historical basis from which examples of exercises of harmony and counterpoint are drawn.[111] Both subjects are usually still taught in a somewhat ahistorical way, thus historically frozen sometime in the Baroque and classical traditions of Western art music of around 1680–1820. In fact, the rules of harmony and counterpoint changed over the different ages, and modern texts on harmony and counterpoint take account of that.[112] Harmony and counterpoint rules are distilled and sometimes dry ideal-typical musical grammar. These types exist in classical music (until about the beginning of the twentieth century) but are presented out of a larger musical context and rarely appear in simple purity in real musical pieces. They are nevertheless an indispensable exercise for analysis and compositional craftsmanship, but for the creative composer especially these are rules he/she has to master in order to be able to break them most effectively in the actual creative process. As will be shown, for the copyright lawyer the rules of harmony and counterpoint are a particularly important example of concepts, techniques and 'ideas'.[113]

Form is the last important element of music. It is also historically the latest, not because musical pieces did not correspond to certain forms (they did, but generally the forms were rather simple ones), but because it was only in the early nineteenth century that the interest in musical analysis and musical forms rose to a scientific level, partly under the influence of the aesthetics of Hegel and German Idealism. The composition teacher, analyst and aesthetician Adolf Bernhard Marx (1795–1866), following Hegel's path, was here of great importance through his textbooks on composition and music theory.[114] The subject of form in music discusses the organisation of whole musical pieces by using

---

Schenkerian analysis 'a composition is seen as the large-scale embellishment of a simple underlying harmonic progression … the same analytical principles that apply to cadences in strict counterpoint can be applied, *mutatis mutandis*, to the large-scale harmonic structures of complete pieces.'

111 See an instructive statistical example to show that the common rule that, first, in the case of root position and first inversion chords the root should be doubled, and in the second place that the fifth, but the third only sparingly, is incorrect for Bach and the Baroque era, De la Motte (2009: 43–44). Here it also becomes apparent that it depends from which composer, which era or which style (Italian, French, German) the rule of harmony in question has been distilled.

112 De la Motte (2009: 7–8); De la Motte (2010: 7).

113 See below under section 4.

114 Cook (1994: 12–13); Dahlhaus (1983: 45).

harmonic, melodic, rhythmic aspects to discover the overall architecture of a piece.[115] For example, there is the binary form, ternary form, and *da capo* form,[116] the sonata form,[117] the symphony, suite, dance (with many sub-categories), variation, the rondo form, concerto, toccata, canon, madrigal, mass, and so on.[118] The aspect of form is an essential starting point for musical analysis. Several types and schools of musical analysis exist.[119]

The elements or building blocks of music are important for an analysis of the protection of music by copyright because these elements are indicators as to what can be protected by copyright in a work of music, and what cannot. This is achieved especially by the so-called idea-expression dichotomy.[120]

3. THE IDEA OF THE 'MUSICAL WORK' IN THE THEORY AND HISTORY OF MUSIC AND ITS SPECIFIC MEANING IN COPYRIGHT LAW

3.1 The Theoretical-Historical Idea of the 'Musical Work'

According to Goehr, music philosophy distinguishes four analytical theories of the musical work. First, the Platonist view: musical works are universals constituted by structures of sounds and exist everlastingly, long before any compositional activity and long after they may have been forgotten. In an Aristotelian view, musical works exist as performances and score-copies. According to the nominalist view, works of music have no form of abstract existence; performances are only classified because they stand in appropriate relations to one another and to score-copies, and

---

[115] See for example Scruton (1997: 309–12).

[116] Knaus and Scholz (1988: 45–65).

[117] An example of a full analysis of pieces in sonata form in Cook (1994: 260) using some classical and early Romantic works.

[118] A.B. Marx, *Die Lehre von der musikalischen Komposition*, vol. 3 (1879: 1–13, and ix–xiv) distinguishes in particular between compositions for independent musical instruments and for vocal compositions, and within the former states as separate sub-species the piano etude, the piano fugue, the variation, the small rondo form, the large rondo form, the sonata form, and mixed forms, for example the sonata-like rondo, and within the latter category (vocal compositions) classifies into the recitativo, the lied (song), and choral compositions.

[119] Cook (1994: 27, 67, 116) on formal and psychological approaches to analysis, Schenkerian analysis and so on.

[120] See below under section 4.

this classification is only linguistic for the convenience of referring to certain classes of particulars. The fourth view is the idealist view of musical works (Croce, Collingwood): works are identified with ideas formed in the composer's mind and are then expressed in an objectified form through score-copies or performances which make the works accessible to the public. The work is, however, the musical idea itself, not its objectified expression.[121] Goehr then characterises the idea of the 'musical work' as a regulative concept, not as a constitutive one: it indicates normatively what should be done in a given artistic genre, not what the fabric of the practice is. The 'musical work' is also an open concept, that is, unbounded, mutable, receptive to continuity, and able to undergo alterations in its definition without losing its identity as new examples come to appear as standard. This is in contrast to closed concepts which refer to their own particular internal, formal, structural or purposeful coherence, for example in justice or property.[122]

From that Goehr proceeds to a controversial historical claim: the regulative concept 'musical work' emerged only around 1800; before that time composers did not really have the understanding of what we today call 'musical work' as a result of nineteenth-century Romantic aesthetics. Therefore Baroque composers like Bach did not intend to compose musical works, but were, and saw themselves as, craftsmen.[123] This view has been criticised by several authors. It has been said that Goehr's argument is based on an overstated idea that the concept of music as a fine art emerged under the duress of the Romantic cult of personality in the early nineteenth century. But one can see from the sources, without being in danger of an anachronistic reinterpretation, that Baroque composers like Bach or Fux considered their productions as autonomous works of art,[124] and the same can also be claimed for the seventeenth century and even earlier periods.[125] Critics also pointed out that the emergence of the idea of the 'work concept' around 1800 and its dominance from then onwards has to be sought not in the means of production or performance but in the way music was experienced by the audience.[126] In this debate the real question is probably (to revert to the

121 Goehr (1992: 14–19).

122 Goehr (1992: 93–94, 102–3).

123 Goehr (1992: 8, 111–15). See also critical discussion of Goehr's claim by Barron (2006: 41–42).

124 White (1997: 97, 101–2) with the examples of passages from Fux's *Gradus ad Parnassum*, and Bach's *Musical Offering*.

125 Butt (2005: 30).

126 Erauw (1998: 112).

four different analytical views of musical works outlined before) 'whether the interaction between ideas held about music and the various musical objects or events at hand *together* generated the various notions of the musical work'.[127]

This argument for a 'Romantic' shift of the understanding of the 'musical work' around 1800 is also relevant to copyright law, because the issue of the interpretation or emergence of the concept of the musical work is intertwined with the issue of authorship.[128] In the discourse on copyright history the argument of the emergence of the concept of the 'Romantic' author, which is claimed to have appeared sometime in the late eighteenth century and which is seemingly responsible for the shaping of the modern copyright laws and their authorship/ownership rules, is well known. Both the 'Romantic' author debate among copyright scholars, initiated mostly by Woodmansee and Jaszi,[129] and Goehr's interpretation of the historical development of the concept of the musical work have common ancestors, particularly Barthes's and Foucault's 'death of the author' idea,[130] although it must be stressed that neither Barthes and Foucault nor copyright scholars elaborating on Barthes's and Foucault's authorship concepts devote any discussion to music.[131] I have criticised elsewhere at length[132] the highly speculative and unsatisfactory critique of the concept of the 'Romantic author' in copyright scholarship that supposedly governs copyright law principles, and is allegedly responsible for a false understanding of authorship in the modern (Internet) world, and purportedly hinders the recognition of work collaborations by copyright law, so there is no need to repeat that discussion here. The real effect of the 'Romantic author' critique of a 'traditional' understanding of authorship is ultimately a rejection of any individual creativity and authorship, hence the individual artist (or group of collaborating artists) should not be able to claim copyright protection. This is precisely in line with the interests of large entertainment enterprises, which normally hold copyright ownership in an individual

---

127 Butt (2005: 38).

128 Butt (2005: 40, 47–48).

129 Especially in Woodmansee (1984: 425); Jaszi (1991: 455).

130 Barthes (1979b: 145); Foucault (1991: 101).

131 Rahmatian (2011: 157). Barthes does, however, talk about music in *Musica Practica*, see Barthes (1979a: 149) – how illuminating that is, must be decided by the reader (an approach that would possibly obtain Barthes's agreement).

132 Rahmatian (2011: 149–82).

author's works anyway, either by way of assignment or through employee's copyright rules, particularly in the music industry.[133] In this way, a neo-liberal justification in the appearance of a sophisticated or even subversive critique has been provided, a typical feature of postmodernist theories.[134]

3.2 The Meaning of the 'Musical Work' in Copyright Law, and the Relevance of 'Recording'

Following Goehr's definition,[135] one could be tempted to say that the open concept of the 'musical work' in music theory is turned into a closed concept of 'musical work' by copyright law since the law transforms the musical work into an object of property. But matters are not quite that simple. In copyright law, a musical work is not conclusively defined, and it would probably have a sclerotic effect if it were. In UK law a 'musical work' is 'a work consisting of music', exclusive of words and dance ('action') intended to be sung, spoken or performed with the music.[136] That limitation only denotes that words and dance[137] are in categories different from 'musical work' (literary work, dramatic work), but does not define 'musical work' further, so this is also an 'open concept'. However, the 'category approach' of copyright systems requires the creation in question to fall into one of the provided legal categories (literary work, dramatic work, musical work, artistic work etc.) as a first prerequisite for protection.[138] Continental European authors' rights systems do not have a category approach; their list of work categories is open-ended, but here the differences between the two protection philosophies are in effect not very significant.[139] The legal meaning of 'musical work' probably comes closest to a nominalist view of

---

133 Rahmatian (2011: 177–80).

134 See, generally in relation to postmodernism, and particularly in relation to Foucault, Mandosio (2010: 70–74).

135 Goehr (1992: 93–94, 102–3).

136 CDPA 1988, s. 3(1).

137 Dance is covered superficially only in the legal literature on copyright. This may be the case because the dance community is rather reluctant about asserting rights, and there is as yet no case law on dance, see Waelde, Whatley and Pavis (2014: 218, 224).

138 CDPA 1988, ss. 1(1) and (2), 3(1). Time will tell whether this remains the case, see a qualifying statement in relation to the UK category approach in *SAS Institute v. World Programming* [2013] EWHC 69, para. 27. See also Chapter 2 by Charlotte Waelde.

139 Rahmatian (2011: 53) with further references to French and German law.

the 'musical work' in music theory, with elements of an idealist understanding.[140]

A musical work in copyright law does not coincide with a work of music in music theory.[141] An illustrative case on this point was *Sawkins v. Hyperion*.[142] The musicologist Sawkins prepared a performing edition of some works of the French Baroque composer Michel-Richard de Lalande (1657–1726). He gathered surviving manuscripts and prints scattered in various libraries world-wide, selected the most appropriate version, and produced a score and a series of parts which would make the works (*grand motets*) playable. He also inserted or re-composed missing material, added transcriptions and a figuring to the bass line or a figured bass altogether, all in all 3,000 editorial interventions.[143] The defendant, a record company which refused to pay Sawkins a royalty or performance fee and was subsequently sued for copyright infringement, claimed, among other things, that Sawkins's editorial interventions did not form part of the music and so he did not create an original musical work which would warrant copyright protection (Lalande's music itself was undisputedly in the public domain).[144] Leaving aside the separate issue of originality in copyright for now,[145] the question was whether the restoration by the musicologist to make Lalande's works of Baroque music performable again amounts to a 'musical work' in the sense of copyright. It does, in the opinion of both the High Court[146] and the Court of Appeal,[147] which shows that the legal/normative category of musical work does not correspond entirely to what composers, musicians and listeners would normally regard as 'music'; for them this would be Lalande's music, restored.[148] In fact, Sawkins attempted to *not* give the impression that he did anything which was not in the spirit of Lalande's work, since a restorer must subject his own artistic intentions to those of

140 See Goehr (1992: 14–19, 93–94, 102–3) and above on this point.

141 See also on this point, Barron (2006: 43–45).

142 *Sawkins v. Hyperion Records Ltd.* [2005] EWCA Civ 565, [2005] RPC 32 (Court of Appeal); [2004] EWHC 1530 (Ch), 2005 RPC 4 (High Court).

143 An extended discussion of this case by Rahmatian (2009: 560–91) that also takes account of the far more detailed facts.

144 *Sawkins v. Hyperion Records Ltd.* [2005] EWCA Civ 565, paras. 24, 42.

145 See below under section 4.

146 *Sawkins v. Hyperion Records Ltd.* [2004] EWHC 1530 (Ch), paras. 54, 58.

147 *Sawkins v. Hyperion Records Ltd.* [2005] EWCA Civ 565, paras. 36, 43, 45, 49–40.

148 Rahmatian (2009: 566).

the artist whose work is to be restored.[149] So the restorative performing edition prepared by the musicologist is not new music independent from Lalande's (for example a variation of it or work inspired by it), which would be considered as a 'musical work' in music theory. When the case was decided, music circles were rather upset, probably because they wrongly assumed that this decision would draw public domain works back into copyright. However, the musical work for which Sawkins could claim copyright is only the narrow area, besides the music by Lalande, that constitutes his own editorial input.[150] Everybody is free to create his/her own performing edition on the basis of the existing manuscripts.[151] This highlights the normative/nominalist aspect of the concept of 'musical work' in copyright law.

However, there is also an idealist aspect to the legal concept of 'musical work'. Music is the sound, not the score for the purpose of copyright protection. Case law is unequivocal here: the impact on the ear is more important than the notes written down.[152] Infringement cannot be determined by a note-for-note comparison of the claimant's and the defendant's work; the notes are essential but not the sole determinants of what is heard.[153] Reproduction of a musical work only occurs (and infringement if a substantial part was reproduced) when the substance of

---

149 See also *Sawkins v. Hyperion Records Ltd.* [2005] EWCA Civ 565, paras. 80, 82 where the court likened Sawkins's work to that of a picture restorer.

150 In copyright law the theoretical rule is clear, and those who raised concerns (also lawyers) in relation to this decision did not seem to have had sufficient understanding of music and/or of UK copyright law. But it is obvious that the application of this principle can cause great problems, because restorations of something that is no longer there in the original, or restorations where there may be several options, are in reality difficult to separate from the original work (here Baroque music) that is in the public domain.

151 *Sawkins v. Hyperion Records Ltd.* [2005] EWCA Civ 565, para. 86: '... the sort of work done by Dr Sawkins should be encouraged. It saves others the time and trouble of re-creation of near-lost works, *but in no sense creates a monopoly in them.* If someone wants to use Dr Sawkins's short cut, they need his permission.' (emphasis added). See also Rahmatian (2009: 585–86, 590).

152 *Austin v. Columbia Graphophone Co* [1917–23] Macg. Cop. Cas. 398: In that case the defendants had deliberately harmonised the plaintiff's material in the same manner as the plaintiff had done, although they had not taken the actual notes used by the plaintiff. By using the plaintiff's methods of harmonisation they had imitated the plaintiff's work and captured the impression the plaintiff's work created and on which the commercial success was based. Hence there was infringement of copyright. This case was referred to approvingly in *Sawkins v. Hyperion Records Ltd.* [2004] EWHC 1530 (Ch), para. 57.

153 *Sawkins v. Hyperion Records Ltd.* [2004] EWHC 1530 (Ch), para. 57.

the original copyright work is taken, not just when identity is achieved.[154] 'Music must be distinguished from the fact and form of its fixation as a record of a musical composition. … But the fixation in the written score or on a record is not in itself the music in which copyright subsists.'[155] Nevertheless, the copyright system of the UK requires fixation or recording of a musical work as a prerequisite of protection.[156] Continental European authors' rights countries do not have such a fixation requirement, so, for example, a piano improvisation is protected by the author's right even if not recorded at all. However, there may well be problems of evidence in an infringement action, so that in effect the situation may not be much different from the UK.[157] But the dualism – (1) the protected music is the perceived sounds, and (2) the score is the reified evidence of the composed musical work[158] – has features of an idealist interpretation of the 'musical work' in the philosophy of music. While the music may first exist as an idea, it must obtain objectified expression through a score or in a performance,[159] whereby the performance, being ephemeral, must itself be fixed, for example on a sound recording (which attracts copyright protection in its own right, separate from the recorded music). Imprecise and shadowy as the score is to depict the music as it is to be performed, the law uses this reification as a shorthand reference to the musical work to attach copyright protection and to turn it into a 'definite' and duration-less property object.

Copyright law was not always so sure about this. In an old case[160] the idea that music is the sound, not the score, was taken to its logical conclusion. Music appeals to the ear, while a sheet of music appeals to the eye, hence the performance of the sheet music (in this case by means of a perforated piano roll[161]) was held not to be infringement of the

---

[154] *Francis Day & Hunter v. Bron* [1963] 1 Ch 587, at 611–612, also with reference to *Austin v. Columbia Graphophone Co* [1917–23] Macg. Cop. Cas. 398.

[155] *Sawkins v. Hyperion Records Ltd.* [2005] EWCA Civ 565, para. 53.

[156] CDPA 1988, s. 3(2).

[157] Rahmatian (2011: 54–55) with further references in relation to French and German law.

[158] Rahmatian (2009: 568).

[159] See Goehr (1992: 18).

[160] *Boosey v. Whight* [1900] 1 Ch 122 (CA).

[161] The piano roll was not considered as a reproduction of the notes in the sheet music, and was therefore held as not infringing copying of the music, *Boosey v. Whight* [1900] 1 Ch 122, at 124.

copyright in the music. Today this would unquestionably be copyright infringement.[162]

It follows from the present law about musical copyright that any change in the score, for example through an editorial intervention, which has an impact on the acoustical event of the performed music itself ('the totality of the sounds produced by the musicians'[163]), is potentially a candidate for copyright protection. There will indeed be copyright protection if that intervention or change is also considered as 'original' in the specific meaning of copyright law.[164] The criterion of originality in copyright law will be discussed now.

4. THE CONCEPTUALISATION OF 'ORIGINAL' MUSIC BY COPYRIGHT LAW AND ITS PROTECTABLE ELEMENTS

4.1 The Meaning of 'Originality' in Copyright in Relation to Works of Music

The requirements for copyright protection of music are that the creation must be a 'musical work', that the musical work must be recorded,[165] and that it must be 'original' in the meaning of copyright law.[166] The traditional British approach to originality was that the music must be the result of the author's *own* skill, labour, effort and judgement, expense and so on.[167] Effectively, the originality requirement acts as a protection for the author against a short-cut or free ride by somebody else, who has not exercised the author's skill and effort. So that person does not have the expenses and has not taken any commercial risk, yet still seeks to take over the author's product at a fraction of the cost. Originality in copyright law means 'not deriving from elsewhere, not being copied'; it does not

---

162 CDPA 1988, s. 17(2).

163 This is the expression used by the court in *Sawkins v. Hyperion Records Ltd.* [2005] EWCA Civ 565, para. 49.

164 That is what *Sawkins v. Hyperion Records Ltd.* [2005] EWCA Civ 565 decided with regard to scholarly editions of music, see especially para. 49. See also for more detail, Rahmatian (2009: 568–69).

165 For work and recording/fixation, see above under section 3.

166 CDPA 1988, s. 1(1) and (2).

167 The classical decisions are *University of London Press v. University Tutorial Press* [1916] 2 Ch 601, at 610, *Ladbroke (Football) Ltd. v. William Hill (Football) Ltd.* [1964] 1 WLR 273.

mean 'creative' or 'artistic'.[168] On this basis, Sawkins's editorial efforts were accepted as being 'original' for the purpose of copyright protection[169] in *Sawkins v. Hyperion*, still the latest principal English case on the subsistence of copyright in musical works. The court specifically pointed out that copyright protection prevents a competitor from making a short-cut.[170]

In the light of recent CJEU/ECJ judgments on the originality criteria in copyright,[171] the classical UK definition of originality may well have to be qualified – to what extent, however, remains controversial. According to some views, the CJEU decisions arguably have not changed substantially the originality principles in UK copyright law,[172] while others detect a sea change.[173] In any case, greater emphasis will have to be placed on 'judgement' and 'choice' when assessing originality in UK law to give effect to the CJEU requirements: the composer/author must apply his/her judgement to make selections and choices when he/she creates the work, and through these choices the author expresses original creative ability and thus stamps his/her personal touch on the work. That would reflect the originality test of 'own intellectual creation' in several EU Directives on aspects of copyright[174] in the interpretation of the CJEU.[175]

---

168 See Rahmatian (2011: 38–41, 52–56), discussing specifically the unfair competition aspect of UK copyright protection, and contrasting it with the authors' rights approach, which insists on a 'personal intellectual creation' or 'the work bearing the stamp of the author' for originality and protection.

169 And they were considered as 'musical works' in the first place, see discussion above under section 3.

170 *Sawkins v. Hyperion Records Ltd.* [2005] EWCA Civ 565, para. 86. See also Griffiths (2013: 774–75).

171 Especially the cases *Infopaq International v. Danske Dagblades Forening* [2009] ECDR 16 (Case C-5/08); *Bezpečnostní softwarová asociace v. Svaz softwarové ochrany v Ministerstvo kultury* [2011] FSR 18 (Case C-393/09); *Painer v. Standard Verlags GmbH, Axel Springer AG, Süddeutsche Zeitung GmbH, Spiegel-Verlag Rudolf Augstein GmbH & Co. KG, Verlag M. DuMont Schauberg Expedition der Kölnischen Zeitung GmbH & Co KG* [2012] ECDR 6 (Case C-145/10); *Football Dataco Ltd and others v. Yahoo! UK Ltd and others*, 1 March 2012 [2012] ECDR 10 (Case C-604/10).

172 See Rahmatian (2013b: 4) for a discussion of why the traditional originality criteria of UK copyright will effectively only need slight adjustment following recent CJEU cases.

173 For example Rosati (2013: 47), Griffiths (2013: 780–83).

174 Directive 96/9/EC (Database Directive), Art. 3(1); Directive 2009/24/EC (Software Directive), Art. 1(3); Directive 2001/29/EC (Information Society Directive), Art. 2(a) (reproduction right); Directive 2006/116/EC (Term Directive), Art. 6 and Recital 16.

Whether this 'new' test moves UK originality closer to the Continental European authors' rights concept of originality is however most doubtful,[176] and the decision of *Sawkins v. Hyperion* shows that. This case has been decided in England and in France on substantially the same facts,[177] and in both countries the courts gave the musicologist Sawkins copyright/authors' rights protection in relation to his performing edition. While the English court could rely on its classical 'skill and labour' originality doctrine, and the principle that copyright protection seeks to prevent making a short-cut,[178] the French court, delivering its judgment a few months earlier, stressed that originality is a relative concept and found no difficulty in attesting the restorer a personal contribution that amounts to genuine creative work. In this way the French court reconciled its decision with the theoretically different originality requirement in French authors' rights law. In French authors' rights law a work is original if it has the mark of intellectual contribution. The element of personal choice played a role in the assessment of the originality of the intellectual contribution,[179] here the preparation of a performing edition.

A composer going about the composing of music in a 'traditional' manner, that is, writing a score (probably irrespective of which kind of notation is used), or recording sound patterns in a broad sense, will almost always fulfil the originality requirement for copyright protection, whichever originality test is applied. However, the law struggles in situations of contributions and joint authorship, for example where different band members are involved. Here it shows that the law has

---

175 See particularly *Infopaq International v. Danske Dagblades Forening* [2009] ECDR 16 (Case C-5/08), para. 45; *Painer v. Standard Verlags GmbH and others* [2012] ECDR 6 (Case C-145/10), para. 94; *Football Dataco Ltd and others v. Yahoo! UK Ltd and others*, 1 March 2012, [2012] ECDR 10 (Case C-604/10), para. 38.

176 See Rahmatian (2013b: 21–22, 24–27).

177 *Sawkins v. Harmonia Mundi*, TGI Nanterre, 1re ch. 19 Janv. 2005: RIDA 1/2006, p. 391. See also, 'Case Comment: *Sawkins v. Harmonia Mundi*' (2006: 118–19).

178 *Sawkins v. Hyperion* [2005] EWCA Civ 565, paras. 36, 42, 86.

179 *Sawkins v. Harmonia Mundi*, n. 177 above, pp. 4–5: 'une œuvre de l'esprit doit porter la marque de l'apport intellectuel et personnel de l'auteur, peu important son degré d'originalité … [le demandeur] a dû procéder *à des choix artistiques personnels et arbitraires à partir de son interprétation personnelle des œuvres* … l'originalité étant relative, il importe peu que les apports soient disséminés …' (my emphasis).

difficulties with the fundamentally performative element in music.[180] The phenomenon of the composer-performer/improvising composer is evidently not a new one – Mozart and Beethoven were among the most celebrated composer-performers of their time.[181] In jazz and pop music one is frequently confronted with that issue today. The courts rightly distinguish between the composition and the performance,[182] in line with the copyright statute,[183] but it becomes a problem to decide when a performance departs so considerably from the composition that it can be regarded as a new, independent musical work. In pop music in particular, a fixed written score that conclusively notes down the composition is uncommon.[184] The typical court cases concern a musical contribution of one band member (a solo, a drum rhythm) which has an effect on the overall acoustic impression of the performed piece. One case said that a contribution must be 'to the creation of the musical works, not to the performance or interpretation of them' and must 'possess significant creative originality'[185] to be considered as original (and co-authorship/co-ownership be awarded with an entitlement to a share in the royalties). A joint author/co-composer needs to provide 'a significant creative input' that 'finds its way into the finished work.'[186] So the band member must qualify as a co-composer, not just as a co-performer, even if the composition is the result of improvisatory takes and versions of all performers through which the work is gradually shaped over a period of time. To arrive at a distinction, the improvisation must tip over into a mere performance, the improvisation must have stopped, the composition completed, and the acoustical rendering must have become merely

---

180 See on co-authorship/co-ownership in music the extensive discussion in Chapter 6 by Alison Firth. See also discussion above under section 1.

181 Obviously one has to distinguish between the composer-performer who composes first and then performs the composition himself, and the composer who composes by means of performance and improvisation. What Mozart really was (since he seemed to have composed everything in his head anyway) is not so easy to decide, but that was before the copyright era in the Habsburg countries.

182 *Hadley v. Kemp* [1999] EMLR 589. Case comment by Arnold (1999: 464); *Coffey v. Warner/Chappell Music* [2005] EWHC 449 (Ch). See also McDonagh (2012: 69–70).

183 Copyright protection of the composition (musical work): CDPA 1988, ss. 1(1)(a) and 3(1); performance (separate rights in performances by the performer, whether this is also the composer or not): CDPA 1988, s. 180(1)(a).

184 However, that was unusually the case in *Hadley v. Kemp* [1999] EMLR 589.

185 *Hadley v. Kemp* [1999] EMLR 589, 643–44, 648.

186 *Robin Ray v. Classic FM* [1998] FSR 622, 636.

performance of the musical work – an artificial categorisation. Here we have again the problem of the law with temporal structures, movements, developments.[187] But there are also problems with distinctions as to modality. Is the contribution of a drummer to songs of a pop group part of the musical work (so it may attract copyright protection in the form of co-authorship/co-ownership), or only performance? Or is it only the player of a melody instrument who would be able to qualify, or the singer? It may depend on each band who writes, or co-writes, the songs ('writing' is here understood as encompassing any process of creation), but a drummer can qualify in the view of the courts, at least 'a good drummer' can as he 'can significantly influence the whole composition'.[188] The drummer's contribution was here part of the composition as performed, not of the performance only.

The cases on joint authorship with regard to musical works display a certain anomaly. To qualify for a share in the copyright the claimant must show that he significantly participated in the creation of the musical composition pursuant to a common design,[189] and his contribution must also be 'original' in the copyright sense, whereby originality is here understood, exceptionally, as demonstrating some artistic ability or creativity.[190] However, neither in the copyright systems, nor in the authors' rights countries does 'originality' require artistic creativity,[191] and that also applies to the possibly new interpretation of originality by the CJEU: 'own intellectual creation' denotes 'choice', which enables a certain authorial individuality to be reflected in the work; artistic ability, or *artistic* creativity, is irrelevant.[192] Another example of a certain inclination towards artistic creativity in assessing originality in cases of jointly composed musical works is *Fisher v. Brooker*.[193] At issue was,

---

187 See above under section 1.

188 *Stuart v. Barrett* [1994] EMLR 448, at 460. In that case the court awarded the drummer a share in the copyright of the songs in question.

189 *Stuart v. Barrett* [1994] EMLR 448, at 460, following *Cala Homes (South) Ltd. v. Alfred McAlpine Homes East Ltd. (No. 1)* [1995] FSR 818.

190 *Hadley v. Kemp* [1999] EMLR 589, 643–44, 648, *Stuart v. Barrett* [1994] EMLR 448, at 460. Less specific in *Brighton v. Jones* [2005] FSR 288 (the case concerned a theatre play, a dramatic work).

191 See Rahmatian (2011: 54–58, 191–93) for a longer discussion of this complex issue in copyright law. The problem here is that now a proliferation of the use of the word 'creativity' exists well beyond the artistic sector, which makes clear distinctions difficult.

192 See discussion above under 4.1.

193 *Fisher v. Brooker* [2006] EWHC 3239 (Ch), [2007] FSR 12, at 255. The Court of Appeal decision of *Brooker v. Fisher* [2008] EWCA Civ 287, and the

among other things, the eight-bar organ solo played by the band member of Procol Harum, Matthew Fisher, on the Hammond organ at the beginning of the song 'A Whiter Shade of Pale' (1967). The defendant, Gary Brooker, claimed that Fisher's organ solo was only an arrangement of an earlier version of the song by the defendant for voice and piano. However, evidence showed that Mr Fisher was at most building upon 'ideas' used in the course of rehearsal, but was not copying Mr Brooker's piano version. The judge decided that the claimant's organ solo introduction was sufficiently different from what the defendant had composed earlier on the piano to qualify in law, 'and by a wide margin, as an original contribution to the work.' Fisher therefore shared the ownership of the musical copyright in the song as a joint author.[194] This case also indicates a bias towards 'artistic creativity' as a requirement to find for originality. Not only does the reference to an original contribution 'by a wide margin' suggest this, but also the judge's consideration as to whether the claimant was entitled to a share in the copyright if his only contribution to the work had been the organ accompaniment to the sung parts.[195] All that ushers in the question 'what is (good) art (or music)?', which is normally carefully avoided when the subsistence of copyright is ascertained,[196] and rightly so, because it is not the courts' business to decide that.

Incidentally, in *Fisher v. Brooker* it was not disputed that the eight-bar organ solo at issue was inspired by J.S. Bach's second movement of the Third Orchestral Suite in D major (BWV 1068, 'Air on the G String') and a second work by Bach, the cantata 'Wachet auf, ruft uns die Stimme' (BWV 140).[197] The claimant's piece was sufficiently independent from its models to attract protection in its own right, but the question of 'inspiration' touches on the problem of the idea–expression dichotomy.

House of Lords decision of *Fisher v. Brooker* [2009] UKHL 41, 1 WLR 1764, did not reverse or specifically discuss the points relevant here and are therefore disregarded.

194 *Fisher v. Brooker* [2007] FSR 12, paras. 40, 42. See McDonagh (2012: 64) for a case comment.

195 *Fisher v. Brooker* [2007] FSR 12, para. 41 (in this case the judge did not have to decide this point).

196 Barron (2002: 379–80, 387–88, 399), discussing the more complicated relationship between copyright and art.

197 *Fisher v. Brooker* [2007] FSR 12, para. 36.

4.2 The Concept of the 'Idea–Expression Dichotomy' in Copyright Law and its Application to Works of Music

The principle in copyright law is that ideas (concepts, methods, techniques) are not protected by copyright, while expressions (the application of ideas as they specifically manifest themselves in the concrete produced work) are.[198] This so-called rule of the idea–expression dichotomy is not uncontroversial.[199] However, despite its ambiguities it is a generally helpful rule for delineating and limiting the extent of the property protection copyright confers,[200] particularly with regard to music.[201] The 'elements' or 'building blocks' of music outlined above[202] are what lawyers would call 'ideas' in copyright law: rhythm, melody, harmony, counterpoint, form, methods of instrumentation in arrangements, and their rules and principles. The problem usually arises in copyright infringement cases of works of literature because of non-literal copying of a pre-existing work (a slavish copy obviously infringes and does not create any difficulties). It appears that notions of 'storylines', 'historical facts', 'central themes' as instances of non-protectable ideas are easier to grasp than non-protectable concepts of music.[203] This is also because with music the matter is more difficult: what is actually copied if the subject-matter of protection is supposed to be the sound, not the score?[204] If 'ideas', that is, building blocks of the craft of music, are taken – and that is entirely inevitable – then the result may well sound similar to the claimant's pre-existing works, and that points towards infringement. Whether there is sufficient similarity is usually ascertained on the basis

---

[198] TRIPs Agreement 1995, Art. 9(2), Directive 2009/24/EC (Software Directive), Art. 1(2), *Designers Guild v. Russell Williams* [2001] ECDR 123, para. 25, *Bezpečnostní softwarová asociace v. Svaz softwarové ochrany v Ministerstvo kultury* [2011] FSR 18 (Case C-393/09), para. 49 (reference to the 'merger doctrine').

[199] Masiyakurima (2007: 555–64).

[200] Rahmatian (2011: 131–35).

[201] A similar discussion, with different examples, can be found in Rahmatian (2005: 285–288), Rahmatian (2009: 574–77), Rahmatian (2011: 133–35).

[202] Above under section 2.

[203] Cases therefore tend to focus on the non-literal copying of literary/dramatic works: *Harman Pictures v. Osborne* [1967] 1 WLR 723, *Ravenscroft v. Herbert* [1980] RPC 193, and more recently, *Baigent v. The Random House Group* [2007] EWCA Civ 247, [2007] FSR 579, CA ('*Da Vinci Code*-case').

[204] *Francis Day & Hunter v. Bron* [1963] 1 Ch 587, at 608, quoting *Austin v. Columbia Graphophone Co* [1917–23] Macg. Cop. Cas. 398, at 409; *Sawkins v. Hyperion Records Ltd.* [2005] EWCA Civ 565, para. 53.

of whether an ordinary reasonably experienced listener may perceive it that way.[205] The test of ascertaining recognisably copied melodies can be deceptive; one major psychological problem is that once a melody is recognised, especially if it is a very familiar tune, the differences between the claimant's and defendant's works are soon perceived as immaterial, and infringement is found potentially too readily.[206] In court trials an assessment of the similarity of two musical works can look like this:[207]

> I have already referred to the fact that the six quavers which form the opening bar of 'Spanish Town' [the plaintiffs' musical work] are … a commonplace series to be found in other previous musical compositions. Our attention was drawn, for instance, to an Austrian dance tune composed in the early nineteenth century by Von Lichnowsky, the opening bar of which is identical with that of 'Spanish Town.' The same sequence of notes is also to be found in a song entitled 'Let Us Sing Merrily,' although in this case there is a difference of tempo. In these circumstances, the fact that 'Why' [the defendants' musical work] begins with an opening bar containing a similar, though not identical, phrase is of no special significance. By itself it would not be sufficient to warrant the inference that, if the phrase was copied, it was copied from the plaintiffs' work rather than some other composition. What is significant is the fact that both in 'Spanish Town' and 'Why' the opening phrase enunciated in the first bar is developed over the remainder of the first eight bars by the use of the same devices or tricks of composition, namely, repetition followed by a pause, followed again by further repetition with a slight variation. It is this circumstance which produces the degree of similarity between the two compositions.

This passage reveals three problem areas when a pre-existing work A containing *ideas* (for example a harmonic progression I–V–I) realised in the *expression* of a distinct melody may be copied and infringed by a work B:

(1) Work B shares the ideas with work A (for example the same harmonic progression), but not the expressions. In that case there is no infringement, but the example is also artificial. Ideas which do not manifest themselves in expressions are in reality impossible. Ideas are

---

205 *Francis Day & Hunter v. Bron* [1963] 1 Ch 587, at 610, 622. As to the reasonable listener standard in the USA, see *Baxter v. MCA* 812 F.2d 421, and critical comments by Keyes (2003–2004: 431–34).

206 Discussion of this problem in Craig and Laroche (2014: 61–65) with a model composition for illustration (with audio file at: http://www.iposgoode.ca/?attachment_id=21753), an invention/fugato-like piece containing melodies by Beethoven, Wagner, Britney Spears and Nirvana interwoven in the new piece.

207 *Francis Day & Hunter v. Bron* [1963] 1 Ch 587, at 615–16.

(abstract) elements of the musical grammar, for example, the harmonisation technique of a bass part 1–2–3 with Ib–Vc–I, types of cadences, a counterpoint part in the form of two notes against one in oblique or contrary motion,[208] figured bass,[209] accompaniment and tune formulae (also ornamentation formulae), rhythmic structures, structures of form (A–B–A form, variation, canon, dance), potentially (but with caution) standards in jazz[210] and so forth. Where a composer invents his own grammar or elements as part of a new composition technique, it could be viewed as expression, because the composer would be in the position of a 'writer who must provide specially vocabulary and syntax for each sentence he writes.'[211] But if that technique becomes a common standard over time (like 12-tone music, which re-used old composition methods anyway), it will probably be considered as an idea. All these 'ideas' in the copyright sense can only enter the acoustically perceivable material world if they assume some representation or reification which is a form of expression in itself, embodied in some kind of fixation.[212] In theory, if the expression merely renders the idea, and does not add anything at all to it, then this expression cannot attract protection.[213] So the chord f–a–c is only the idea 'F-major chord' rendered acoustically or in writing. But what is the situation with an extremely standard harmonic progression vi–ii–V–I? The concept (vi–ii–V–I) will be an unprotectable idea, but its realisation (and there are several possibilities to do that) potentially could be. Distinctiveness or idiosyncrasy in the application of this harmonic progression (especially in combination with rhythmic and melodic elements) tends towards copyright protection.[214]

So what aspect of the material infringes (*expression* taken from a pre-existing work which is also a substantial part of it) and what aspect is

---

208 See above under section 2.

209 Discussion of the figured bass in *Sawkins v. Hyperion Records Ltd.* [2004] EWHC 1530 (Ch), para. 15. See also Rahmatian (2009: 574).

210 Craig and Laroche (2014: 48) on borrowing (in jazz and generally) and the potential artificiality of the interpretation that copyright requires.

211 Instructive in Adorno, *Philosophie der Neuen Musik* (2003b: 101).

212 See also *Donoghue v. Allied Newspapers* [1938] 1 Ch 106, at 110.

213 This is the 'merger doctrine' (especially in the United States): if there is only one way of expressing an idea, no protection is given, because otherwise any protection of the expression would in fact give protection to the idea, see for example *Kregos v. Associated Press*, 937 F.2d 700, 705 (CA-NY, 2nd Cir. 1991). Now also at EU level in *Bezpečnostní softwarová asociace v. Svaz softwarové ochrany v Ministerstvo kultury* [2011] FSR 18 (Case C-393/09), para. 49.

214 *Francis Day & Hunter v. Bron* [1963] 1 Ch 587, at 616 (in the passage following from the quote above).

available to all (*idea*, such as concepts of harmonic progression in principle)? It is a legal/normative decision by the courts whether vi–ii–V–I really manifests only an 'idea' and does not (also) contain an expression: thus the 'idea' is not merely detected, it is *made*.[215] The 'idea' is conceptually a kind of Kantian thing-in-itself or *Ding an sich* that is incapable of being observed,[216] being an abstraction deduced (or reduced) from its physical manifestation/representation or 'expression'. Thus what we perceive is either a manifestation of the 'idea' (no protection) or a manifestation of an expression, based partly on the idea but something added to it (copyright protection).[217] Which is which, is ultimately decided by the court in the individual case. However, some guidance as to which elements constitute unprotectable ideas provides descriptions in music theory and analysis of a conceptual framework of a specific piece, for example:[218]

> The materials that mark the two thematic areas of [Beethoven's piano sonata] Op. 49/2 are not only similar texturally (that is obvious) but melodically too: Fig. 128 shows this. And there is also a rhythmic similarity between the upper parts of bars 3 and 27. On the other hand the two themes are distinct harmonically in that the A theme is quite discursive with its implied V^7 of IV, whereas the B theme hugs its tonic closely (everything is either a D major chord or resolves directly to one).

What is characteristic here is that this description is a 'reverse-engineered' abstraction of the expression for the purpose of research and analysis, but it is not the expression itself, because nobody would be able to perform the music on the basis of this description.[219] That non-reversibility indicates that the description does not denote the actual protectable expression but the underlying unprotectable idea or part of it.[220]

---

215 As Lord Hailsham put it in *L.B. Plastics v. Swish Products Ltd.* [1979] RPC 551, 629: 'it all depends on what you mean by "ideas"'.

216 Kant, *Prolegomena zu einer jeden künftigen Metaphysik* (*Prolegomena to any future Metaphysics*) § 13, note II (1995: 47).

217 See also *Designers Guild v. Russell Williams* [2001] ECDR 123, para. 25: '[E]very element in the expression of an artistic work … is the expression of an idea on the part of the author.' (per Lord Bingham).

218 Cook (1994: 266).

219 But one would be able to on the basis of the extract of the score in fig. 128 that has been mentioned.

220 See also Rahmatian (2011: 134–35), and Rahmatian (2005: 287) with different examples, including one from a letter by Mozart describing in words the

(2) Work B shares the ideas with work A, and takes over a part of the expressions of the work A. If that part is also a substantial part (or sufficient to make the individuality of the original author appear in the section taken), then there will be infringement. But, as the quotation above from *Francis Day & Hunter* shows, the more commonplace a phrase or melody is, although capable of being copyright-protected in principle, the more it tends to be shifted towards unprotectable ideas, or alternatively, the more it is regarded as a work not originating from the claimant but from somewhere else, typically with no definite pedigree. In either case infringement would be denied. In that connection the blunt nature of the instrument 'copyright' reveals itself particularly well: work B sharing a substantial part of expressions in work A indicates infringement, but not necessarily 'stealing' in a musical/aesthetic sense. The concepts of copyright cannot accommodate creative musical borrowing (whether or not transformative), as it always occurred in musical history and as it appears currently widely in music sampling, for example in hip hop music.[221]

(3) Work B shares the ideas with work A, and deliberately takes over a part of the expressions of work A as a basis for a new work, for example an arrangement (adaptation) of work A in the form of an orchestration or a variation work. The part taken over in work B is certainly a substantial part, and if there is no permission (licence) from the copyright owner of work A, then there will be infringement. However, work B is sufficiently independent and original (in the copyright sense) that it attracts copyright in its own right to the extent to which it does not infringe work A (in the same way as an unauthorised translation of a novel into another language). For example, if, by comparison with the original protected work, an arrangement exhibits a sufficient degree of originality, then it is capable of being a separate copyright work and obtains protection, and the degree of originality is no different from what is required to establish copyright in any other work.[222] Where work B was only inspired by work A, there is no infringement at all.[223] The separate nature (and copyright protection) of orchestral arrangements, for example, is not in doubt as

realisation in his composition of a dramatic scene in the *Abduction from the Seraglio*.

221 Arewa (2005–2006: 547, 550, 558, 579–86, 610–12, 615–18, 624–28, 630–34).

222 *Fisher v. Brooker* [2007] FSR 12, para. 44.

223 *Fisher v. Brooker* [2007] FSR 12, para. 36, leaving aside that J.S. Bach's music is not protected by copyright anyway.

such,[224] but what is simple adaptation and what is sufficiently independent work (or contribution) is a matter of fact and degree,[225] and is ultimately decided by the court in each individual case. We are also confronted here again with the issue as to when a musical performance of work A departs so significantly from the canon of acceptable performances that it could be regarded as an independent new work B,[226] being an adaptation or arrangement of work A, and therefore attracting copyright as a composition in its own right.[227]

5. COPYRIGHT TRANSFORMING THE WORK OF MUSIC INTO A 'MUSICAL WORK' AND PROPERTY RIGHT: DOES THAT REFLECT THE COMPOSERS' AND PERFORMERS' IDEA OF MUSIC?

Music is an entirely time-dependent process, a temporal structure; it reflects the inner awareness of time, is abstract and ephemeral, and naturally cannot be possessed and allocated. However, that is what the law in its property system, that is, its copyright system, seeks to do when it grants protection for 'music'. The law transforms the music into discernable and static entities, 'musical works', to which legal rights can attach, in some ways like a ladle having scooped water from a flowing brook to make the water controllable and capable of being owned. The emphasis on the notation, the writing or fixation as a prerequisite for copyright protection, underlines this, although the law acknowledges that the written notes are not the music; the music is the performed sound. The sound recording counteracts the fleeting nature of music today, far more than the classical written score could ever do:[228] music becomes an available object and is no longer a fashioned period of time only. The 'musical work' is a normative definition, overlapping, but not coinciding with, what musicians regard as music. This definition uses aspects of the

---

224 *Godfrey v. Lees* [1995] EMLR 307, *Beckingham v. Hodgens* [2002] EWHC 2143 (Ch), [2002] EMLR 45.

225 As one can see from the reasoning of *Fisher v. Brooker* [2007] FSR 12, paras. 41–42.

226 Compare the discussion in Chapter 3 by Martin Parker Dixon on the interpretation of J.S. Bach's music by Glenn Gould, turning Bach into '*Gould's* Bach'. With Gould's interpretation of Mozart's piano music this is definitely true, in various ways.

227 *Coffey v. Warner/Chappell Music* [2005] ECDR 21.

228 Ashby (2010: 28–33).

elements of music, such as melody, harmony, counterpoint, form, but not systematically, and these building blocks of music are designed to create music, not legal protection, so they are of limited use as a basis for establishing copyright protection. Copyright law also divides composition from performance and allocates different rights to either, although in reality one precipitates the other and they are often inseparable in the creative process, for example in improvisation. As a result, authorship and entitlement (copyright ownership, especially to found claims to royalties) become difficult to ascertain, particularly in the usual scenario of collaboration of several composers/performers or 'musicians'.[229]

The legal transformation of music into 'musical works' by copyright law and the factual transformation of music into recorded past musical performances by sound recordings are essential to the commodification and commercialisation of music.[230] Copyright reflects the composers' and performers' idea of music only very imperfectly. However, it is doubtful whether copyright law intends to reflect fully the nature of music and music performance in its protection mechanism for music. What it does, and it seems that this is the predominant concern, is to create a notional black box of property into which the art of music is squeezed to render it a controllable object of property that can be owned, defended against infringers, transferred against payment, and commodified in other ways, for example (increasingly) in the form of speculation. Therefore the law apparently does not need to have a too-sophisticated understanding of the object of protection, the music. Whether the art of music making suffers through this treatment is secondary because once the music is an object of property, a price can be put to it and a commercial value allocated which is essential to business and commercialisation. The copyright-protected musical work is then similar to a share in a company, not expressing the true quality of the enterprise and its products, but having a notional value, perceived or fixed by the market (for example the stock exchange) at a given time, and largely independent from any intrinsic and possibly non-pecuniary values of the company. So the black box of copyright property may not have to contain much 'art' or 'music' at all, and discussions about whether the quality of modern music of all styles is promoted or damaged by copyright and the music business can become redundant, because these aspects can be relegated to aesthetic quibbles of an irrelevant elite of artists and art critics. The cultural industries

229 See Chapter 6 by Alison Firth.
230 Rahmatian (2005: 274–75, 285, 288) with further references.

effectively have operated on this basis for a long time.[231] Even an empty shell is perceived as valuable, so long as it is alienable against money. Obviously, one cannot blame copyright for that: copyright is just a tool, used and shaped by human actors. Which task copyright is supposed to fulfil depends on them. If copyright is meant to be a commodification device for music, then it plays its role well. If copyright is understood as a gentle protective support for the unique art form of music and its creators, then it needs substantial retuning.

BIBLIOGRAPHY

Adorno, Theodor W. (2003a), *Musikalische Schriften I-III: Klangfiguren, Quasi una fantasia, Musikalische Schriften III* (Gesammelte Schriften Band 16), Frankfurt am Main: Suhrkamp.

Adorno, Theodor W. (2003b), *Philosophie der neuen Musik* (Gesammelte Schriften Band 12), Frankfurt am Main: Suhrkamp.

Arewa, Olufunmilayo B. (2005–2006), 'From J. C. Bach to Hip Hop: Musical Borrowing, Copyright and Cultural Context', 84 *North Carolina Law Review*, 547–645.

Arnold, Richard (1999), 'Are Performers Authors?', 21 *European Intellectual Property Review*, 464–69.

Ashby, Arved (2010), *Absolute Music, Mechanical Reproduction*, Berkeley and Los Angeles: University of California Press.

Barron, Anne (2002), 'Copyright Law and the Claims of Art', 4 *Intellectual Property Quarterly*, 368–401.

Barron, Anne (2006), 'Introduction: Harmony or Dissonance? Copyright Concepts and Musical Practice', 15(1) *Social & Legal Studies*, 25–51.

Barthes, Roland (1979a), 'Musica Practica', in Stephen Heath ed. and trans., *Image-Music-Text*, Glasgow: Fontana/Collins, pp. 149–54.

Barthes, Roland (1979b), 'The Death of the Author', in Stephen Heath ed. and trans., *Image-Music-Text*, Glasgow: Fontana/Collins, pp. 142–48.

Benjamin, Walter (2007), 'Über Sprache überhaupt und über die Sprache des Menschen', in Hartmut Böhme and Yvonne Ehrenspeck (eds), *Aura und Reflexion. Schriften zur Kunsttheorie*, Frankfurt am Main: Suhrkamp, pp. 95–110.

Bent, Margaret (1997), 'Polyphony of Texts and Music in the Fourteenth-Century Motet: *Tribum que non abhorruit/Quoniam secta latronum/Merito hec patimur* and Its "Quotations"', in Dolores Pesce (ed.), *Hearing the Motet. Essays on the Motet of the Middle Ages and Renaissance*, New York and Oxford: Oxford University Press, pp. 82–103.

Brendel, Alfred (2001), *On Music. Collected Essays*, London: Robson Books.

[231] A famous critic of this state of affairs was Adorno, as is well known. See for example, Horkheimer and Adorno, *Dialektik der Aufklärung* (1986: 118–29) (the section on the cultural industry – '*Kulturindustrie*' – is likely to have been written mostly by Adorno).

Butt, John (2005), 'The Seventeenth-century Musical Work', in Tim Carter and John Butt (eds), *The Cambridge History of Seventeenth-Century Music*, Cambridge: Cambridge University Press, pp. 27–54.

Butt, John (2010), 'Do Musical Works Contain an Implied Listener? Towards a Theory of Musical Listening', 135(1) *Journal of the Royal Musical Association*, 5–18.

Case Comment: *Sawkins v. Harmonia Mundi* (2006), 37 *International Review of Intellectual Property and Competition Law*, 116–22 [no author].

Coker, Wilson (1972), *Music and Meaning. A Theoretical Introduction to Musical Analysis*, New York: The Free Press.

Cook, Nicholas (1992), *Music, Imagination, and Culture*, Oxford: Oxford University Press.

Cook, Nicholas (1994), *A Guide to Musical Analysis*, Oxford: Oxford University Press.

Cooke, Deryck (1973), *The Language of Music*, London: Oxford University Press.

Craig, Carys and Laroche, Guillaume (2014), 'Out of Tune: Why Copyright Law Needs Music Lessons', in Courtney Doagoo, Mistrale Goudreau, Madelaine Saginur and Teresa Scassa (eds), *Intellectual Property for the 21st Century. Interdisciplinary Approaches*, Toronto: Irwin Law, pp. 43–71.

Da Vinci, Leonardo (2001), *Leonardo on Painting*, Martin Kemp (ed.), New Haven and London: Yale University Press (Yale Nota Bene).

Dahlhaus, Carl (1983), *Analysis and Value Judgment*, Siegmund Levarie trans., New York: Pendragon Press.

Dahlhaus, Carl (1988), 'Musiktheorie', in Carl Dahlhaus (ed.), *Einführung in die systematische Musikwissenschaft*, Laaber: Laaber Verlag, pp. 93–132.

Daniélou, Alain (1949), *Northern Indian Music*, vol. 1, London: Christopher Johnson, Calcutta: Visva Bharati.

De la Motte, Diether (1993), *Melodie. Ein Lese und Arbeitsbuch*, München; Kassel, Deutscher Taschenbuch Verlag; Bärenreiter Verlag.

De la Motte, Diether (2009), *Harmonielehre*, 15th ed., Kassel-Basel: Bärenreiter.

De la Motte, Diether (2010), *Kontrapunkt*, 8th ed., Kassel-Basel: Bärenreiter.

Devlin, Keith (2000), *The Language of Mathematics. Making the Invisible Visible*, New York: W.H. Freeman and Co.

Donington, Robert (1992), *The Interpretation of Early Music*. New rev. ed, New York and London: W.W. Norton & Co.

Erauw, Willem (1998), 'Canon Formation: Some More Reflections on Lydia Goehr's Imaginary Museum of Musical Works', 70(2) *Acta Musicologica*, 109–15.

Foucault, Michel (1991), 'What Is an Author?', in Paul Rabinow (ed.), *The Foucault Reader*, London: Penguin, pp. 101–20.

Franklin, Benjamin (1968), *The Papers of Benjamin Franklin*, Leonard W. Labaree (ed.), vol. 12, New Haven and London: Yale University Press.

Freud, Sigmund (1957), 'On Narcissism: An Introduction', in James Strachey (ed.), *The Standard Edition of the Complete Psychological Works of Sigmund Freud*, vol. 14 (1914–1916), London: The Hogarth Press, pp. 73–102.

Fux, Johann Joseph (1971), *The Study of Counterpoint from Johann Joseph Fux's* Gradus ad Parnassum, in Alfred Mann ed. and trans., New York and London: W.W. Norton.

Gadamer, Hans-Georg (2003), *Truth and Method. Second, revised Edition*, Joel Weinsheimer and Donald G. Marshall trans., New York: Continuum.

Goehr, Lydia (1989), 'Being True to the Work', 47(1) *The Journal of Aesthetics and Art Criticism*, 55–67.
Goehr, Lydia (1992), *The Imaginary Museum of Musical Works. An Essay in the Philosophy of Music*, Oxford: Clarendon Press.
Gowers, Timothy (2002), *Mathematics. A Very Short Introduction*, Oxford: Oxford University Press.
Griffiths, Jonathan (2013), 'Dematerialization, Pragmatism and the European Copyright Revolution', 33(4) *Oxford Journal of Legal Studies*, 767–90.
Gülke, Peter (1989), 'Rousseau und die Musik oder Von der Zuständigkeit des Dilettanten', in Peter Gülke (ed.), *Jean-Jacques Rousseau: Musik und Sprache*, Leipzig: Reclam, pp. 331–522.
Hamilton, Andy (2007), *Aesthetics and Music*, London and New York: Continuum.
Hanslick, Eduard (1902), *Vom Musikalisch-Schönen. Ein Beitrag zur Revision der Ästhetik der Tonkunst*, 10th ed., Leipzig: Verlag von Breitkopf und Härtel.
Hegel, Georg Wilhelm Friedrich (1986), *Vorlesungen über die Ästhetik I* (Werke 13), Frankfurt am Main: Suhrkamp.
Hoffmann, Ernst Theodor Amadeus (Wilhelm) (1988), *Schriften zur Musik. Singspiele*, Berlin und Weimar: Aufbau Verlag.
Horkheimer, Max and Adorno, Theodor W. (1986), *Dialektik der Aufklärung*, Frankfurt am Main: Fischer Taschenbuch Verlag.
Hornbostel, Erich Moritz von (1986), *Tonart und Ethos. Aufsätze*, Leipzig: Reclam.
Hudson, Alastair (2013), *The Law of Finance*, 2nd ed., London: Sweet & Maxwell.
Husserl, Edmund (2000), *Vorlesungen zur Phänomenologie des inneren Zeitbewußtseins*, Martin Heidegger (ed.), Tübingen: Max Niemeyer Verlag.
Husserl, Edmund (2009), *Ideen zu einer reinen Phänomenologie and phänomenologischen Philosophie*, Hamburg: Felix Meiner Verlag.
Jankélévitch, Vladimir (2003), *Music and the Ineffable*, Carolyn Abbate trans., Princeton and Oxford: Princeton University Press.
Jaszi, Peter (1991), 'Toward a Theory of Copyright: The Metamorphoses of "Authorship"', 1991(2), *Duke Law Journal*, 455–502.
Kames, Lord Kames (Henry Home) (1970), *Elements of Criticism*, vol. 1, Hildesheim, New York: Georg Olms Verlag (facsimile edition of the first edition of 1762).
Kant, Immanuel (1974), *Kritik der Urteilskraft* (Werkausgabe, Band 10), W. Weischedel (ed.), Frankfurt am Main: Suhrkamp Verlag.
Kant, Immanuel (1995), *Prolegomena zu einer jeden künftigen Metaphysik, die als Wissenschaft wird auftreten können*, Stuttgart: Reclam.
Karolyi, Otto (1987), *Introducing Music*, Harmondsworth: Penguin.
Kepler, Johannes (2002), 'Harmonies of the World. Book Five', in S. Hawking (ed.), *On the Shoulders of Giants: The Great Works of Physics and Astronomy*, Philadelphia, London: Running Press, pp. 635–723.
Keyes, J. Michael (2003–2004), 'Musical Musings: The Case for Rethinking Music Copyright Protection', 10 *Michigan Telecommunications and Technology Law Review*, 407–44.
Kivy, Peter (1991), *Music Alone. Philosophical Reflections on the Purely Musical Experience*, Ithaca and London: Cornell University Press.
Kivy, Peter (1995), *Authenticities: Philosophical Reflections on Musical Performance*, Ithaca, London: Cornell University Press.
Kivy, Peter (2007), *Music, Language, and Cognition and Other Essays in the Aesthetics of Music*, Oxford: Oxford University Press.

Knaus, Herwig and Scholz, Gottfried (1988), *Formen in der Musik*, vol. 1, Wien: Österreichischer Bundesverlag.

Kristeller, Paul Oskar (1952), 'The Modern System of the Arts: A Study in the History of Aesthetics (II)', 13(1) *Journal of the History of Ideas*, 17–46.

Kubik, Gerhard (1988), *Zum Verstehen Afrikanischer Musik*, Leipzig: Reclam.

Lear, Jonathan (1981), 'A Note on Zeno's Arrow', 26 *Phronesis*, 91–104.

Mandosio, Jean-Marc (2010), *Longévité d'une imposture: Michel Foucault*, Paris: Éditions de L'Encyclopédie des Nuisances.

Mankiw, N. Gregory (2012), *Principles of Economics*, 6th ed. (International edition), Mason O: South Western, London: Cengage Learning.

Marx, Adolf Bernhard (1868), *Die Lehre von der musikalischen Komposition, praktisch theoretisch*, Erster Theil, 7th ed. Leipzig: Breitkopf und Härtel.

Marx, Adolf Bernhard (1879), *Die Lehre von der musikalischen Komposition, praktisch theoretisch*, Dritter Theil, 5th ed. Leipzig: Breitkopf und Härtel.

Masiyakurima, Patrick (2007), 'The Futility of the Idea/Expression Dichotomy in UK Copyright Law', 38(5) *International Review of Intellectual Property and Competition Law*, 548–72.

Mattheson, Johann (2011), 'Der vollkommene Kapellmeister' (extracts), in Frieder von Ammon and Elisabeth Böhm (eds), *Texte zur Musikästhetik*, Stuttgart: Reclam, pp. 76–92.

McDonagh, Luke (2012), 'Case Comment: Rearranging the Roles of the Performer and the Composer in the Music Industry: the potential significance of *Fisher v. Brooker*', 1 *Intellectual Property Quarterly*, 64–76.

Nettl, Bruno (1983), *The Study of Ethnomusicology. Twenty-nine Issues and Concepts*, Urbana and Chicago: University of Illinois Press.

Padovan, Richard (1999), *Proportion. Science, Philosophy, Architecture*, London and New York: E. & F.N. Spon.

Rahmatian, Andreas (2005), 'Music and Creativity as Perceived by Copyright Law', 3 *Intellectual Property Quarterly*, 266–93.

Rahmatian, Andreas (2009), 'The Concepts of "Musical Work" and "Originality" in UK Copyright Law – *Sawkins v. Hyperion* as a Test Case', 40(5) *International Review of Intellectual Property and Competition Law*, 560–91.

Rahmatian, Andreas (2011), *Copyright and Creativity. The Making of Property Rights in Creative Works*, Cheltenham, UK and Northampton, MA, USA: Edward Elgar.

Rahmatian, Andreas (2013a), 'A Fundamental Critique of the Law-and-Economics Analysis of Intellectual Property Rights', 17(2) *Marquette Intellectual Property Law Review*, 191–229.

Rahmatian, Andreas (2013b), 'Originality in UK Copyright Law: The Old "Skill and Labour" Doctrine under Pressure', 44 *International Review of Intellectual Property and Competition Law*, 4–34.

Roederer, Juan G. (2008), *The Physics and Psychophysics of Music. An Introduction*, 4th ed., New York: Springer.

Root-Bernstein, Robert S. (2001), 'Creativity and Scientific Thinking', 34(1) *Leonardo*, 63–68.

Rosati, Eleonora (2013), 'Towards an EU-wide Copyright? (Judicial) Pride and (Legislative) Prejudice', 1 *Intellectual Property Quarterly*, 47–68.

Rousseau, Jean-Jacques (1997), 'Essay on the Origin of Languages in which Something is said about Melody and Musical Imitation', in Victor Gourevitch (ed.), *The Discourses and Other Early Political Writings*, Cambridge: Cambridge University Press, pp. 247–99.

Schopenhauer, Arthur (2008), *Die Welt als Wille und Vorstellung*, München: Deutscher Taschenbuch Verlag.
Schumann, Robert (1982), *Schriften über Musik und Musiker*, Josef Häusler (ed.), Stuttgart: Reclam.
Scruton, Roger (1997), *The Aesthetics of Music*, Oxford: Oxford University Press.
Stambaugh, Joan (1964), 'Music as a Temporal Form', 61(9) *The Journal of Philosophy*, 265–80.
Toulmin, Stephen and Goodfield, June (1968), *The Fabric of the Heavens*, Harmondsworth: Penguin.
Vaughn, Kathryn (2000), 'Music and Mathematics: Modest Support for the Oft-Claimed Relationship', 34(3/4) *Journal of Aesthetic Education*, 149–66.
Wackenroder, Wilhelm Heinrich (2011), 'Das eigentümliche innere Wesen der Tonkunst und die Seelenlehre der heutigen Instrumentalmusik', in Frieder von Ammon and Elisabeth Böhm (eds), *Texte zur Musikästhetik*, Stuttgart: Reclam, pp. 122–32.
Waelde, Charlotte, Whatley, Sarah and Pavis, Mathilde (2014), 'Let's Dance! – But Who Owns It?', 36(4) *European Intellectual Property Review*, 217–28.
Wellek, Albert (1963), *Musikpsychologie und Musikästhetik. Grundriss der Systematischen Musikwissenschaft*, Frankfurt am Main: Akademische Verlagsgesellschaft.
White, Harry (1997), '"If It's Baroque, Don't Fix It": Some Reflections on Lydia Goehr's "Work-Concept" and the Historical Integrity of Musical Composition', 69(1) *Acta Musicologica*, 94–104.
Whittall, Arnold (2003), *Exploring Twentieth-Century Music*, Cambridge: Cambridge University Press.
Wiora, Walter (2000), 'Der Grundbegriff Kunstwerk. Versuch einer wissenschaftlichen Klärung', 31(1) *International Review of the Aesthetics and Sociology of Music*, 7–51.
Woodmansee, Martha (1984), 'The Genius and the Copyright: Economic and Legal Conditions of the Emergence of the "Author"', 17(4) *Eighteenth-Century Studies*, 425–48.

5. Who wrote Duke Ellington's music? Authorship and collective creativity in 'Mood Indigo'

Björn Heile

Musical copyright law is subtly informed by often tacit aesthetic preferences. For instance, it privileges melody over harmony. As the entry on 'melody' of the Music Copyright Infringement Resource (Columbia Law School and USC Gould School of Law 2014) has it:

> Melody is overwhelmingly the single most important feature of a musical work in evaluating the merits of copyright infringement claims. The entire corpus of judicial opinions in the area of music copyright infringement dwells on melody as the single most idiosyncratic element of the works in question, and almost entirely the locus of the economic worth of a song.[1]

The corresponding entry on harmony only describes the phenomenon in musical terms; its value and relevance in adjudicating copyright infringement claims is not even considered. Indeed, a judgment in a case between the estates of Duke Ellington and Billy Strayhorn (very close to the matters discussed here) argues that '[h]armony is a derivative creation almost by definition. A composer generally creates a harmony to accompany a particular melody, as opposed to developing harmony in the abstract.'[2] Although this confident pronouncement is only true of a very narrow selection of musical styles (whereas in many others melody

---

[1] http://mcir.usc.edu/glossary/M-R/Pages/Melody.html, accessed 14 September 2014.

[2] *Tempo Music, Inc. v. Famous Music Corp.*, 838 F. Supp. 162, Dist. Court, SD New York (SDNY 1993). Significantly, though, the judgment goes on to state that '[t]he Court is not convinced that harmony is unprotectable as a matter of law. While we agree that melody generally implies a limited range of chords which can accompany it, a composer may exercise creativity in selecting among these chords.' Cf. the very interesting and subtle commentary on Music Copyright Infringement Resource (http://mcir.usc.edu/cases/1990-1999/Pages/

largely arises from harmony or is inextricably bound up with it), there are fairly sound reasons for privileging melody over harmony in this way: harmony is often relatively anonymous; note, for instance, the importance of stock harmonic progressions such as I–vi–IV–V in popular music (Moore 2004: 334–35), to say nothing of even more ubiquitous progressions such as in the Blues. While the precise origins of these harmonic phenomena are unclear and they can therefore be legitimately regarded as being in the public domain, the same cannot be said about other widespread harmonic progressions, such as the so-called rhythm changes based on Gershwin's 'I Got Rhythm', which act as the foundation for countless jazz tunes. Composers have claimed copyright for pieces based on rhythm changes without in turn paying royalties to Gershwin (or his estate), on the basis that the tunes are contrafacts (although whether Gershwin was really the first to ever use the progression associated with his song must remain doubtful). Nevertheless, as will be seen, harmony can be a more 'idiosyncratic element' of a composer's or performer's style and more unequivocally reveal their 'authorial signature' than melody. A commonly cited example in jazz would be the individual harmonic language of pianist McCoy Tyner, which is instantly recognisable, whereas his melodic style is much less characteristic (Givan 2007).

Likewise, copyright is primarily concerned with composition, rather than performance: a tune can be protected by copyright, a particular way of playing or singing it cannot. Indeed, as Auslander (2008: 147–58) discusses in detail, performance is not subject to copyright at all under US law (although he neglects to mention that this is actually an anomaly of the US system, since, for example, under UK law there are performers' rights). As a result, improvisation in particular is relegated to a lower status, if indeed it is recognised at all (the Music Copyright Infringement Resource has no entry on it). A fixed (recorded) improvisation would obtain copyright protection as a musical work, but improvisation as such is not recognised by copyright specifically as a separate artistic activity. Finally, and most importantly for my purposes, copyright recognises the achievement of individual named authors (or composers) but not collective forms of creativity (Frith and Marshall 2013: 18, fn. 14).

Whether legal practice followed and adopted the aesthetic concepts in vogue during the inception of copyright law during the eighteenth and nineteenth centuries, as most commentators appear to (often tacitly) assume, or whether, conversely, it created the basis for the concept of the

---

tempofamous.html, accessed 2 October 2014), which is rather more musically literate than the judgment itself.

musical work and for the insistence on originality as its distinguishable criterion, as Anne Barron (2006a) contends, matters relatively little for my purposes. What does matter is that copyright law is not neutral when it comes to aesthetic values: it is informed by aesthetic preferences just as it has an impact on artistic practices (Kretschmer and Kawohl 2013).

In the following I want to discuss some of the aesthetic ramifications of key concepts surrounding musical copyright law. As a musicologist without legal training, my objective is not to attribute copyright or uncover copyright infringement in particular or, indeed, to debate legal concepts and practice in general, but rather to demonstrate how complex such notions as authorship and originality, on which copyright law rests, can be in musical practice.

My example is drawn from the music of Duke Ellington, or, to avoid a simplistic attribution of authorship, music associated with Duke Ellington. This is hardly a radical test case of a musician or group of musicians for whom the very idea of copyright is anathema and where there is hardly any overlap between the values enshrined in copyright law and those held by the musicians and the communities in which they are operating. On the contrary, Ellington is as close to a traditional authorial figure as one can get in the field of jazz and popular music. He is routinely considered as America's or the twentieth-century's greatest composer, an accolade which does not seem to allow any doubts about the authorship of 'his' works or their originality. Unlike a lot of modern jazz, which primarily results from the creative and often improvised interactions between individuals in a collective, the music played by the Duke Ellington Orchestra was largely or fully notated, and the scores (or 'book' as it is often called in big band parlance) were mostly composed by Ellington. This puts the band at one extreme within the overall spectrum of big band swing. Count Basie's band, for instance, relied on generally simpler arrangements, so-called 'head arrangements' (because they can be remembered without notes) often based on riffs – simple rhythmic motifs which could be sung to musicians or communicated in verbal instructions without the need for notation – and placed a greater emphasis on improvisation (DeVeaux and Giddins 2009: 215–16). Other bands relied on 'books' which had, however, little to do with their leaders: a large proportion of the repertoire of many big bands during the swing era of the 1930s consisted of the work of such composers and arrangers as Fletcher Henderson. Indeed, one of the most interesting features of a crucial event in the history of big band swing, the 'battle of the bands' at the Savoy Ballroom on 11 May 1937, in which Chick Webb's band defeated Benny Goodman's, is that both played a number of the same arrangements by Henderson as well as Edgar Sampson who worked for both bandleaders (Giddins 1998: 139–40).[3] In other words, what is unusual about the Duke Ellington Orchestra is not that they played from scores (although they may have relied on them more than many other bands), but that their repertoire was so dominated by the work of their leader. Partly as a result, that work is also clearly associated with Ellington's name and established his fame – whereas Henderson, despite being one of the most influential composers in the history of jazz, remained a comparatively obscure figure known only to jazz fans and experts.

Yet, despite the importance of Ellington's individual stylistic signature for the music of his Orchestra, it can be very difficult to identify in detail what exactly Ellington contributed to the music that is associated with his name and often registered to him. Some of the most astute thoughts about Ellington's legacy come from his biographer James Lincoln Collier. Considering first his work as a songwriter he comments:

> [T]he central melodic ideas of virtually all of Ellington's best known songs originated in somebody else's head. 'Black and Tan Fantasy', 'Black Beauty', and 'East St Louis Toodle-Oo' were primarily the work of Bubber Miley. 'Creole Love Call' was written by King Oliver; 'Caravan' and 'Perdido' by Juan Tizol. 'Mood Indigo' was worked out mainly by Lorenzo Tio, Jr. 'Do Nothing till you Hear from Me' was adapted from 'Concerto for Cootie', the main theme of which was written by [Cootie] Williams; 'Don't Get Around Much Anymore', 'I Let a Song Go Out of My Heart', and 'I'm Beginning to See the Light' came from Hodges melodies; 'In a Sentimental Mood', 'Sophisticated Lady', and 'Prelude to a Kiss' were adapted from Otto Hardwick melodies; 'I Got It Bad' was adapted from something Mercer [Ellington] wrote; 'Satin Doll' and 'Take the "A" Train' were written by Billy Strayhorn. Of all the songs on which Ellington's reputation as a songwriter – and his ASCAP royalties as well – is [sic] based, only 'Solitude' appears to have been entirely his work (Collier 1993: 302).

Evaluating Ellington's status as a composer he writes:

> By 'composer' we usually mean somebody who makes up more or less complete works of music that are written down or, today, at least organized on a piece of tape by the creator. Ellington rarely wrote out a composition in

---

[3] Ken Burns's influential, if controversial, TV documentary *Jazz* (Burns 2001) memorably dramatises the battle by contrasting both bands' performances of Sampson's 'Don't Be That Way' – incidentally a composition based on 'rhythm changes'. The only band to comprehensively defeat Webb's was Ellington's, by the way.

complete form, and in many, perhaps most, instances, the work existed on paper only in scraps and pieces, which have long since disappeared.

> Furthermore, like that of the songs, the provenance of much of the work is obscure. The men in the sections worked out a lot of the voicings, although in the main from chords supplied by Ellington. Tom Whaley and Juan Tizol [Ellington's main copyists] often made alterations as they extracted the parts. A great many contrapuntal or answering lines were suggested by members of the band … Phrases, snatches of melody, came from everywhere. And, of course, after 1939 Billy Strayhorn contributed a great deal. (Collier 1993: 303).

Will Friedwald (quoted in Santacroce 2014) makes a similar observation, homing in, however, on the crucial question of credit:

> Irving Drake described Ellington's orchestra as a musical kibbutz, in that it was this kind of collective. There were, say, you know, five or six really talented composers apart from Ellington in that orchestra and often, you know, they worked with Ellington in developing his tunes and he would work on developing things that they came up with, and there was a lot of back and forth in it. To a great degree, they were credited and compensated and to a certain degree, they were not.

When it comes to credit and compensation, the most aggrieved party was arguably Billy Strayhorn, mentioned only in passing by Collier above. Strayhorn was a composer and arranger of a similar stature to that of Ellington – some of the Orchestra's greatest hits, including their signature tune 'Take the "A" Train' are his – but he has arguably never been given his full due, either in fame or fortune. The received wisdom was that Strayhorn and Ellington collaborated so closely and that their styles were so similar – or rather that they were able to mimic each other's style so perfectly (more often Strayhorn imitating Ellington than the other way around) – that their individual contributions were indistinguishable. The record was put straight in an important book by Walter van de Leur who, through a meticulous analysis of both composers' styles and working methods, argues convincingly that Strayhorn had a distinct voice and approach as a composer and that his contributions can be traced quite precisely – and that they indeed often remained anonymous and uncredited, either deliberately or through the negligence of the company employed, Tempo Music Inc. (van de Leur 2002: 100–116).[4] In the process, van de Leur (2002: 107) dispels some of the myths, partly also

[4] It is therefore no surprise to hear of cases contested between the estates of Ellington and Strayhorn, such as the one cited above in note 2.

propagated by Collier: 'The perennial anecdotes about music written on shirtsleeves notwithstanding, Ellington (like Strayhorn), for the larger part of his career, relied on written scores and parts, a practice he started somewhere in the early thirties as a result of the increasing complexity of his music and the growing number of voices in his band.'[5]

I want to concentrate on a much earlier period in Ellington's career, before Strayhorn joined the enterprise and muddied the waters even further. My focus is on 'Mood Indigo' (1930). The piece was the Orchestra's first hit which made them famous, although their reputation and exposure had increased gradually during the preceding three years when they were employed at the Cotton Club, the formative period for the band and for Ellington as composer and leader. In his autobiography, the Duke, who had a penchant for tall tales as much as for great tunes, summed up the composition of the piece thus (Ellington 1976: 78–79):

> [In 1930], in the fall, we had a six-piece recording date. … On this occasion, as usual, the night before was the time for me to write and think music. I already had three tunes and, while waiting for my mother to finish cooking dinner, I began to write a fourth. In fifteen minutes, I wrote the score for 'Mood Indigo'. We recorded it, and that night at the Cotton Club, when it was almost time for our [regular radio] broadcast, Ted Husing, the announcer, asked, 'Duke, what are we going to play tonight?' I told him about the new number, and we played it on the air, six pieces out of the eleven-piece band. The next day, wads of mail came in raving about the new tune, so Irving Mills [the band's manager, publisher and occasional lyricist] put a lyric on it, and royalties are still coming for my evening's work more than forty years later.

In an interview (quoted in Nicholson 1999: 113), he further clarified that Mills had changed the title to 'Dreamy Blues' to give it wider appeal, although it soon reverted. It was recorded first for Okeh Records on 14 October 1930, then for Brunswick on 17 October and a third time, with a larger band, for RCA Victor on 10 December 1930, although the band is given different names each time (the first two also appeared under the original title 'Dreamy Blues').[6] To complicate matters, the recordings are

---

[5] Van de Leur's research is focused on the Duke Ellington Collection at the Smithsonian. Unfortunately, I have not been able to access the Collection for this research.

[6] http://www.depanorama.net/ (accessed 19 September 2014). There is a little uncertainty about dates. According to Ellington's own account (quoted above), the piece was recorded and broadcast live on the same day, although most other accounts suggest that the broadcast took place on the following day (then, again, it is also possible that it occurred after midnight, therefore

significantly different (my observations are based on Brunswick 4952, the second and most widely disseminated recording).

Somewhat contradicting his own account of a composition that was quickly jotted down, he gave it a loose programme on another occasion (quoted in DeVeaux and Giddins 2009: 227):

> It's just a little story about a little girl and a little boy. They're about eight and the little girl loves the little boy. They never speak of it, of course, but she just likes the way he wears his hat. Every day he comes by her house at a certain time and she sits in her window and waits. … Then one day he doesn't come. 'Mood Indigo' just tells how she feels.

What Ellington, not uncharacteristically, fails to acknowledge in any of these accounts is that the piece or the inspiration for it was not entirely his. As practically all commentators point out, he learned the melody for the piece from his clarinettist Albany (Barney) Bigard. As was already pointed out, this was common practice in Ellington's band, in which many of the catchiest melodies were provided by the players associated with them. Bigard (1988: 64–65) claimed, however, that he had to sue Ellington to get a cut of the royalties: 'We didn't think anything of it and, all of a sudden, it began to get popular and that was that. I missed the boat for 28 years on royalties. I didn't get a dime. It was all under Ellington's and Mills's names'. Although he has received credit, he claimed to have sold the rights to Mills 'for twenty-five or fifty dollars' and that he received royalties only following the court case (of which there aren't any known records) (Bigard 1988: 65).

In any case, the story doesn't quite end there. Bigard (1988: 64) further claimed to have learned the tune from his teacher, Lorenzo Tio (Jr.):

> My old teacher, Lorenzo Tio, had come to New York and he had a little slip of paper with some tunes and parts of tunes that he had written. There was one I liked, and I asked him if I could borrow it. He was trying to interest me in recording one or two maybe. Anyway, I took it home and kept fooling around with it. It was just the second strain. There was no front part on what Tio gave me. I changed some of it around, for instance the bridge on the second strain, and got something together that mostly was my own but partly Tio's.

Indeed, Al Rose claims that the melody was the signature tune of Armand Piron's orchestra, of which Tio was a member (quoted in Tyle 2014). In that case, Tio or his heirs would presumably deserve credit and a share of

---

technically falling on the next day, although informally taking place on the same night). This need not concern us further.

the proceeds as well. Indeed, his daughter claimed to have had 'a business arrangement' with Ellington (Tyle 2014), although what that amounted to is anyone's guess.

As if the origin and authorship of the tune were not complicated enough, it is not entirely certain what exactly he contributed. The piece is in an ABA' (or ternary) form, with a contrasting middle section sandwiched between statements of the main melody or theme. Unusually for Ellington, who tended to prefer to modulate to often distant keys in his middle sections (with a particular preference for the key of the flattened sixth, also a favourite of romantic composers such as Schubert), the middle section stays in the same key. Indeed, again uncharacteristically, it features much the same harmonic progression as the outer sections, making the piece appear like a set of variations or succession of choruses[7] (although the contrast in melodic material, character and instrumental sound makes the three-part division clear enough).

In the quotation above, Bigard speaks of a 'second strain' which suggests that he is referring to the B section, although the term is not very clear. He goes on to say that:

> Duke figured out a first strain and I gave him some ideas for it too. He wrote out a three-part harmony for the horns, we added my second strain and recorded it. [Arthur] Whetsol [the trumpeter] had the lead, I had the second and [Joe] Ticky Sam [Nanton, the trombonist] had the third. (Bigard 1988, 64)

While this confirms Bigard's (or Tio's) authorship of the B section, Bigard also makes a partial claim for the A section. However, his recollection obviously cannot be trusted: if with 'lead', 'second' and 'third' he is referring to the voices in the opening three-part harmony, he is clearly misremembering – all commentators are agreed that the clarinet plays the bottom part, and this is unmistakable on the recording. How far his testimony can be trusted in other matters is an open question.

In any case, the admission that he contributed the 'second strain', presumably the B section, relativises the importance of his contribution substantially (his partial claim for the A section notwithstanding). Songs or pieces are typically identified by their A section and this is where we would normally look for a tune – name any Ellington hit number and

---

[7] Since jazz standards are frequently based on the choruses of Tin Pan Alley songs, the term 'chorus' tends to refer to the pattern established by the opening of a piece, which is typically 32 bars long and in a regular chord progression, which is then repeated. The melodic material of the opening may or may not be taken up in later choruses, although it's typically restated at the end.

what comes to mind is its opening melody. On one level, 'Mood Indigo' is no exception: the A section (see Figure 5.1)[8] is far more memorable and justly famous; the B section (see Figure 5.2), by contrast, is undeniably attractive and effective but not particularly 'special'. The problem is, however, that the A section does not qualify as a 'tune'. Almost uniquely for a jazz standard, it is, as Bigard hinted at, in fact a three-part chorale, and, although the top part functions as a melody, its effect is almost solely due to the accompanying harmony.

The B section, by contrast, conforms much more to standard expectations of a 'tune'. A feature on the piece on National Public Radio seemingly correctly identifies Bigard's contribution as exactly that melody (Santacroce 2014). By contrast, DeVeaux and Giddins (DeVeaux and Giddins 2009: 227) appear to identify what they simply call 'the melody' as the top line of the chorale of the A section when they state that Ellington 'cast the whole thing in a daringly original arrangement' (which can only refer to the opening), also suggesting that he added 'a memorable bridge'.[9] Despite these discrepancies, no-one seems to admit to any uncertainty as to what is meant by the 'tune' or 'melody' that Bigard contributed. Interestingly, the vocal version, recorded in 1940 with Ivie Anderson as singer, does not feature the melody of the B section at all; after a short piano introduction, Anderson sings the top line of the chorale accompanied by lush horns (Ellington's band had grown to what became full big band line-up in the intervening years).

---

[8] The transcription of Figure 5.1 follows Darcy James Argue http://musicalexchange.carnegiehall.org/profiles/blogs/arranging-ellington-the-ellington-effect (accessed 18 September 2014). Argue corrects the influential transcription by Gunther Schuller (1986: 343). Presumably following Irving Mill's original publication of the sheet music version of the tune, many transcriptions and arrangements are in A flat major, but the original is definitely in the more common B flat major. I wish to thank Jamie Fyffe, Peter Elsdon and Bill Sweeney, whose sharp ears confirmed the accuracy of Argue's transcription. Figure 5.2 is my transcription.

[9] 'Bridge' refers to a contrasting section within the opening theme, in this case bars 9–12 (coming after the bars shown in Figure 5.1), before the opening is restated (the theme is a classic AA'BA form, albeit in 16 slow, rather than the conventional 32 up-tempo bars). The section, which features a dialogue between trumpet and trombone which loosens the chordal texture of the opening, is indeed 'memorable'. The term 'bridge' is sometimes used more loosely to refer to any kind of contrasting or transitional section, potentially even an entire middle section, but, given their standing, it is safe to assume that DeVeaux and Giddins are employing the term in its technical sense here. What makes them think that Bigard contributed the first eight bars and Ellington contributed the bridge is anyone's guess, though.

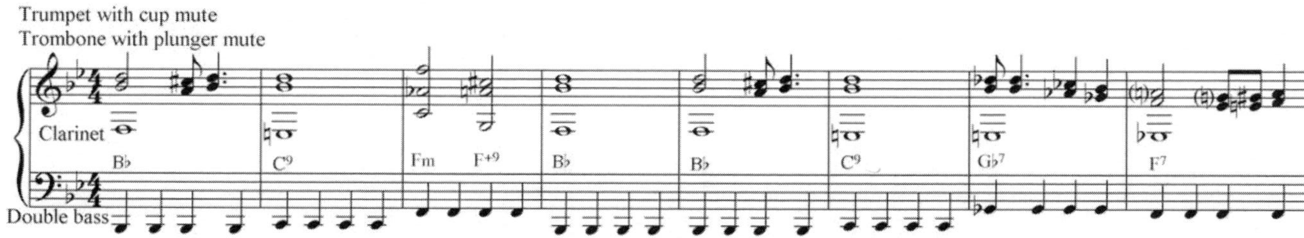

Figure 5.1 *Ellington/Bigard, 'Mood Indigo', beginning, Brunswick 4952, 17 October 1930*

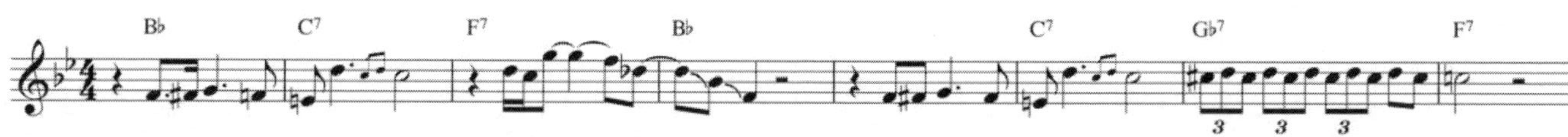

Figure 5.2 *Ellington/Bigard, 'Mood Indigo', B section, Bigard's solo, Brunswick 4952, 17 October 1930*

If Bigard's (or Tio's) contribution did consist of the melody of the B section as I assume, their role would be rather limited. Despite its undeniable charms, the clarinet tune is fairly unremarkable. Since the B section is based on the same harmonies as the A section, it appears rather like an instrumental solo on a chorus (and is often described as such).[10] These solos are often improvised, and in that case the improvising musician has no rights at all. Many comparable examples, from the work of the Duke Ellington Orchestra and others, come to mind. Maybe the most compelling is Ray Nance's trumpet solo on Billy Strayhorn's 'Take the "A" Train'. This solo became such an integral part of the piece that it was usually repeated almost note by note in every performance, whether by Nance or his successors in the Ellington band, notably Cootie Williams. There is no evidence that anyone else (including Strayhorn) wrote the solo, so the most likely assumption has to be that Nance improvised or wrote it. This makes the solo a part of the performance practice of the piece, rather than its composition, and, consequently, Nance has not been credited, although he or his descendants could presumably claim copyright as a (performing) composer.[11] For a listener, however, his contribution to 'Take the "A" Train' is not substantially different from Bigard's to 'Mood Indigo': both play instrumental solos whose melodies contribute to the character of the piece in question. Yet,

---

[10] A good example here is Schuller (1989, 307, fn. 41) who, when discussing solos which may not be entirely 'spontaneous' (i.e. improvised), comments that: 'a previously worked-out "solo" might have been so successful – as in the case of Barney Bigard's famous clarinet chorus in 'Mood Indigo' – that it could not be improved upon and thus would become an integral part of the composition'. Note that Schuller seems to assume that Bigard's solo was an addition to the piece during performance, not its starting point (he never mentions the tune's genesis) and that he indeed regards it as a 'chorus'. He may have worked on the first Okeh recording, in which Bigard's solo is followed by one by Arthur Whetsol (trumpet), thus strengthening the impression of a succession of solo choruses, rather than a tripartite form with a solo in the middle section, or potentially the later Victor recording, in which the sequence is reversed – although that later recording is usually regarded as inferior. The Brunswick recording is unique in featuring only a solo by Bigard.

[11] Indeed the fact that Williams and other trumpeters typically copy Nance's solo is usually regarded as an act of homage, upholding Nance's 'moral right' (in an untechnical sense) as author in an informal, communitarian way. A counter-example can be seen in the dispute between guitarist Pat Metheny and saxophonist Kenny G about the latter's appropriation of the music of Louis Armstrong. Essentially, without using the term in its legal sense, Metheny claims that Kenny G has breached the moral rights inherent in Armstrong's legacy. See Whyton (2013: 57–81).

in Bigard's case the melody came at the beginning of the creative process, in Nance's near the end – more than that, considering the distinction between composition and performance informing musical copyright, Nance's solo is not even a part of 'Take the "A" Train' at all, even though millions of people have got to know the piece with this solo and may love it partly because of that.

Returning to 'Mood Indigo', what Ellington did was to write a piece around Bigard's (or Tio's) melody. This method contrasts with other pieces co-written with his band members. For instance, 'Caravan' is clearly based on its haunting opening melody, contributed by valve trombonist Juan Tizol. Similarly, the main theme in 'Concerto for Cootie' was suggested to Ellington by the composition's dedicatee, trumpeter Cootie Williams. In 'Mood Indigo', by contrast, Ellington seems to have built a piece around the melody which only appears in its middle section.

According to all accounts, the most original aspect of the piece is its opening chorale. Ellington emphasised the fact that it is indeed an integral three-voice structure, and not a tune with harmonic accompaniment, by having the players perform in front of the band like featured soloists in live or filmed performances (there is a host of footage featuring the piece, from widely different periods and involving various players). But what is even more revolutionary is its arrangement. Here is Ellington's (1976: 80) own account again:

> When we had made 'Black and Tan Fantasy' with the growl trombone and growl trumpet, there was a sympathetic vibration or mike tone. That was soon after they had first started electrical recording. 'Maybe if I spread those notes over a certain distance', I said to myself, 'the mike tone will take a specific place or specific interval in there.' It came off, and gave that illusion, because 'Mood Indigo' – the way it's done – creates an illusion. To give it a little additional lustre for those people who remember it from year ago, we play it with the bass clarinet down at the bottom instead of the ordinary clarinet, and they always feel it is exactly the way it was forty years ago.

At that time, big band arrangement tended to be sectional, pitting reeds (clarinets and saxes) against brass (trumpets and trombones) and typically using instrumental sections in blocks. 'Mood Indigo' was originally scored for a comparatively small band; nevertheless, combining instruments from different families in this manner was already unusual (and became a hallmark of Ellington's style), and the use of mutes adds a particular colour. According to a commonly held view, espoused by David Baker (quoted in Santacroce 2014) and John Edward Hasse (1995: 142), the most original feature is that the arrangement is 'upside down', with the lowest instrument (the trombone) on top. Again, this is actually not quite so clear: many other commentators seem to hear the trumpet carrying the top line; this is very difficult to distinguish, but the register (up to a high F) is very high for a trombone and it is difficult to see how even a star player such as Joe 'Tricky Sam' Nanton could have played it with such control and with soft dynamics.[12]

Whatever the exact instrumentation, the arrangement creates a completely unprecedented sound: the brass fragile and soft, the clarinet warm and rich. Overall, the notes are all in a relatively narrow middle range that was perfect for the still relatively rudimentary technology of the time, but, with the exception of the trumpet (which is, however, muted), none of the instruments is playing in its own respective middle range, which can often be relatively dull and inexpressive. (Ellington's oft-repeated claims regarding the 'mike tone' are less clear, however: although such low-frequency hums are common on old records, I cannot hear anything like that in this recording.)

The way Ellington appears to have approached the task of integrating Bigard's tune was to base the entire composition on its harmonic progression, so that the tune would appear like a solo chorus or one of a sequence of variations. That progression could hardly be simpler: a cadence I–ii–V–I in B flat Major, followed by a variation as a turnaround to the beginning (I–ii–bVI7–V7) (see Figure 5.1). In Ellington's hands, this basic progression is embellished by a rich and sophisticated chromaticism, which lends the piece its languid and sensuous quality and which is almost entirely lacking in the tune itself. Concentrating on the top line, the first instance of this chromaticism is so inconspicuous as to be hardly noticeable: from its opening D, the melody briefly touches on C sharp, a chromatic neighbour note. This same note becomes more prominent in the following bar when it becomes an additional leading note on dominant harmony, leaning into its goal, the D of the ensuing tonic, and, with the previous F, outlining a particularly expressive and

12 My expert listeners Jamie Fyffe, Peter Elsdon and Bill Sweeney hear the trumpet carrying the top line, as Argue's transcription indicates as well. The portamenti caused by the trombone's slide are the giveaway, which can be identified with the second voice. Hasse (1995: 210) cites Ellington pointing out that sustaining the high D 'haunted trumpet players for many years … to the extent that they never wanted to play the lead part.' This is somewhat confusing, since although the top line does indeed centre on D, thereby providing further confirmation that it is played by the trumpet (contrary to Hasse's own assertion), this is in no way a challenge for a trumpet (although it is for a trombone whose range is generally an octave lower). Hasse does not provide a source.

sinuous diminished fourth.[13] Arguably the most radical instance, however, comes two bars later, after a restatement of the opening motif, when the melody slides chromatically downwards, and again the crucial note is C sharp or, rather its enharmonic equivalent D flat, this time harmonised with a G flat dominant seventh chord. This last chord appears entirely foreign in B flat major and it is resolved (if that is the word) by sinking chromatically to the dominant, an F seventh chord. Probably the best explanation is that it is a tritone substitution for C (this harmony is shared with the B section, but it seems more likely to have started life in the A section, where its chromaticism is more of a piece with the surrounding music). If so, it is an early example, since that phenomenon is largely associated with the bebop of the early 1940s, and it is more typically used as a substitute for the dominant, not ii, or a secondary dominant replacing ii, as in this case.

One striking aspect of Ellington's mastery of chromatic harmony here is its economy. The melody consists of only very few notes, and Ellington gets some of the most astonishing effects by re-harmonising C sharp (a note that is foreign in the key) and its upper neighbour D. The surprising ways in which the former is coloured harmonically have already been explained, but the latter is also interesting. Although it mostly appears as the third of the tonic B flat major, as one would expect, in the second bar of the tune, it features as the ninth over C major (II, replacing its minor parallel ii at this point), another surprising and expressive harmonisation, particularly for the time (these harmonic devices would become more commonplace in later decades). The astonishing arrangement and harmony of this section clearly reveal Ellington as the composer, even if Bigard did contribute the melodic line (which, to repeat, I regard as unlikely; the more persuasive assumption appears to be that he contributed the melody of the contrasting middle section).

In some respects, then, we have come full circle. Although early on I relativised Ellington's claim to authorship of 'Mood Indigo', on the grounds that 'the melody' (whatever that means exactly) was provided by his clarinettist Barney Bigard and/or Bigard's teacher, Lorenzo Tio, later on I suggested that what makes the piece special is clearly Ellington's work. Among these features are the fact that its main theme is a chorale, the way that chorale is arranged and the subtle chromatic harmonies employed. In terms of an aesthetic judgement of originality, these aspects

13 Conventionally, in a dominant–tonic progression such as this, the leading note is the third of the dominant which resolves to the root of tonic. Here, this relation is doubled a third higher, creating added tension. The result is an altered dominant chord.

arguably outweigh the 'ownership' of any of the melodies employed, whether it is the top line of the opening chorale or the clarinet solo in the B section. Yet, as the opening quotation suggests, it is the melodic content on which most judgments on copyright hinge, whereas harmony and arrangement are typically afforded a lower status – an assessment that jars with Ellington's artistry or indeed any kind of composition of a sophistication beyond mere tune smithery. As pointed out, the harmony is far more 'idiosyncratic' than any of the melodies.[14] Likewise, his art is revealed not least in the subtle arrangement, another craft that is typically afforded a lower status than musical (particularly melodic) invention by copyright law. Note, too, that, if Bigard had improvised the melody of section B or contributed it to the performance rather than the composition proper (as Nance did with his solo to 'Take the "A" Train'), he would have found it extremely difficult to establish copyright claims to that work. More important even than any distinction between the competing claims of melody and harmony, musical invention and arrangement, or

---

[14] Again, the commentary on *Tempo Music vs. Famous Music* on the *Music Copyright Infringement Resource* is worth quoting at length:

> The Court's statements raise nice questions too about how musicians create new and derivative musical works, and whether assembling the harmonic and melodic components is, at least for some genres, more simultaneous than the Court's discussion here suggests. It may be worth pondering, for instance, whether Mozart or Bach conceived their melodic lines independent of the harmonies they set them to. Or, does the relationship between melody and harmony in the conception of Classical works depend more on the genre of the work involved (e.g. Theme-and-variations, fugue) than upon the approach of a particular composer (or group of composers associated chronologically and stylistically)? Is it more likely that a jazz melody sooner than a Classical one would be conceived and fixed independent of a harmonic setting? What holds the attention of listeners when they hear new jazz harmonizations of well-known tunes; outré settings that wild-eyed church organists (yes, they exist) use to renew shopworn hymn tunes; a series of variations on a well-known theme? What do these examples suggest about the potential value of harmony to the aesthetic and financial value of a musical work?

(http://mcir.usc.edu/cases/1990-1999/Pages/tempofamous.html, accessed 2 October 2014)

There is a rare acknowledgement here that questions of musical technique (and therefore what aspects of a style are characteristic and copyrightable) are style-specific and that generalisations about the role of melody and harmony in music lack any kind of credibility or legitimacy, although the section does not go nearly far enough. Distinctions between classical and jazz music are not nearly fine-grained enough; every period, genre or composer and, in some cases, piece have their specific stylistic conventions.

composition and performance is the fundamental insight that, when it comes to individual contributions to a collective creative effort, there will always be more shades of grey than black and white and unequivocal attribution is more the exception than the rule. Among creative people such as the Duke Ellington Orchestra, ideas would have constantly circulated and the musicians would have spurred one another to ever newer inventions. In other words, all the aesthetic preferences enshrined by copyright as outlined above seem peculiarly ill-suited for this kind of music.

In a celebrated account, the sociologist (and amateur jazz pianist) Harold Becker (2008: 1) argued more than thirty years ago:

> All artistic work, like all human activity, involves the joint activity of a number, often a large number, of people. Through their cooperation, the art work we eventually see or hear comes to be and continues to be. The work always shows signs of that cooperation. The forms of cooperation may be ephemeral, but often become more or less routine, producing patterns of collective activity we can call an art world.

It may come as no surprise that a sociologist would emphasise the collective nature of creativity, but, less predictably, similar views have emerged in psychology, where the notion of 'distributed creativity', according to which 'creativity is embedded in social groups, and … creative products emerge from collaborative networks' (Keith and DeZutter 2009: 81), has been gaining ground.[15]

There is no absolute contradiction between approaches which prioritise individual achievement and those which emphasise collective endeavour. These are complementary perspectives, and musical styles, cultures and practices vary in terms of the relative importance of either side. Nor should the practical difficulties or epistemological uncertainties surrounding creative processes be used as an excuse to deny proper acknowledgement, credit and reward to individual achievements. As my discussion above has shown, it is possible to clarify some of individual original contributions that have gone into a masterwork and lucrative hit tune such as 'Mood Indigo'. As I have also pointed out, there are suggestions that Ellington himself did not always treat his collaborators fairly and such behaviour should not be condoned. Nevertheless, what is required is a change of emphasis from the normative assumption according to which creative products emerge primarily from the work of named individuals,

---

15 For related approaches in music, see, for example Born (2005) and Clarke, Doffman and Lim (2013).

on which copyright is largely based, to one according to which they are primarily the result of collective endeavour, in which individual contributions can often no longer be identified. What such a model could look like in concrete terms is hard to say. Jason Toynbee (Toynbee 2010) has used Reggae as an example of 'social authorship' which has developed largely due to the absence of an effective system of copyright enforcement, arguing for the adoption of a system similar to the GNU General Public License (GPL) used in open source software. Yet, his somewhat utopian depiction of the Jamaican music scene is difficult to reconcile with his own admission of the poverty of musicians and their exploitation by producers who not only retain profits and rights but also credits. Moreover, virtually all of his claims have been comprehensively rebutted by Johnson Okpaluba (2010, 374–86), who has pointed out that 'the lack of an adequate copyright environment and the lack of any direct involvement of the major record companies in Jamaica has meant that the vast majority of pre-1990s recordings and rights have been entirely appropriated by the global major record companies with little or no revenue finding its way back to the original artists or producers' (375–76, fn. 8), that there is little evidence that the flourishing of Jamaican music is related to the lax copyright regime, that most major artists have welcomed more effective copyright protection, and that the economic and legal structure of the music business is so distinct from that of software engineering so as to invalidate the comparison with the GPL license.

The wholesale rejection of any form of copyright protection seems thus tantamount to throwing out the baby with the bathwater. While Okpaluba's arguments against the adoption of the GPL license in music are clearly well made, this is not to say that a more developed equivalent of the model that takes the economic structures and working practices of the music industry into account may not hold promise in the future, particularly at a time when the primary economic value of recordings is increasingly that of acting as promotion for live performances. In the meantime, a more enlightened and musically informed legal practice that considers all aspects in which creativity finds an original expression, including such means as harmony, arrangement and production, and which recognises performance on a comparable level with composition, would be possible within the confines of the current overall system (for a fuller discussion of possible revisions to British copyright see Barron 2006b and Bently 2009).

To complicate matters further, one way in which Ellington achieved his unique vision and sound was precisely by giving his musicians the freedom and encouragement they needed in order to provide their individual ideas. As is well known, Ellington chose musicians with very distinctive or even idiosyncratic qualities, such as a unique sound (the growl effects produced by Nanton and Whetsol in pieces such as 'Mood Indigo' are cases in point), and he wrote music specifically for them rather than for their instruments, even writing their names rather than the instrument in his scores. He was also famously indulgent towards his musicians, rarely reprimanding or disciplining, let alone firing them, and generally paying well. This may go some way in explaining their relative loyalty. Indeed, his leadership style has been the subject of studies in management (for example Humphreys, Ucbasaran, and Lockett 2012). In other words, if Ellington did not always directly and personally create the music played by his Orchestra, he was largely responsible for creating the conditions under which it could be created. What he is credited for in this sense is as a bandleader, more than as a composer, and his name is used more as a brand name than as an authorial signature. This would set him on a par with other bandleaders, such as the aforementioned Benny Goodman, Chick Webb or Count Basie (the two first-named also enjoying high profiles as performers). Ellington's case is, however, more complex since his work as a composer cannot be separated from his role as bandleader or, indeed, his activities as a performer. Ultimately, his artistry is to be found in the way he managed to combine these various roles. As a bandleader, he attracted and inspired some of the most creative musicians of his day, whose work he embraced and made his own (more or less legitimately). Directing them and performing with them clearly honed his compositional style and abilities, and his own compositions are to a certain extent a product of these influences. A sensitive approach to his work needs to be mindful of the different roles Ellington performed and the contributions made by his musicians and other collaborators. This includes a subtle understanding of the inextricable relation between individual authorship and collective or distributed creativity. As I have also pointed out, the music of the Duke Ellington Orchestra is hardly unique in this regard, and in specific ways, all music and indeed artistic activity is subject to these complementary if frequently competing forces. Any discussion of copyright has to be informed by the same principles and needs to remain cognisant of the contingency of all claims to individual creative contributions.

BIBLIOGRAPHY

Auslander, Philip (2008), *Liveness: Performance in a Mediatized Culture*, London: Routledge.

Barron, Anne (2006a), 'Copyright Law's Musical Work', *Social & Legal Studies* 15 (1), 101–27.

Barron, Anne (2006b), 'Introduction: Harmony or Dissonance? Copyright Concepts and Musical Practice', *Social & Legal Studies* 15 (1), 25–51.

Becker, Howard Saul (2008), *Art Worlds*, 25th anniversary ed., updated and expanded, Berkeley, CA, London: University of California Press.

Bently, Lionel (2009), 'Authorship of Popular Music in UK Copyright Law', *Information, Communication & Society* 12 (2), 179–204.

Bigard, Barney (1988), *With Louis and the Duke: The Autobiography of a Jazz Clarinetist*, New York: Oxford University Press.

Born, Georgina (2005), 'On Musical Mediation: Ontology, Technology and Creativity', *Twentieth-Century Music* 2 (1), 7–36.

Burns, Ken (2001), *Jazz*, documentary miniseries, PBS.

Clarke, Eric, Doffman, Mark, and Lim, Liza (2013), 'Distributed Creativity and Ecological Dynamics: A Case Study of Liza Lim's "Tongue of the Invisible"', *Music and Letters* 94 (4), 628–63.

Collier, James Lincoln (1993), *Duke Ellington*, Macmillan/McGraw-Hill School Pub.

Columbia Law School, and USC Gould School of Law (2014), *Music Copyright Infringement Resource*: http://mcir.usc.edu (accessed 1 October 2014).

DeVeaux, Scott Knowles, and Giddins, Gary (2009), *Jazz*, New York: W.W. Norton.

Ellington, Duke (1976), *Music Is My Mistress*, New York: Da Capo Press.

Frith, Simon, and Marshall, Lee (2013), 'Making Sense of Copyright', in *Music and Copyright* (ed. Simon Frith and Lee Marshall), pp. 1–18, Hoboken: Taylor and Francis.

Giddins, Gary (1998), *Visions of Jazz: The First Century*, Oxford: Oxford University Press.

Hasse, John Edward (1995), *Beyond Category: The Life and Genius of Duke Ellington*, New York: Da Capo Press.

Humphreys, Michael, Ucbasaran, Deniz, and Lockett, Andy (2012), 'Sensemaking and Sensegiving Stories of Jazz Leadership', *Human Relations* 65 (1), 41–62.

Keith, R., and DeZutter, Stacy (2009), 'Distributed Creativity: How Collective Creations Emerge from Collaboration', *Psychology of Aesthetics, Creativity, and the Arts* 3 (2), 81–92.

Kretschmer, Martin, and Kawohl, Friedemann (2013), 'The History and Philosophy of Copyright', in *Music and Copyright* (ed. Simon Frith and Lee Marshall), pp. 21–53, Hoboken: Taylor and Francis.

Nicholson, Stuart (1999), *Reminiscing in Tempo: A Portrait of Duke Ellington*, Evanston, IL: Northwestern University Press.

Okpaluba, Johnson (2010), '"Free-Riding on the Riddim"? Open Source, Copyright Law and Reggae Music in Jamaica', in *Copyright and Piracy* (ed. Lionel Bently, Jennifer Davis, and Jane C. Ginsburg), pp. 374–86, Cambridge: Cambridge University Press.

Santacroce, Lou (2014), 'Mood Indigo', NPR.org. http://www.npr.org/2000/11/06/1113561/npr-100-mood-indigo (accessed 21 September 2014).

Schuller, Gunther (1986), *The History of Jazz*, New York, Oxford: Oxford University Press.

Schuller, Gunther (1989), *The Swing Era: The Development of Jazz, 1930–1945* (*The History of Jazz*, vol. 2), New York, Oxford: Oxford University Press.

Toynbee, Jason (2010), 'Reggae Open Source: How the Absence of Copyright Enabled the Emergence of Popular Music in Jamaica', in *Copyright and Piracy* (ed. Lionel Bently, Jennifer Davis, and Jane C. Ginsburg), pp. 357–73, Cambridge: Cambridge University Press.

Tyle, Chris (2014), 'Mood Indigo (1930)' http://www.jazzstandards.com/compositions-1/moodindigo.htm (accessed 1 October 2014).

Van de Leur, Walter (2002), *Something to Live For: The Music of Billy Strayhorn*, Oxford: Oxford University Press.

Whyton, Tony (2013), *Jazz Icons: Heroes, Myths and the Jazz Tradition*, Cambridge: Cambridge University Press.

6. Music and co-authorship/co-ownership

Alison Firth

INTRODUCTION

To establish copyright, one needs to identify a work and an author. The musical work embodies expressive content. It is the subject-matter of copyright, the personal intellectual creation[1] of its composer, or 'author' in copyright parlance.[2] It must satisfy the requirements of fixation in material form, in countries where that is required. In cases of joint authorship it is especially important to identify the work in question and to distinguish it from related antecedent (or later) works.[3]

Identifying the author, or all the authors, of a work enables the parameters of its copyright to be drawn. In particular, authorship may establish *qualification*, the link between the work and the country providing legal protection. The *duration* of copyright in musical works is derived from the life of the author or authors, being calculated in the EU as 70 years from the death of the longest-surviving author.[4] Most obviously, authorship is key to *ownership* of copyright. Exercise of the

---

1 See Chapters 2 and 4.

2 Sherman refers to the work's 'persistent and longstanding function … as shorthand for the output of an author': Brad Sherman 'What Is a Copyright Work' (2011) 12 *Theoretical Inquiries* 1 at 99. Referring to Foucault's exploration 'What is an author', Sherman at 120–21 describes the work as occupying a 'pivotal (but largely unexplored) position in copyright law'.

3 Richard Arnold 'Reflections on "The Triumph of Music": copyrights and performers' rights in music' [2010] IPQ 153 at 159.

4 In the EU, 70 years *post mortem auctoris* for musical works: Directive 2006/116/EC on the term of protection of copyright and certain related rights, Art 1. Directive 2011/77/EU amended the earlier directive in various respects, including a mandatory provision that the term of copyright in co-written works consisting of words and music be calculated by reference to the composers of both music and libretto/lyrics: Art 1(1).

economic rights of reproduction, adaptation, communication to the public, etc. will be the privilege of the author or someone claiming through the author. The author or authors will enjoy *moral rights* in favour of identification of themselves as authors[5] and maintenance of the work's integrity. For all these purposes, correct recognition of authorship is crucial. This chapter discusses joint authorship and its legal consequences.

Copyright is a non-registered right; much of our understanding of the legal issues of co-authorship derives from decided cases, where ownership disputes have required the court to interpret and apply the law. Very often, this solves the problem of identifying the work – the version in issue is usually that which has been recorded or performed to popular acclaim[6] – and leaves the court to identify the authors.

JOINT AUTHORSHIP IN UK LEGAL HISTORY

The UK's Copyright Act 1911, s 16(3) defined a 'work of joint authorship', for the purposes of calculating duration of copyright, as meaning

> a work produced by the collaboration of two or more authors in which the contribution of *one* [*each*] author is not distinct from the contribution of the other author or authors. [emphasis added, 'each' replaces 'one' in current legislation]

The 1911 Act formed the basis for copyright law throughout the then British Empire as well as in the United Kingdom. Thus, case-law of Commonwealth countries may assist in the interpretation of UK provisions, and vice versa.[7] The definition of 'work of joint authorship' in the current UK statute – s 10(1) of the Copyright Designs and Patents Act

---

5 Attribution of authorship was recognised by Mummery LJ as significant to Fisher's claim to have jointly composed the recorded version of 'A Whiter Shade of Pale' in *Brooker v Fisher* [2008] FSR 26 at [77].

6 For problems, see Luke McDonagh 'Rearranging the Roles of the Performer and the Composer in the Music Industry: the potential significance of *Fisher v Brooker*' [2012] IPQ 64 at 71–73.

7 See, for example, Louise Longdin 'Collaborative Authorship of Distance Learning Materials: cross-border copyright and moral rights problems' [2005] EIPR 4.

1988 (CDPA) – is identical,[8] save that 'each' replaces 'one', as shown in the quotation above. Joint authorship as enshrined in statute has thus enjoyed more than a century of stability in the UK, although the application of the law in particular cases continues to be worked out.

Prior to 1911, there was statutory provision for *collective* literary works, such as magazines or encyclopaedias, which vested copyright in the editor or publisher who commissioned contributions from individual authors.[9] However, statute also contemplated that a *single* work might have multiple authors; for example, s 1 of the Dramatic Literary Property [i.e. Copyright] Act[10] referred to 'the author or authors, or the survivor of the authors'. This joint authorship of a single work fell to be explored by the courts.

In *Levy v Rutley*,[11] the plaintiff commissioned a playwright, Wilks, to write a play about the supposed adventures of Charles II after his escape from the battle of Worcester. As well as suggesting the subject of the drama, Levy had subsequently caused a scene to be inserted and other minor changes made in order to render the play more attractive to audiences. After Wilks's death, Levy complained that the defendant Rutley had made unauthorised use of the play. Levy's interest in the copyright, and the duration of that copyright, depended crucially on Levy being regarded as a joint author. However, the court held that neither his suggestion of the subject-matter, nor the subsequent changes, rendered Levy a co-author of the play.

Byles J considered that Levy's 'small part' was insufficient to establish joint authorship of the play as a whole, in the absence of a pre-concerted joint design. He stressed that to hold otherwise would cause great uncertainty:

> … so many persons as may have contributed separate, scenes or portions of a dramatic piece might each have separate and concurrent actions for penalties against a person who may have represented the whole or particular parts of it,

---

8 However, copyright term is now calculated by reference to the last of the co-authors to die, as opposed to the first to die under the 1911 Act. This switch was achieved by the Copyright Act 1956.

9 Section 18 of the Literary Copyright Act 1842, described as 'ill-drafted' by the editors of *Copinger & Skone-James on Copyright*, para 5-31.

10 Dramatic Literary Property Act 1833, 3 & 4 Wm. 4, c. 15. See Ronan Deazley (2008) 'Commentary on Dramatic Literary Property Act 1833', in *Primary Sources on Copyright (1450–1900)*, eds L. Bently and M. Kretschmer, www.copyrighthistory.org.

11 (1870–71) LR 6 CP 523.

> without any means on his part of knowing that there was a plurality of authors, or who they were.

Concurring, Keating J stated

> … though it may not be necessary that each should contribute the same amount of labour, there must be a joint labouring in furtherance of a common design.

The absence of such cooperation in the 'design', 'execution' or 'improvement' of the work was fatal to Levy's case. What is interesting here is that Keating J recognises that cooperation might occur at the various stages of creation and perfection of a dramatic work.

A third judge, Montague Smith J, referred to an earlier case of *Marsh v Conquest*[12] (in which he had been involved as advocate) as having disposed of any argument that Levy had become author or proprietor of the copyright by employing Wilks to write the play. He also posited that

> If, when the piece was brought to the plaintiff, he had said to Wilks, 'This thing requires to be remodelled, and you and I will do it together,' and Wilks had assented, possibly a case of joint authorship might have been set up.

This case established the idea of common design, and that of significant but not-necessarily-equal contributions, as hallmarks of joint authorship. The later statutory definition, with its emphasis on the blending of authorial contributions so that they cannot be distinguished, keeps this line of legal reasoning separate from the law relating to collective works.

JOINT AUTHORSHIP IN OTHER LEGAL SYSTEMS

At this point, it is interesting to note that differentiation of collaborative output into divisible (collective) and indivisible (joint) works appears more clearly in some civil law jurisdictions than others; for example Art 8(1) of Germany's Copyright Act provides

---

[12] (1864) 17 Common Bench Reports (New Series) 418; 144 ER 169, 'the earliest recorded case on joint authorship': Lior Zemer *The Idea of Authorship in Copyright* (Ashgate 2007), p. 190, n. 15.

> Where several persons have jointly created a work without it being possible to separately exploit their individual shares in the work, they are joint authors of the work.[13]

Belgium is also said to make the distinction but not France.[14] In fact, Art L113-2 of the French intellectual property code identifies three kinds of multi-author work: the 'Work of collaboration', in which more than one natural person has participated (with no requirement of indivisibility); the 'Composite work', which incorporates pre-existing works without the collaboration of the authors of the earlier works; and the 'Collective work', a species of edited work where individual contributions are merged.

In the US, *Levy v Rutley* was influential. However, in the absence of statutory codification (prior to 1976), US law on co-authorship and co-ownership has had a troubled century, with divergent and difficult interpretations of the requirement of collaborative intent. Balganesh has pointed out[15] that such intent could be directed to the process of collaboration itself (the means by which the work is produced), to the end result (in the form of a joint work), or to the legal consequences (in the form of shared ownership). None of these variants seems sufficient on its own for a finding of joint authorship in the US. The courts furthermore seem to require that each author's contribution be separately eligible for copyright. Balganesh refers to scholarship on the philosophy of action and behavioural economics in order to reframe shared intentionality.

Zemer, writing in 2007, commented on rejection by the English Court of Appeal in *Beckingham v Hodgens* of intention to create a joint work as

---

[13] Copyright Act of 9 September 1965 (Federal Law Gazette Part I, p. 1273), as last amended by Article 8 of the Act of 1 October 2013 (Federal Law Gazette Part I, p. 3714), translation by Ute Reusch available at http://www.gesetze-im-internet.de/englisch_urhg/englisch_urhg.html. See, to similar effect, Art 11(1) of Austria's Federal Law on Copyright in Works of Literature and Art and on Related Rights, available in English translation at http://www.wipo.int/wipolex/en/text.jsp?file_id=124839#JD_AT091EN_A11.

[14] Lionel Bently and Brad Sherman *Intellectual Property Law* (OUP 2014), p. 131, n. 55. Nonetheless, the ability of a joint author to use her or his own contribution independently under French law depends upon divisibility. Mark Perry and Tomas Margoni 'Ownership in Complex Authorship: a comparative study of joint works' [2012] EIPR 22 (cited by Bently and Sherman) compare Italian and US law.

[15] Shyamkrishna Balganesh 'Unplanned Coauthorship' (2014) 100 *Va L Rev* 1683.

a 'touch-stone' of joint authorship.[16] At the time, intention seemed also to be a key test in Canadian law,[17] but since then the Canadian Federal Court has rejected it.[18]

Thus, there is considerable divergence in the treatment of joint works under the copyright laws of different countries. This chapter will concentrate on UK cases, as representative of a relatively stable and uniform Commonwealth tradition.

The UK statutory definition stresses two important aspects, collaboration between authors and blending of their authorial contributions. These will be considered further below; although conceptually separate, they may be evidentially linked.

EVIDENCE – AN ASIDE

Before looking in more detail at modern UK law and cases on joint authorship and musical works, one should note that, in every case, availability and quality of evidence is crucial. A party's cause and the quality of the court's decision-making can be greatly assisted by good recollection, record-keeping and version control.[19] A well-informed judge helps enormously, too.[20] For example, in *Stuart v Barrett*[21] the claimant drummer Stuart was found to be a straightforward and conscientious witness; he assisted the court in listening to recordings put in evidence. The judge had a good ear for music and the willingness to listen. This benefited both parties.

---

[16] Lior Zemer 'Is Intention to Co-Author an Uncertain Realm of Policy?' (2007) *Columbia J L & the Arts* 611, citing *Beckingham v Hodgens* [2003] EWCA Civ 143; [2004] ECDR 6.

[17] *Neudorf v Nettwerk* [2000] RPC 935 – requirement of intent introduced through US caselaw; said to ensure that editors do not become authors.

[18] *Neugebauer v. Labieniec* [2009] FC 666, 75 CPR (4th) 364, discussed by David Vaver 'Recent Copyright Law Developments: more reform?' (2010) IPJ 103 at 104. Vaver regards the requirement that the authors' contributions be 'independently copyrightable' as 'wrong in principle'; it also sits ill with indivisibility.

[19] By contrast, see *Brown v Mcasso* [2005] EWCC 1; [2005] FSR 40, where the disputed issue of which version of the rap lyrics had been presented to Mr Brown occupied a lot of the court's time.

[20] In *Brooker v Fisher* [2008] EWCA Civ 287; [2008] FSR 26 at [1], Mummery LJ referred to the 'musically literate' trial judge (Blackburne J).

[21] [1994] EMLR 448 Thomas Morison QC, sitting as a deputy High Court judge.

In *McPhail & others v Bourne & anor*,[22] Morgan J had to contend with evidence that was potentially affected by witnesses' 'self-serving reconstruction in the period between the relevant events and the time of the trial', confusion, and parental loyalties. Ultimately, the claim to set aside a settlement agreement relating to band-written songs failed. (It was for the claimant to make out their case on the balance of probabilities.)

Experts may be called, perhaps to explain contemporary genres to judges. In *Brown v Mcasso*,[23] HHJ Fysh explained that in assessing joint authorship, the court could take account not only of the facts, but also of 'the views of experts in the field in question – in this case, persons having general musical expertise and who are knowledgeable about the genre of music in issue in particular'. Judges do not always find their evidence of assistance. In *Brown*, the experts did not seem terribly familiar with rap. Furthermore, the judge took the view that they had applied too high a standard of originality in assessing Mr Brown's contribution.[24]

Nonetheless, expert evidence and the playing and discussing of works in court can be vital. Lewison J was trial judge in *Barrett v Universal-Island Records Ltd*;[25] one part of the case involved the contribution of an instrumental bridge between verses of a song 'Who the Cap Fit' (based on the Bob Marley composition 'Man to Man'). Lewison J was invited to listen to the two songs on his own; neither was played or discussed in court, nor was expert evidence addressed to them. He stated

> I am quite unable, on my own and without expert assistance, to reach any conclusion about whether the bridge was an original composition; a question of interpretation or performance; or part of an overall arrangement of the song as a whole.

Finally, in many music copyright cases, some of the litigants appear in person without professional representation. In those circumstances, court etiquette demands that the advocate for the represented party assist the court in appreciating legal aspects of the case from both sides. This occurred in *Bamgboye v Reed*,[26] a case heard in the Queen's Bench Division. (Normally, copyright cases are assigned to the Chancery

22 [2008] EWHC 1235 (Ch).
23 [2005] EWCC 1; [2005] FSR 40 at [42].
24 at [45].
25 [2006] EWHC 1009 (Ch); [2006] EMLR 21.
26 [2002] EWHC 2922 (QB).

Division of the High Court.) The judge Hazel Williamson QC (sitting as a Deputy Judge of the High Court) put it thus, at [34]

> There is always a heavy burden on counsel appearing against litigants who do not have legal representation because they have to help the court to see both sides of the case. In an area of law as complex as copyright this is particularly important, and I would say that Mr Harbottle has discharged this burden on counsel admirably.

MUSICAL VERSUS OTHER FORMS OF WORK, AND PERFORMANCE

The Copyright, Designs and Patents Act 1988 treats music and words of a song or opera as separate works: '"musical work" means a work consisting of music, exclusive of any words, or action, intended to be sung, spoken or performed, with the music'.[27] As Arnold has pointed out, this does not actually define what is meant by 'music', but that may be understood by reference to ordinary usage: 'the essence of music is combining sounds for listening to'.[28]

Returning to what music is *not*, in the UK, words and accompanying music are treated separately. By contrast, in many Continental jurisdictions song, opera, etc., are considered composite works; the author of the music and the author of the lyrics being seen as joint authors. For example, in *Hellenic Society for the Protection of Copyright & others v MacMan Tourist Publishing Technical SA*,[29] the music, but not the words of the song 'Let's Go to Jamaica' had been used without consent by defendants in a television advertisement. The Greek lower courts had dismissed the claim of the author of the lyrics, but the Greek Supreme Court held that finding to be in violation of Art 7(1) of the 1993 Copyright Act, on cooperative works.[30] Article 7(1) governs works created with the direct collaboration of two or more authors.

---

[27] CDPA, s 3(1).

[28] Arnold 'Reflections on "The Triumph of Music"', citing Mummery LJ in *Sawkins v Hyperion Records* [2005] 1 WLR 3281 at [53], [55]–[56]. See, also, Andreas Rahmatian 'The Concepts of "Musical Work" and "Originality" in UK Copyright Law – *Sawkins v Hyperion* as a Test Case' (2009) IIC 560 at 565–69.

[29] [2004] ECDR 32 (Case 1251/2003, Court of Arios Pagos (Supreme Court), Greece).

[30] Art 7(2) and (3) deal with collective and complex works respectively.

> More specifically, in the event that for the creation of a work two or more authors act jointly, in such a manner that each one of them influences the work of the others and all together influence the final result (as is the case of the poet of a poem set to music and of the composer of its music), those authors become co-owners of the relevant copyright (pecuniary and moral rights included).[31]

Although words and music are considered distinct under UK law, clearly the rhythm and feeling of lyrics informs music and *vice versa*. In *Brown v Mcasso Music Production Ltd*,[32] the claimant Loxley Brown, an expert in 'dancehall reggae' and rap, was called in to give a more authentic 'feel' to a rap number previously composed and recorded by the defendant's employees for the purposes of an advertisement. He was held to be a joint author of the later version of the rap. The special place of lyrics in rap, over a 'structural' 'music bed', was mentioned and HHJ Fysh stated 'The music is a base line [probably: 'bass line'] having a distinct contributory harmony but whose existence is driven by the vocal imperative'.

In *Hayes v Phonogram Limited & others*,[33] a claimant who had contributed rap lyrics to a pre-existing 'house' piece was held not to be entitled to participate in the commercial success of later 'house' versions without rap lyrics.

The UK approach to words and music has caused problems, in that copyright in words and music would usually expire at different times. The Copyright and Duration of Rights in Performances Regulations 2013[34] overcame this by introducing a new category 'Works of co-authorship' for the purposes of calculating duration of copyright (new s 10A CDPA and amended s 12(8)). Otherwise, the distinction between words and music has been retained.

The definition of 'musical work' also excludes action, such as dance or dramatic gesture. A 'musical' show may contain musical, literary and dramatic works (dance and mime are considered forms of dramatic work under CDPA, s 3(1)).

---

31 *Hellenic Society for the Protection of Copyright & others v MacMan Tourist Publishing Technical SA* [2004] ECDR 32 at [4.1].

32 [2005] EWCC 1; [2005] FSR 40, appealed but not on the issue of joint authorship [2005] EWCA Civ 621; [2006] FSR 24.

33 [2002] EWHC 2062 (Ch); [2003] ECDR 11.

34 SI 2013 No. 1782, in force from 1 November 2013, http://www.legislation.gov.uk/uksi/2013/1782/pdfs/uksi_20131782_en.pdf, implementing Directive 2011/77/EU [n. 4, above].

Prof Charlotte Waelde's chapter[35] considers the role of performance in the context of dance. Clearly, musical and dramatic works are designed to be performed and a good performance adds immeasurably to the impact of music or drama. Arnold goes further to argue that in some cases the performance defines the work; particularly so when 'fixation' is achieved by recording performance.[36]

It is often difficult to draw a clear line between musical performance and authorship/composition.[37] For example in relation to one of the disputed songs in *Stuart v Barrett*, the judge found that, although Stuart's off-beat drumming made an 'obvious and significant' contribution (to performance, we infer) he had 'tinkered with' a pre-existing composition rather than making an authorial contribution. In relation to other songs, collectively written albeit often inspired by Barrett's lyrics or 'bits & pieces', Stuart the drummer and other band members were held to have jointly composed the music.

In *Hadley v Kemp*,[38] the claimant band members had 'interpreted' songs on their instruments. However, the evidence suggested to the judge that the band's songs had not been collectively written.[39] Rather, the first defendant Gary Kemp had

> … composed at home, with a guitar and sometimes a piano. In this way for each song he developed, and fixed in his musical consciousness, the melody, the chords, the rhythm or groove, and the general structure of the song from beginning to end. Usually at the same stage he wrote the entire lyrics for the song. When Mr Kemp had created a song in this way, and not before then, he presented it to the other members of the band.

Although the contributions of the other musicians were significant to the success of the recordings, they were not 'of the correct kind' to constitute authorship:

---

[35] See Chapter 2. See, also, Charlotte Waelde, Sarah Whatley and Mathilde Pavis 'Let's Dance! But Who Owns It?' [2014] EIPR 217.

[36] For example Louis Armstrong's work, discussed by Arnold 'Reflections on "The Triumph of Music"' at 153, citing Tim Blanning *The Triumph of Music: Composers, Musicians and Their Audiences, 1700 to the Present* (Allen Lane 2008; pbk edition Penguin 2009).

[37] Andreas Rahmatian *Copyright and Creativity: The Making of Property Rights in Creative Works* (Edward Elgar 2011), p. 191, a matter of fact and degree. See, also, Rahmatian 'The Concepts of "Musical Work"' at 573–76.

[38] [1999] EMLR 589.

[39] Thus enabling the court to distinguish *Stuart v Barrett.*

> … contributions by the plaintiffs, however significant and skilful, to the performance of the musical works are not the right kind of contributions to give them shares in the copyrights.

As Arnold has argued, this decision is problematic, especially in relation to band member Steve Norman's saxophone solos, which were not composed by Kemp. In one recorded song, the sax solo extended to 16 bars, 9 per cent of the piece.[40] This aspect of the case would likely be decided differently after the decision of the House of Lords in *Fisher v Brooker*.[41]

In *Coffey v Warner*,[42] the court rejected an attempt to define a work by reference to what had allegedly been taken by the defendants – 'voice expression' (in effect, 'timbre'), 'pitch contour' ('the general shape of the pitches to which … words … [were] sung' rather than the notes themselves) and 'syncopation' of or around [a phrase]. Again, these were seen as aspects of performance rather than of composition.

CASES ON JOINT AUTHORSHIP – MUSE, AUTHOR, EDITOR, CRITIC?

Copyright is an unregistered right, as mentioned above; we get to hear about the cases only when collaborators fall out and resort to the courts. Rightly, judges say that each case is decided on its own facts, that joint authorship is a matter of 'fact and degree'.[43] But looking at the body of cases that have been decided, can any patterns be discerned in UK joint authorship claims? Does it make a difference at what point in the creation of the work the alleged contribution was made, or in what form?

---

40 Arnold, 'Reflections on "The Triumph of Music"' at 159; Richard Arnold 'Are Performers Authors? *Hadley v Kemp*' [1999] EIPR 464. Richard Arnold 'The Myth of the Auteur: performers as authors' in *Yearbook of Copyright & Media Law III*, eds Eric Barendt *et al.* (OUP 2000).

41 [2006] EWHC 3239 (Ch), [2007] FSR 12; [2008] EWCA Civ 287, [2008] FSR 26; [2009] UKHL 41, [2009] FSR 25. McDonagh 'Rearranging the Roles of the Performer and the Composer'.

42 *Elizabeth Coffey v Warner/Chappell Music Ltd* [2006] EWHC 449 (Ch); [2005] FSR 34 at [5]–[6].

43 For example *Brown v Mcasso* [2006] EMLR 3; [2005] FSR 40.

Recalling Keating J's comments in *Levy v Rutley*, one may consider the different stages of creation of a work – design, execution[44] and improvement. Clark, Smyth and Hall,[45] writing of joint authorship of dramatic works, remark:

> It is essential that there be a substantial contribution to forming the written dialogue *qua* author, rather than *qua* muse, *qua* critic or *qua* editor. [citations omitted]

This suggests that a claimant may struggle to establish joint authorship where their contribution comes at the initial design stage ('muse') or improvement ('critic', 'editor') stages. However, joint authorship at the 'improvement' stage was expressly contemplated in *Levy*, if in collaboration with the author of the draft.

Staying with non-musical works for a moment, the provision of ideas and information at the 'design' stage (to the person executing them into written expression) *may* support a claim to authorship if accompanied by subsequent scrutiny, editing and approval by the originator of the ideas. This is borne out by the Indian case of *Heptulla v Orient Longman Ltd.*[46] Maulana Azad, a leader of the Indian independence movement, and Prof Humayun Kabir were held to be joint authors of Azad's autobiography. Kabir took notes of Azad's reminiscences (in Urdu), rendered them into English prose, and went through them with Azad, who made many changes and decided what ultimately would be published (all but a section which was to wait until 30 years after his death).[47]

An extreme example of editor as joint author from the Polish Supreme Court[48] has been noted by Kolczynski and Antas. Here the court held

---

[44] Note that here we are considering the intellectual task of conceptualising and developing the work into its expressive form, rather than any mere physical labour of execution. See, for example, Jane C. Ginsberg 'The Concept of Authorship in Comparative Copyright Law' (2003) 52 *DePaul L Rev* 1063 at 1072; *Robin Ray v Classic FM* [1998] FSR 622.

[45] Robert Clark, Shane Smyth and Niamh Hall *Intellectual Property in Ireland* (3rd ed., Bloomsbury Professional (Ireland) 2010), p. 275.

[46] [1989] FSR 598, BN Kirpal J, HC Delhi.

[47] See, also, *Cala Homes (South) Limited & others v Alfred McAlpine Homes East Limited* [1995] FSR 818 (prompts/sketches plus direct responsibility for content of final architectural drawings made initiator a joint author with draughtsmen).

[48] Case II CSK 527/10, noted by Kolczynski, Janusz and Przemyslaw D. Antas 'A Person Making Editorial Changes to a Scientific Paper Is Entitled to Claim the Joint Authorship of Such a Work: Judgment of the Polish Supreme Court of May 25, 2011 in Case II CSK 527/10' [2012] EIPR 419.

that significant deletions from a scientific paper rendered the editor a joint author. The decision is controversial, although original selection and arrangement is indeed seen as conferring authorship in the context of collections and databases.

In music co-authorship cases, the claimant is rarely 'muse' or initiator. The person initiating the work has usually been credited already with its sole creation and other contributors are seeking to displace that. The initiator may be a forceful member of a band who wishes to retain control, the paradigm being Gary Kemp of Spandau Ballet.[49] In *Bamgboye v Reed*, the power struggles occurred in the context of a recording studio where Mr Bamgboye had learnt his skills. The claimants' usual problem, therefore, is to establish that they participated sufficiently in 'execution' and/or 'improvement' to be considered co-authors.

In *Bamgboye*[50] and *Stuart*,[51] the claimants made their contributions during the stage of 'execution' of the works. To use another distinction that can be found in the literature, their contributions were contemporaneous with the contributions of other collaborators, rather than sequential.[52]

In *Stuart*, the band created most of the disputed songs by what was later described[53] as 'collective jamming'.

> Someone started to play and the rest joined in and improvised and improved the original idea. The final piece was indeed the product of the joint compositional skills of the members of the group present at the time.[54]

The band worked up musical ideas or 'bits and pieces' provided by Barrett and other band members into viable numbers that were eventually recorded on tape. The court held that the plaintiff drummer was joint author of the music:

> I listened to some of the tapes produced in Court and I am in no doubt about the significance of the drum part to the whole of the work. The work is given

---

[49] *Hadley v Kemp* [1999] EMLR 589. The fact that ultimate control of expression was retained by the author in *Brighton v Jones* was a significant factor in preventing a contributor making suggestions in rehearsals from being regarded as a joint author: [2004] EWHC 1157 (Ch); [2004] EMLR 26.

[50] *Bamgboye v Reed* [2002] EWHC 2922 (QB).

[51] *Stuart v Barrett* [1994] EMLR 448.

[52] See, for example, Longdin 'Collaborative Authorship of Distance Learning Materials' at 7.

[53] *Hadley v Kemp* [1999] EMLR 589 at 641.

[54] *Stuart v Barrett* at 458.

> shape and drive by the drummer and a good drummer, as I accept the plaintiff is, can significantly influence the whole composition. In fact, the plaintiff has composed songs and is the copyright owner of them.

In *Hadley*, as outlined above, Gary Kemp's compositions were largely complete as to words, melody and piano or guitar accompaniment before he revealed them to the band. Although the court's findings can be criticised in denying all claims from the other band members, this is an example where Kemp withheld from any common design or collaboration in composition. It is also an example where the alleged contributions from others were sequential rather than contemporaneous.

Hadley might be thought to suggest that a musician who can show that they were there from the outset (or nearly so in Bamgboye's case) is in a better position than a latecomer who adapts, amends, or embellishes a pre-existing work in rehearsal or performance. However other cases, many successful, involved musical contributions made after an arguably complete work was in existence. A contributor who alters or edits a pre-existing work may be a joint author of the resulting 'improvement', provided that the contribution is significant/original and the element of collaboration in furtherance of a common design is present.

However, in the absence of such collaboration, the fresh copyright in the later version will belong solely to the subsequent contributor. That person will, however, require a licence from the copyright owner in the earlier version of the work to exercise the later copyright without infringement.[55] In *Redwood Music v Chappell* the author of the earlier work, a song entitled 'Zing!' was not involved in later arrangements. Those arrangements had the requisite degree of originality to attract fresh copyright, but this belonged to the arranger, not to the owner of copyright in the first version. Such a claim by the earlier copyright holder was expressly rejected by the court.

Sawkins v Hyperion[56] may be regarded as a related case, although the parts added by Sawkins were not so much improvement as reconstruction of the partially lost works of Lalande. Here Lalande was long dead, so there was no question of collaboration with the earlier composer, or infringement of his copyright.

---

[55] See, for example, *Brighton v Jones* [2004] EWHC 1157 (Ch); [2005] FSR 16 at [77]: Jones would require a licence in respect of a draft opening script authored by Brighton and used in Jones's play once an earlier implied licence had been revoked.

[56] [2005] EWCA Civ 565; [1982] RPC 109.

SERIES OR PARALLEL CONTRIBUTIONS AND THE NOTION OF 'NOT DISTINCT'

Before considering the cases on co-authorship of altered works, a third possible distinction may be introduced, relating to the position of the contribution within the work. Collaborators' contributions may be placed

- either in 'parallel' with other contributions, as where a piano accompaniment is devised for a song and runs through the song alongside the vocal part;
- or in 'series',[57] as where an instrumental solo is inserted between verses of a song.

Bamgboye's contributions included drum, bass-line, bass-line variant which became melody, and cymbal effects. They were 'in parallel', as were Stuart's contributions. The band contributions in *Hadley* were both. In *Fisher v Brooker*, the organ solo in 'A Whiter Shade of Pale' was 'in series'.

This positioning does not, however, seem to affect the outcome of the cases. It is submitted that this is because 'not distinct' in CDPA, s 10(1) has been interpreted in most of the cases in the musical (and possibly commercial) sense. It doesn't matter that 'series' contributions are temporally separable, if they form an integral part of the work. However this was mentioned in *Hadley v Kemp*[58] as a 'footnote' as a possible additional objection to Norman's claim to joint authorship by virtue of saxophone improvisations or 'fills'.

Likewise it makes no difference that 'parallel' contributions are technically separable, on different instruments, staves, bars, tracks of a recording, etc.

For example, in *Beckingham and Hodgens* the violin part contributed by Beckingham ('Bobby Valentino') was clearly integral to the later version of the work. The judge commented that it depended upon what was already there, and would sound odd and lose meaning if played on its own.[59]

---

57 Please note that this concept is different from that of 'serial collaboration' promoted by Jaszi, for example in Peter Jaszi 'On the Author Effect: contemporary copyright and collective creativity', in *The Construction of Authorship: Textual Appropriation in Law and Literature*, eds Martha Woodmansee and Peter Jaszi (Duke University Press: 1994).

58 At 650.

59 *Beckingham v Hodgens* [2003] ECDR 6 at [46].

'IMPROVEMENT' CASES

The most common form of 'improvement' or editorial contribution, at least in successful claims, is by addition. The first in time of the cases where additions were in issue was *Godfrey v Lees & others*.[60] Godfrey was a classically trained pianist. In 1969 he was invited to live with the defendants, who had established their pop group about three years previously. He was to make orchestral arrangement of group-written songs (thus his contributions were 'parallel'). Unpaid, he travelled with the band to gigs, conducted the orchestral arrangements for the recording and organised a tour. On the criteria of *Stuart v Barrett* he was found to be joint author of six arranged works. He had made significant and original contributions, pursuant to a common design. In relation to four of the works, his contributions were held to be substantial. In relation to two others, his piano and organ accompaniments were just enough to secure joint authorship. However, it does not matter if the contributions were equal in 'quantity, quality or originality'.[61]

In view of the circumstances and delay in asserting Godfrey's claim to authorship, he was held to be estopped from revoking a gratuitous implied licence for the band to use his arrangements. The court considered it would be unconscionable to allow him to revoke the licence, given that he had not asserted his claim previously, and the band had relied on using the arrangements in achieving hard-earned success. Thus, Godfrey's claims failed overall. In this case, as in *Stuart*, one sees the court taking a critical stance on delay.

The next case to be decided was *Hadley v Kemp*,[62] already mentioned above. Despite a general approach among the band of sharing everything with each other and their manager, Kemp had been credited with composition of all the band's songs except one (Steve Norman's 'Motivator'). For a number of years, his publishing company paid half the royalties it received to the band's operating company. The dispute arose after Kemp decided to stop these payments. Other members of the band (lead vocalist Tony Hadley, drummer John Keeble, saxophone, guitar and percussion-playing Steve Norman, though not Kemp's bass-playing younger brother, Martin Kemp) sued for breach of contract and later put forward claims to co-authorship of the music.

---

60 [1995] EMLR 307.

61 *Godfrey v Lees* [1995] EMLR 307 at 325.

62 [1999] EMLR 589.

Although the band had fallen out by then, Park J mentions as a 'heartening feature' of the case that they retained great respect and admiration for each other's artistic abilities. He rejected the contract claims on the basis that there had been no binding agreement for publishing royalties to be paid.

As for the co-authorship claims, it was not a 'collective jamming' case on the evidence. Kemp's songs were held to have existed as musical works by the time he presented them to the rest of the band.[63] Could *Hadley* therefore be regarded as an 'addition' case, with the performed contributions of the other musicians being added to the songs as presented? Although many passages might appear to support this, the better answer appears to be 'no'.

Crucially, the judge regarded the pre-existing works not as Kemp would have sung and played them to the band (who then would have added to them), but rather as he had mentally devised them for the whole group, which he was able to convey to the band.

> Of course there was a marked difference between (a) the sound of the song sung by Mr Kemp to the accompaniment of himself on an acoustic guitar, and (b) the sound of the song sung by Mr Hadley with the backing of the whole Spandau Ballet band. But that does not mean that the whole band were creating a new and different musical work. Rather they were reducing Mr Kemp's musical work to the material form of a recording. After all, when Mr Kemp devised the song he devised it for performance, not by himself as a solo artist, but by Mr Hadley and the whole band. A composer can 'hear' the sound of his composition in his mind before he ever hears it played. Beethoven could hear his music in this sense even when he was deaf. *When Mr Kemp was devising his songs the sound which he had in his musical consciousness must surely have been the sound they would have when performed by Spandau Ballet*, not the sound they would have when sung by Mr Kemp alone to the accompaniment just of his own guitar. [emphasis added]

This may seem a speculative finding, but it enables one to make sense of the decision that the recorded versions of (all but one of) the songs were composed by Kemp. Park J went on to say that his view was informed by the expert evidence of a Mr Guy Protheroe and he cited factual evidence

---

[63] Notwithstanding CDPA, s 49(4): 'References in this Act to the time at which … a … musical work was made are references to the time … at … which it was first reduced to writing or some other material form.' Copyright had not by then attached insofar as they had not been written out or recorded on other material form.

in support, such as the rapport between Kemp and Keeble, who testified 'I knew what was in his [Kemp's] head'.

In relation to one song, 'Glow', Park J did find co-authorship by percussionists – that Keeble and Norman were joint authors with Kemp. Here the decision can be regarded as one of addition.

Beckingham v Hodgens[64] involved a professional fiddle player who acted as session musician for a recording, and added a four-bar violin part to the song 'Young at Heart'. The new part was used in the introduction and repeated three times during the song, which had previously been recorded by Banarama. This led to 50 per cent share in music copyright of that recorded version being attributed to the claimant. As in *Stuart*, the granting of an equal share in copyright was made in the absence of any evidence pointing towards a different division, although it appears rather generous in this case.

Although there had, again, been a long delay, the circumstances here were different from *Godfrey*. The 'Bluebells' had disbanded two years after the song was recorded. The song had later been used in a television commercial and enjoyed a consequent revival. Although the defendants had originally enjoyed a gratuitous implied licence to use the song, it was not unconscionable for Beckingham to revoke it when he did, in 1993.

There is little sign of the courts' being inhibited in finding co-authorship by the fact that unequal contributions might be rewarded by equal shares of copyright. If this had been a problem, it was solved by the decision in *Bamgboye v Reed*.[65] Hazel Williamson QC held, at [42]:

> Mr Harbottle submitted – and in my judgment this must be right – that there is no requirement that joint authorship necessarily involves equality on a 50:50 basis. It would be possible for there to be, as it were, a joint ownership in unequal shares in principle.

Bamgboye had claimed 50 per cent; this was reduced to 33 per cent. Since then the courts have been willing to compensate for differences in contribution by estimating shares of copyright and therefore rewards.

Brown v Mcasso is the rap case outlined above.[66] Brown's contributions may be regarded as additions or improvements.

---

64 [2003] ECDR 6.

65 [2002] EWHC 2922 QB.

66 *Brown v Mcasso Music Production Ltd* [2006] EMLR 3; [2005] FSR 40.

The final 'addition' case is *Fisher v Brooker*.[67] The disputed work was the recorded version of 'A Whiter Shade of Pale' released in 1967 by Procul Harum. It had an initial contribution from Brooker in the form of a pre-composed song with four verses and piano accompaniment. Brooker's music was inspired by JS Bach's 'Air on the G String' and Keyboard Concerto No 5 in F Minor. By contract, Brooker had assigned his rights in the song, and any future 'arrangements', to Essex Music. Subsequently, Fisher became involved and added Hammond organ elements inspired by JS Bach's 'Wachet Auf' – a 'parallel' accompaniment running through the song and serial elements in the form of an eight-bar introduction, repeated between verses and notably in the form of an improvised 'solo'. The later version was recorded and released.

In his decision, Blackburne J elaborated on the court's distaste for late claims. The first problem of delay is whether the passage of time has rendered a fair trial impossible. Here, the significance and immediate success of the work, the clear recall of its creators and the fact that interviews about it had been given down the intervening years meant that fair trial was possible.[68] The second aspect, whether delay had made it unconscionable for Fisher to assert his claims, was litigated all the way to the House of Lords.

Blackburne J did not spend much time on analysis of the law of joint authorship, but rather on the evidence, which included expert evidence from a Mr Oxendale, who identified the keyboard concerto source. The judge held that Fisher's contributions were sufficiently significant and original to make the recorded version a new work and not a 'mere arrangement'. Fisher and Brooker were joint authors of this work and the judge estimated their contributions and therefore shares in the fresh copyright at 40 per cent (Fisher) and 60 per cent (Brooker).

He took the view that the defendants had not suffered detriment from the delay, so that Fisher's claim to copyright was not barred, although he could not claim that the defendants had been unjustly enriched in the intervening period. They were protected by an implied licence, which was revocable and had been revoked by the claim.[69] The judge also refused to grant an injunction. The Court of Appeal upheld the findings of fair trial and co-authorship and the refusal of injunctive relief. Mummery LJ engaged in interesting and valuable discussion on implied

67 [2006] EWHC 3239 (Ch), [2007] FSR 12; [2008] EWCA Civ 287, [2008] FSR 26; [2009] UKHL 41, [2009] FSR 25.

68 [2006] EWHC 3239 (Ch), [2007] FSR 12 at [14]–[24]; upheld [2008] EWCA Civ 287, [2008] FSR 26 at [36]–[44].

69 Distinguishing *Godfrey v Lees* [1995] EMLR 307.

licences.[70] Essex Music had impliedly licensed the development, performance and recording of the earlier song while Fisher impliedly licensed recording and exploitation of the later version.

However, the Court of Appeal disapproved the judge's declaration that Fisher was co-owner of copyright, given the long period during which Fisher failed to assert his interest. The copyright declaration was later restored by the House of Lords. Any future attempt by Fisher to block exploitation of the song through injunction could be dealt with on its merits, including questions of delay. In its final decision the House of Lords considered that much argument on the contractual nexus of the case was undermined by failure to develop the relevant points before Blackburne J.

THE 1, 2, 3 OF JOINT AUTHORSHIP

Judges and commentators tend to identify three main ingredients of joint authorship. However, they differ somewhat in their recipes. A common starting point is the case of *Robin Ray v Classic FM*:[71]

> A joint author is accordingly a person
>
> (1) who collaborates with another author in the production of a work;
> (2) who (as an author) provides a significant creative input; and
> (3) whose contribution is not distinct from that of the other author;
>
> He must contribute to the 'production' of the work and create something protected by copyright which finds its way into the finished work.

References to 'work' and 'protected by copyright' indicate that the fundamental requirements as outlined by Andreas Rahmatian[72] apply to the contribution – it must be in a form recognised as 'work', have originality, be expression,[73] and be fixed/recorded in material form. However, it need not be 'protected by copyright' in its own right; rather it

---

[70] At [101]–[103].

[71] [1998] FSR 622 at 636: adapted by the editors of *Copinger & Skone-James on Copyright* at 4-34; applied in *Brighton v Jones* to construct a modified triptych: (1) significant but not necessarily equal contributions; (2) contributing to the creation of the work and not of a different kind (for example not testing, performance); (3) direct responsibility for the form of the work.

[72] See Chapter 4.

[73] For example *Ray* at 636: 'A joint author must participate in the writing and share responsibility for the form of expression in the … work.'

is integrated into the joint creation. The joint author must contribute in a manner which is 'significant'. This is a difficult term, not found in the statute. Put another way, not *de minimis*. For example, in *Fisher* the court appears to have doubted[74] that the organ accompaniment would be significant alone, but combined with the solo it certainly was.

The *Ray* definition, while not specifically mentioning the phrase 'common design', contains two relevant elements: 'collaboration', and the 'production of the work'. This suggests the first aspect of Balganesh's analysis, collaboration as a joint process, a means to a common goal, here the 'finished work'. This is reinforced by the Court of Appeal's discussion in *Beckingham v Hodgens*:[75]

> Plainly, for there to be a collaboration at all, the parties must have a common design to produce the work. Those authors who reach the threshold of a 'significant and original' contribution in furtherance of that common design should, in my view, be entitled to call themselves a co-author. Any other test introduces undesirable problems of proof for which I can see no basis in the Act.

As noted before, the court in *Beckingham* rejected a submission that there should further be an intention to create a joint work.

The phrase 'common design', though not subjected to much analysis in the UK cases, emphasises in 'improvement' cases that there must be both collaboration and 'significant and original' input from the author of earlier material *and* from the author of later material. If the earlier author, whose input is beyond question, is long-deceased (*Sawkins*) or absent (*Redwood Music*) then the question is merely whether the input of the later author is sufficiently original to make them sole author of a fresh work. If the earlier author remains very much in charge of improvement, resisting a collaborative approach, then they remain sole authors of the improved material (*Hadley*, *Brighton*).

Bently and Sherman's[76] three-part test is consistent with all the above. Put briefly, they argue that:

1. each author must contribute to the making of the work, a contribution which is 'significant', 'original' and of the appropriate kind;

---

[74] At [41].

[75] [2003] EWCA Civ 143 at [48], per Jonathan Parker LJ (violin part added to pop song, contributor a joint author of resulting work).

[76] Bently and Sherman *Intellectual Property Law*, pp. 130–33.

2. there must be collaboration, according to a common design, cooperation or plan 'which unites the authors'; and
3. the contributions must not be distinct or separate.

AND, FINALLY, SOME QUESTIONS

i. Can Joint Authorship be Determined or Displaced by Agreement between Collaborators?

Agreements between collaborators as to who shall be credited and so forth clearly have evidential relevance – for or against joint authorship, or as admissions of another's claim or contention. Once a work has been published, CDPA, s 104(2) provides a statutory presumption that the authors are those named. If collaborators turn their minds to it, later disputes may be averted. However, it is submitted that the editors of Copinger are correct,[77] that an agreement cannot as a matter of principle determine the issue of authorship. One can determine by agreement in advance to share the consequences and benefits of authorship – copyright[78] and its rewards – but this does not displace the objective, legal, question of authorial contribution.

ii. Can Joint Authorship Expire?

The answer here is 'no'. In *Fisher v Brooker*, a claim brought 38 years after the creation of the works was able to succeed, at least in England. The court pointed out that the Limitation Act, which governs claims to ownership of real property, does not apply to copyright. However, there were doubts whether the claim would have succeeded in Scotland due to different rules on 'prescription of action'.

iii. What is the Nature of Co-Ownership of the Copyright in Jointly Authored Works?

The owners of copyright will enjoy 'undivided shares'; Ben Macfarlane[79] discusses this concept by analogy with a consignment of grain. One may

---

77 Copinger & Skone James, *On Copyright* (16th ed., Sweet and Maxwell 2013) at 4-38.

78 Copyright may be assigned in advance of creation: CDPA, s 91.

79 Ben Macfarlane *The Structure of Property Law* (Hart 2008), pp. 239–40, 533.

not own any particular section within the granary, although they may sell grain in proportion to their interest. There are two possibilities: joint ownership, which carries with it a law of survivorship, so that copyright passes to the surviving author on the death of one co-owner, or 'tenancy in common' whereby each can bequeath or assign their own share. It is thought[80] that most copyrights will be held under tenancy in common rules, although there may be exceptions, for example when spouses jointly create a personal work.

In any event, consent for exploitation is required from all co-authors, so all have control, regardless of extent of their shares: CDPA, s 173(2). This is a result of the decision in *Cescinsky v Routledge*.[81]

iv. Are Band Members Considered Partners and therefore Entitled to Joint Ownership of Band-Written Songs as Partnership Property?

This was raised in *Stuart v Barrett* but not decided, since the claimant was held to be co-author. However, it was accepted that the band membership were in partnership; a partnership at will as there was no formal agreement. It was also accepted in *Hadley v Kemp* that the band had originally been in partnership, but later they used a corporate vehicle. In *Coward v Phaestos*,[82] copyright in software was considered as a partnership asset of a husband-and-wife business, despite no mention in a deed of partnership.

CONCLUSION

Joint authorship under UK law depends upon collaboration of musical co-authors, and significant, original contributions from them towards the finished work. The contributions must be merged, so that they are not distinct. They must be of the correct kind, contributions towards the expressive form that is protected by copyright. Music cases over the last twenty-odd years have contributed significantly to the understanding of the law in general. The cases on modern, popular music have been criticised as not representative of current compositional methods, but most have been decided by musically literate judges with the benefit of

80 A representative view can be seen in the UK response to AIPPI Q194b, available at https://www.aippi.org/download/commitees/194/GR194uk.pdf.

81 *Cescinsky v George Routledge & Sons* [1916] 2 KB 325.

82 *Coward v Phaestos* [2012] EWHC 1292 Ch D.

relevant expert evidence. They demonstrate particularly that collaborative authorship may occur even when one co-author did not participate in the original conception of the work.

7. For the benefit of all musicians? The Musicians' Union and performers' rights in the UK

John Williamson

INTRODUCTION

This chapter aims to trace the development of one strand of music copyright (performers' rights) in the UK from a new perspective – that of industrial relations between the music profession, broadcasters and the recording industry.

Specifically, it will draw on my work on the history of the British Musicians' Union (MU),[1] to highlight the Union's importance in lobbying for the rights of performers throughout a period when performers were barely recognised in UK law. Indeed, the chapter will argue that the Union has played a pivotal and rarely recognised role in propagating discussions around copyright. In doing so, it aims to fill a gap in the literature, re-examining and supplementing the story of copyright in the UK from the perspective of musical workers. Previous accounts of the bundle of rights associated with recordings have tended to focus on the perspectives of the author (see Wallis 2004) and the recording industry (see Greenfield and Osborn 2004; Laing 2004), while studies of performers' rights have been mostly interested in the legal and economic issues surrounding them (see Arnold 1998, 2008; Taylor and Towse 1998; Towse 2004).

In teasing out the implications of the MU's interventions, much can be revealed about not only the nature of the Union and its members, but also the processes, lobbying and negotiations that have seen performers' rights grow to such an extent that in 2014 they fall only narrowly short of those granted to authors.

1 This is part of an AHRC/ESRC funded project, 'The Musicians' Union: A Social History'. More details can be found at http://www.muhistory.com.

The chapter will show that for large parts of the twentieth century, performers' rights were an important bargaining tool for the Union and can be viewed as part of the wider industrial relations process within the recording industry and broadcasting. These accounts show the extent to which future legislation was shaped by negotiations between those parties with an interest in the rights of performers: the musicians themselves (represented by the Union), broadcasters[2] and the record companies. To contextualise this, I will also detail the social, industrial and economic factors which determined the Union's negotiating power at various points and explain how these have played a significant part in the expansion of copyright in sound recordings in the UK.

Central to understanding this is an explanation of the Union's relationships with other parties interested in copyright across the music industries, notably music publishers, record companies and collecting societies. I will argue that the Union's stance on copyright evolved from one of disinterest to one of playing an important part in cross-industrial campaigns for the extension and expansion of music copyright in recent years.

The main focus will be on a period spanning 43 years (1946–89) during which the Union was initially able to extract payment for non-featured performers[3] on recordings and use its considerable influence in the pursuit of legal recognition of such performers. I will do this in three parts. The first will introduce the work of the Union and the notion of performers' rights in sound recordings. The second will provide an account of the evolution of performers' rights, highlighting the role of the Union in both advancing the concept and delaying its eventual recognition in UK law. This will be detailed in three phases: from 1911–1925, from 1926–1988 and the period since 1989. These are not arbitrary divisions, but have been chosen to coincide with the events which can be seen to have framed the Union's interest in copyright matters: the inclusion of sound recordings in the Copyright Act of 1911, the very limited recognition of performers in the Dramatic and Musical Performers' Protection Act (DMPPA) (1925), and the combined effect of the Copyright, Designs and Patents Act (CDPA) (1988) and a report into

---

2 The BBC had a monopoly on radio broadcasting in the UK until the launch of Independent Local Radio (ILR) in 1973. Independent television was launched in 1955.

3 The non-featured performers are those whose names are not associated with the recording or already contracted to or paid in some way by the producer. Initially they were engaged as hired hands and played a flat fee covering all possible uses of their performance.

Collective Licensing by the Monopolies and Mergers Commission (MMC) in the same year,[4] which irrevocably changed the nature of the relations between the Union, record companies and broadcasters. While the MU's power was greatly diminished, it has, nevertheless, remained an important actor in the expansion of both performers' rights and musical copyright more generally in the subsequent decades.

Having shown the Union's importance in the recognition of performers in UK copyright legislation, the final part will reflect critically on its role. This will examine the problems caused, both within the Union and in its relations with the broadcasters and recording industry, by the pursuit of outcomes that benefit some individual members in an organisation that is built around notions of collective action. It will argue that the industrial relationship between the Union and the record companies shifted from being one that used a shared interest in copyright as a means of protecting their differing interests, to one where it has become much harder to distinguish their interests in copyright.

1. INTRODUCING THE MUSICIANS' UNION AND PERFORMERS' RIGHTS

Before making explicit the connection between the Musicians' Union and the rights of performers, it is worth saying a little about both the MU and the rights of performers more generally.

The Union was formed as the Amalgamated Musicians' Union (AMU) by Joseph B. Williams in 1893 at a time when workers (both in general and in the music profession) were becoming increasingly organised and unionised. It merged with the National Orchestral Union of Professional Musicians (NOUPM) in 1921 to form the Musicians' Union and, while its subsequent history has been underpinned by a largely consistent ideology, this has been variously compromised by its fluctuating membership and influence over employers.

This ideology stems from the type of musical employment in which its members were engaged from the early years of the Union. The first members of the AMU were predominantly pit musicians who played in theatres, music halls and cinemas, and it was this cadre of musicians, and their working conditions, that became the initial focus of the Union's policies, which were dominated by issues related to pay and conditions.

---

4 The report was published in 1988 and implemented by the government the following year.

This is significant as it shaped the Union's thinking even after new technologies (recording, radio and the talkies[5]) radically changed the nature of musical employment in the UK during the 1920s and 1930s. It informed what Thornton calls an 'ideology of liveness' (Thornton 1995: 41) that the Union has maintained throughout its history, wherein it has privileged the act of playing live over that of recording.[6] This worldview was to maintain a huge influence over the Union's attitudes towards the overlapping issues of copyright, broadcasting and the public performance of records.

In addressing such issues, the Union's negotiating power has fluctuated depending on a host of factors, including what Batstone identifies as the 'the disruptive power' (Batstone 1988: 220) of trade unions which is dependent on the 'centrality of an occupational group' (ibid) to any manufacturing process or service provision. In this respect, the MU has been central to the recording industry throughout their parallel histories, thus forcing the industry to negotiate on favourable terms to ensure musicians continued to make records. Similarly, broadcasters (especially the BBC) were reliant on MU members' work for large parts of its output, and were equally wary of incurring the Union's displeasure. It was in this context that the Union was able, in the period after 1925, to play a part in greatly enhancing the rights of performers in the UK.

These rights can be viewed as part of the wider development of copyright in musical recordings that began with the Copyright Act (1911). Faced with the technological changes that allowed musical performances to be fixed, the Act recognised 'neighbouring rights' in sound recordings. Arnold describes these as 'similar to, but less than full copyright' (Arnold 1997: 10), where the 'object protected is derivative from a literary or musical work and particularly where the "author" is a corporation, as with record companies and broadcasting organisations' (ibid). However, while the authors were assigned some protection, no efforts were made in the 1911 legislation to allow performers on recordings any control over unauthorised use of their performances.

This was addressed in the Dramatic and Musical Performers' Protection Act (DMPPA) (1925), which was instigated by the record companies, worried that unauthorised recordings could be made from broadcasts, thereby 'breaking the contracts between the artists and the gramophone companies' (ibid: 14). However, the Act merely served to

---

[5] *The Jazz Singer* was the first film to be shown in the UK (in 1928) with sound, thus removing the need for cinema orchestras.

[6] This could be seen in the Union's famous 'Keep Music Live' campaign that began in the 1960s at a time of rapid expansion of the recording industry.

criminalise the activity of producing illicit recordings, which were punished by small fines, from which neither the performer nor record company would benefit. While the Act recognised the rights of performers, with no civil remedies available to performers, it offered very little in the way of actual protection.

This was to remain the case for over sixty years, and Arnold notes that throughout this period, legislatures in the UK and beyond resisted giving proprietary rights and civil remedies to performers. In spite of a raft of changes to existing legislation[7] and a number of copyright reviews,[8] it was only in the CDPA of 1988 that performers were given civil remedies (ss. 180 *et seq.*, 191I, 194), allowing them to prevent unauthorised use of their performances. In assigning these rights to performers, the Act granted rights well short of full copyright to performers, but this was to be the starting point for a number of amendments to the CDPA that have brought performers' rights more in line with copyright as a whole.

The importance of the Union in this story lies in the lengthy period between the first fixation of musical performances and the performers' right to equitable remuneration becoming enshrined in legislation. This meant that for most of the twentieth century, performers' rights were largely an industrial relations issue, and it was here that the Union played a critical role.

2. THE MU AND ITS THREE PHASES OF INVOLVEMENT IN UK COPYRIGHT LAW

In examining the attitude of the Union towards performers' rights (and copyright more generally), it is helpful to view its stance in the three previously identified phases: the first (prior to 1925) where the Union had still to fully recognise the importance of copyright; the second where it co-operated with record companies and broadcasters to protect the rights of performers; and the third (after 1988) when the outcomes of such industrial relations processes were superseded by the eventual recognition of performers in new legislation. Simultaneously, the approach of the Conservative governments of 1979–1997 to both trade unions and the private sector greatly undermined the power the Union had previously enjoyed in relation to the recording and broadcasting industries.

---

[7] A new Copyright Act was passed in 1956 and the Dramatic and Musical Performers' Protection Act was updated in 1958.

[8] Notably the Gregory Report in 1952 and the Whitford Report in 1977.

Phase 1: A Growing Concern? (1911–1925)

In the period leading up to and immediately after the passing of the Copyright Act (1911), there was little evidence in either the AMU's publications[9] or Executive Committee minutes of the time to suggest that copyright was of any concern to its members. This was presumably because none (or very few) of those involved in recording prior to 1911 were likely to be AMU members. Where music was being recorded, it was largely by music hall acts and singers, the majority of whom were either not unionised, or were members of other trade unions, usually the Variety Artistes' Federation (VAF).

Indeed, any public discourse around the legislation, which protected sound recordings for a period of fifty years, was largely between the composers of the music, music publishers and the 'mechanical' music industry (i.e. the record companies), as illustrated by a series of exchanges in *The Times* between George Bernard Shaw, William Boosey (of Chappell Music) and J. Drummond Robertson (the general manager of the Gramophone Company) which highlighted the position of each of the parties, and offers some insight into the subsequent emergence of performers' rights.

The correspondence shows that the issues at stake went beyond what should be covered by copyright legislation and for how long. It also questions to what extent, and by whom, composers should be compensated from the reproduction of their works by the record companies. Two themes that were to reappear throughout twentieth-century musical copyright debates emerged in the letters.

The first concerned the primacy of the composer. Here, the publishers argued that the record companies were profiting from the works of composers without compensating them, in the way to which they were accustomed from sales of sheet music. For the publishers, Boosey argued that recordings were 'copies of a work. They are the means by which the work is performed, just as much as sheet music' (*The Times*, 4 May 1911: 7), whereas Robertson presented a more pluralistic version of the production process, arguing that a record is 'a combination of the author's work, the performers' talent and the mechanician's skill' (*The Times*, 2 May 1911: 10). While he went on to claim that the record companies 'never opposed paying to the author a contribution for the use of his work in the future' (ibid), their stance was one which sought to

---

[9] The *Musicians' Report and Journal* was the Union's magazine for members.

dilute and diminish the position of the composer in the copyright of recordings. This is important, as it shows that the first claims for the rights of performers were being made, not by the Musicians' Union or other musicians' organisations, but by record companies, as a means of tactically undermining the position of the other interested parties, the composers and music publishers.

The second claims related to the industrial power of the record companies. Boosey noted the Gramophone Company's[10] large profits and how they happily paid singers (i.e. the featured performers) and dividends to shareholders while still refusing to pay composers. Shaw argued 'we, being artists, are poor and politically insignificant. They, being industrialists, are rich and can bully governments' (*The Times*, 4 May 1911 7).

In setting out the position of the record companies, music publishers and artists, this correspondence was arguably the beginning of industrial relations in the British music industries. At this juncture, the MU was not a major participant in such debates, but its addition to the power dynamic in subsequent years meant that it was to be at the centre of all the subsequent changes to musical copyright in the UK. These relationships between the Union, the record companies, broadcasters, music publishers and the government are therefore central to understanding the major developments in British copyright where it concerns performers.

If the Copyright Act (1911) was of little immediate interest to the AMU, then the formation, by music publishers, of the Performing Right Society (PRS) in 1914 to collect royalties from public performance of records on behalf of composers was to change this and bring copyright matters onto the Union's agenda for the first time. In 1918, the Society made what McFarlane calls 'a serious diplomatic blunder' (McFarlane 1980: 100) when it decided to set tariffs for venues hosting live performances based on the number of musicians employed in performing them.[11] Believing that this would discourage promoters and venues from using as many musicians for performances, the Union used this threat to jobs as a reason for boycotting works registered by PRS (see Davison 2012).

---

[10] The Gramophone Company was the largest record producer in Britain at the time (see Martland 1997; Gronow and Saunio 1998).

[11] Performing Right Society (now PRS for Music) presently collects from venues and promoters based on the basis of ticket revenue, making payments conditional on the size of the audience rather than the ensemble.

Although the dispute was ultimately resolved[12] and the means of determining PRS's tariffs changed, this was only after the Society had succeeded in taking out an injunction against the Union (see McFarlane 1980: 100; Ehrlich 1989: 16), with Boosey,[13] now the first President of the Performing Right Society, referring to the Union as 'the spoilt darlings of the musical profession' (quoted in Peacock and Weir 1975: 70). Boosey remained a fervent anti-Unionist, and relations between the Union and the Society when under his leadership were rarely good.

This dispute, however, did illustrate the Union's growing power within the music industries, and it was little surprise that it was to become increasingly interested and involved in copyright. Though the Union was rarely proactive in such matters, it became increasingly quick to react to and seek advantage from the actions of the record companies. The first instance of this was in the wake of the Dramatic and Musical Performers' Protection Act in 1925.

It is worth noting that the Act was instigated not by the Union but by the Gramophone Company, and introduced to Parliament as a Private Members' Bill by Sir Martin Conway, whose biography reports that he received a 'magnificent gramophone' from the company in return (Evans 1966: 245). This is arguably the first occasion in which the record companies could be seen to conflate their interests with those of the performers to suit their own lobbying purposes.

Phase 2: Mutual Dependency? The MU and the Recording Industry 1926–1988

With the Act establishing the notion of a limited performers' right in UK law, the Union sought to capitalise on the record companies' advances while becoming increasingly concerned by the threat to employment posed by the growing recording industry. In the period immediately after the legislation, both the Union and the record companies found themselves facing problems, which were to produce joint solutions in the form of two new organisations and the eventual monetisation of public performances of recorded music to the benefit of both parties.

For the MU, the technological changes of the 1920s forced a range of means of protecting members from the growing threat of unemployment. The devastating impact of the talkies on the employment of cinema orchestras coupled with the economic downturn of the late 1920s and

---

[12] JB Williams was appointed to a consultative position with PRS as part of the resolution – for more detail on this dispute see Davison (2012: 252).

[13] By this point Boosey had become the first President of PRS.

early 1930s meant that the Union's membership shrank[14] in proportion with the declining job market. Many strategies were employed to protect employment, but in 1929, the Union was increasingly focused on the crumbs of comfort offered by the recognition of performers in the 1925 legislation. The Union saw this as a possible route towards ending the talkies – by claiming that the use of recorded music on the films was in contravention of the DMPPA. To make this claim, the Union, with the co-operation of several major bandleaders,[15] formed the Musical Performers' Protection Association (MPPA)[16] in 1928.

The MPPA used the limited recognition of performers in the Act to claim that musicians should 'secure the advantages due to them through a proper organisation' (*Melody Maker*, January 1929: 12) and declared among its objectives 'to control the reproduction by mechanical means (such as gramophone records, sound films and the like) of the works and performances of its members' (ibid). It did not, however, aim to ban the use of the recordings, but rather to control and 'collect for its members, fees and subscriptions' (ibid) by way of compensation.

The Union placed considerable emphasis on the role of the MPPA and although it had recruited 5,200 members[17] by July, Union leaders lamented the apathy of those members who did not recognise the extent of the threat to their livelihoods posed by new technologies. For example, Fort Greenwood[18] told the *Melody Maker* that 'we ought to have the signature of every musician in the country' (May 1929: 518) and that 'we really must do better than this. The importance of controlling the copyright in mechanical music should be obvious' (ibid). More significantly, he set out the Union's view that it would be impossible to continue obstructing the onward march of technology and that 'the wiser course is to seek to control it and turn it to our advantage if possible' (ibid).

---

[14] Union membership in 1928 was over 20,000 strong; by 1934 it was under 7,000.

[15] Jack Payne and Jack Hylton were among those dance band leaders involved in both the MPPA and the Union's Dance Section, which was formed in 1930.

[16] The MPPA was a limited liability company set up by and controlled by the Union to ensure its activities were exempt from existing trade union legislation.

[17] Becoming a member merely involved signing up, there was no subscription. The vast majority of members were in London.

[18] Greenwood was London branch secretary of the MU and a former leader of the London Orchestral Association (LOA).

Although the MPPA was not to become a significant association in its own right, the ethos it established was to underpin the Union's approach to technological developments and performers' rights for the remainder of the twentieth century.

However, it was not only the Union that was facing difficulties and seeking legal justification to set up a new organisation. In 1934, the record companies formed Phonographic Performance Limited (PPL) to collect revenue from public performance of recordings after the Gramophone Company won a court case against a Bristol restaurateur, Steven Carwardine,[19] who had been playing records manufactured by the company on his premises. It was another move by the record companies that was to provide an opportunity for the Union.

The context is again important. During the 1920s, the recording industry had grown rapidly, but by the end of the decade this was tempered by fears on the part of the record companies over how the advent of radio would affect sales of records. This, along with the economic crisis, meant that record sales were in sharp decline[20] and according to McFarlane, record companies were 'casting around anxiously for an additional form of income to bolster their sagging profits' (McFarlane 1980: 132).

This involved a number of strategies, including reorganisation[21] of the companies, the formation of the International Federation of Phonographic Industries (IFPI) in 1933 as an international trade body, and the pursuit of the test case by the Gramophone Company against Carwardine. The ruling in the latter stated that the record company had a full copyright in its sound recordings, which included the right to control public performances of the record, distinct from the copyright of the author. Buoyed by this success, the record companies moved quickly, with EMI and Decca, the two largest record companies in the UK, forming Phonographic Performance Limited (PPL) in May 1934.

PPL set about maximising their income by negotiating with the BBC and setting tariffs for other music users, but faced a number of barriers, not least the fear that an appeal would be launched against the *Carwardine* ruling by those users of recorded music resistant to paying for it or

---

[19] *Gramophone Company Ltd v. Stephen Carwardine & Co.* [1934] Ch. 450 (Ch.D.).

[20] The turnover of two major record companies, the Gramophone Company and Columbia Records, had each 'plummeted by 90%' (Gronow and Saunio 1998: 57) prior to their merging to form EMI in 1931.

[21] The Gramophone Company and Columbia Records merged in 1931 to become subsidiaries of Electrical and Musical Industries (EMI).

who felt that the record companies were profiting unfairly from their recorded works. To avoid such problems they rapidly moved to reach agreements with some of the groups most likely to challenge the ruling, notably the musicians who played on the records and the music publishers, both of whom were unhappy at the proceeds of this apparent rights' grab going exclusively to the record labels.

Aware of the need to act on the concerns of musicians,[22] SJ Humphries, one of the directors of PPL, wrote to *The Times* shortly after their first meeting on 6 April 1934, stating their intentions, and proposing that 'although no legal right of the performing artist can be admitted, the claim that recognition should in some way be given to the artist in public performance is just and reasonable' (13 April 1934: 10). PPL set up a committee to negotiate with the Incorporated Society of Musicians (ISM), the MU, VAF and Actors' Equity on behalf of musicians, with limited success.

As part of these negotiations PPL offered 20 per cent of their net income to be distributed among musicians who played on records on an *ex gratia*[23] basis. While this was broadly agreeable to all parties, there was some debate as to how this would be distributed. The MU proposed a means of distributing the money using the MPPA to those of its members who had performed on records, but were subsequently 'astounded to find out' (*The Musicians' Report and Journal*, July 1935: 4) that PPL had decided to pay the musicians directly.

If the MU was somewhat peripheral to the initial discussions with PPL, this changed over the following decade as negotiations continued between the two parties on a range of issues. Union membership recovered from its 1936 low, a result of intensive recruitment among dance musicians, the expansion of the BBC orchestras, and the increased demand for live music at the end of World War II. In addition, recording was, for the first time, affecting an increasing number of MU members. Meanwhile, with PPL still nursing anxieties about their own legal status, it was in the interests of both parties to reach a more robust and lasting agreement.

This was duly finalised in 1946 and was integral to the future development of the British recording industry, with the arrangements,

---

22 Frank Eames, the General Secretary of the ISM, wrote to *The Times* (27 March 1934: 10) highlighting the mutual interests of record companies and musicians in limiting the public performances of records.

23 Meaning 'for favour' – PPL made it clear that this was a voluntary arrangement on their part and in making the payment they were not accepting the principle of a performer's right.

albeit with various modifications, enduring until the late 1980s. Described by *Melody Maker* as 'one of the Union's most sensational victories' (17 May 1947: 1), the agreement satisfied both parties. For the record companies, it removed the threat of a recording strike in the UK[24] and laid the foundations for four decades of relatively cordial industrial relations in the recording industry.

The deal itself continued the *ex gratia* payments to performers, but widened them and increased the overall amount paid by PPL, some of which was now paid directly to the MU. The changing nature of recordings was reflected in a separation between featured and non-featured performers, the latter being the frequently unaccredited musicians (later referred to as session musicians) who played on the recordings. PPL offered to pay 20 per cent of its net income to the record companies for the named performers,[25] and 10 per cent (rising after two years to 12.5 per cent) of its net income to the MU on behalf of the non-featured musicians.[26]

The money this was to generate was, however, only one of the factors that made this a 'sensational' result for the Union. It also gave the Union a large degree of control over the public performance of recorded music, which was achieved through a number of restrictions placed, at the behest of the Union, in the licences PPL issued allowing the use of records in public places.

These restrictions included provisions that no records could be played or be permitted to be played at 'at any theatre, music hall, dance hall, or other place of entertainment' (MU, *Executive Committee Report to Conference*, 1947: 23) where there was either 'a trade dispute directly affecting the rights or interests of musicians' (ibid) or 'where records were played in complete or partial substitution for musicians employed' (ibid). A further restriction on records being played 'where musicians could, having regard to the size and nature of the theatre, music hall, dance hall or other place of entertainment, be employed' (ibid) ensured

---

[24] This was of particular concern in the wake of the American Federation of Musicians (AFM) strike, which prevented all recording between 1942 and 1944. The strike centred on the same issues as were now becoming prominent in the UK – the compensation of non-recording musicians by record companies for loss of work or income. For a detailed account see Roberts (2014).

[25] Usually those in a contractual relationship with the record company involved.

[26] Those musicians who would have simply been paid a fee for taking part in the recording as part of a large ensemble or backing group.

through its ambiguity that almost every venue in the country could, theoretically, be prevented from playing records.

A year after the MU/PPL agreement and under pressure from the Union, PPL concluded a separate deal with the BBC which put equally draconian restraints on the broadcasting of recorded music. This resulted in the establishment of needletime, a restriction on the number of hours of recorded music that could be played on air. This was initially set at 28 hours per week across the BBC's radio and television networks, although this was reduced to 22 hours before gradually being negotiated upwards in a series of agreements (as documented by Witts 2014, Cloonan 2014). Here the Union was able to use its power over PPL to ensure that firstly the BBC, and latterly independent television and radio, provided both a continual stream of income and a source of employment for musicians.

Through these two agreements, the MU had successfully made itself an indispensable partner for the recording industry, despite their different interests in the curtailment of public performance of records. For the MU, this was to ensure its members were not replaced by recorded music, and while its rhetoric often saw it opposing *all* recordings, which were variously described in its publications as 'a grave threat, a serious danger and an ever-present menace' (Thornton 1995: 42) it was willing to compromise and allow tightly controlled use of recordings on radio, television and in public places.

The position of the record companies was perhaps more conflicted. When submitting evidence to the Copyright Committee in 1909, the Gramophone Company believed that public performances would generate additional sales for their records, arguing, 'public performances of records, in our view are a great advertisement for the music' (Board of Trade, 1952: 10). While this position held when the BBC began using recorded music in 1927,[27] the slump in the record business changed their attitude. For PPL, reaching an agreement with the MU was a price worth paying as evident in subsequent events.

After an initial raft of complaints by MU members about PPL's failure or inability to police the use of records in public places, the mutual benefits of the agreement became apparent. After a series of meetings between them, the Union accepted that PPL could not stop *all* public uses of records but that they would 'do everything possible to ensure records will not be used in substitution for a band or orchestra' (*Report of Proceedings, Delegate Conference* 1949: 16). Given the relatively small

[27] The record companies approved free use of records for the BBC on the grounds that it would boost sales.

sums generated for the record companies via PPL, especially in their early years, it was perhaps unsurprising that they were unwilling or unable to commit extensive resources to policing the use of their members' records. As this has gradually become a more significant source of revenue[28] for the industry, the record companies have latterly shown considerably more interest in PPL and their collection procedures.

Around the same time as PPL made the commitment to ensuring the protection of the employment of live musicians, the Union issued an instruction to members that forbade them from recording for any record companies that were not members of PPL, helping create a *de facto* monopoly for PPL-affiliated companies within the recorded music market.[29] These additional arrangements meant that the Union and the record companies were effectively hostages to each other's fortune for the duration of the 1946 agreement, something that was evident in their close co-operation when dealing with potential disruption to it from legislation and the broadcasters.

This was apparent when the first serious challenge to their post-war agreements emerged in the form of the (Gregory) Copyright Committee. This was set up by the government in 1952 to review copyright in the UK, and though both the MU and PPL submitted evidence to the tribunal, they were dissatisfied with its recommendations. The Tribunal was mostly concerned with PPL's ability, at the behest of the MU, to refuse licences for the playing of records. It accepted that in some cases, this was justified, but that in others, PPL were being unreasonable. In addition to recommending a series of exemptions from the reach of the PPL/MU agreement,[30] the Commission recommended the setting up of a Performing Right Tribunal (PRT) to adjudicate on disputes over licences, and rejected the MU's attempts to enshrine a performers' right in law. Instead, it recommended a slight strengthening of the Dramatic and Musical Performers' Protection Act.

The period between the publication of the report in 1952 and the Royal Assent being given to the Copyright Act of 1956 was one in which the MU and PPL lobbied furiously to protect their existing agreement, the

---

28 It has become more significant as sales of recorded music have decreased, and in 2014 income from broadcasters and other music users passed US$1 billion in a year for the first time (http://www.ifpi.org/music-for-broadcast-and-public-performance.php (accessed 30 December 2014).

29 A small number of record companies refused to join PPL, but all the major recording companies were members.

30 Mainly for what the report termed 'Social Service' societies, including, for example, YMCA and YWCA premises, see Board of Trade (1952: 73–74).

loss of which, Hardie Ratcliffe, the Union's General Secretary, said would be 'a most disastrous occurrence' (*minutes of Executive Committee meeting*, 3 and 4 July 1955). Ratcliffe wrote extensively of the 'Copyright Bill Dangers' (*The Musician*, November 1955: 8) and lobbied members of Parliament, while encouraging Union members to write to their MPs to prevent what he saw as a range of 'monstrous' proposals (ibid).

When the Act was finally passed, it was not the outcome that the Union or record companies had wanted, but it was not disastrous either. A tribunal was duly established and performers' rights remained absent from the statute books. However, it did recognise PPL's right to collect performance royalties and did not challenge their agreement with the MU, despite allowing some exemptions and offering a mechanism, through the tribunal, for challenging their operation. This, along with a new Dramatic and Musical Performers' Protection Act in 1958, ensured stable relations between PPL and the MU for a further thirty years. While a number of challenges to the status quo were to emerge from broadcasters, the Union was willing to place its case for statutory performers' rights on the back burner while being secure in a position that enabled it to influence and control the use of recorded music.

Although referrals to the PRT were infrequent, its existence was to provide an opportunity for broadcasters and act as a restraint on the Union and PPL. This was evident in the first case referred to it involving Manx Radio in 1965, which set (for the Union and PPL) some unwelcome precedents.[31] This was important in light of later and potentially larger threats to the Union's influence over broadcasting in the form of pirate radio[32] in the 1960s and the advent of commercial radio in the UK, which was accelerated by the election of the Heath government in 1970.

In the case of the pirates, a period of negotiation involving the government and other interested parties (including PPL and the Union) resulted in legislation in the form of the Marine &c. Broadcasting (Offences) Act (1967).[33] This outlawed the pirate stations, but forced PPL (and the Union) to concede a greater allocation of needletime to the

---

[31] The tribunal awarded Manx Radio a needletime allowance of six hours a day (or 50 per cent of its airtime), which was considerably more than the Union had wanted.

[32] These stations (for example Radios Caroline, Luxembourg and Scotland) were based offshore (broadcasting from ships) or overseas in order to circumvent legislation. They predominantly broadcast a diet of the type of pop music that needletime prevented the BBC from playing in any great quantity.

[33] This is covered in more depth in Barnard (1989).

BBC, which allowed it to launch a pop music station, Radio 1, in the same year. While this was not an ideal outcome for the Union, it was, along with PPL,[34] able to extract not only more money from the BBC but further guarantees of employment, which became increasingly important in the context of threats to employment in the BBC orchestras.[35]

The second threat to the MU and PPL agreement, from commercial radio, was the one that ultimately untangled the complex web of industrial relations in the recording industry. The Union's power had hinged largely on the BBC maintaining a monopoly in radio broadcasting, and with the emergence of Independent Local Radio (ILR) in 1973 this began to wane. A combination of a fear of industrial action and a public service ethos meant the BBC management generally supported the MU's stance on the importance of maintaining employment for musicians within the Corporation, but this type of concern for the welfare of musicians was, unsurprisingly, less prevalent in the commercial sector. The independent stations that launched in 1973[36] did so only after the MU's opposition was weakened by the imposition of not only needletime restrictions, but also levies on their advertising income and a forced commitment to the employment of musicians. By 1980, claiming that the stations were unable to make a profit, and with a more sympathetic government in power,[37] the Association of Independent Radio Contractors (AIRC) referred the original agreement to the PRT in 1980. Although they failed with this challenge, it started a chain of events, including an appeal in 1986[38] that culminated in the referral of PPL to the Monopolies and Mergers Commission in 1988.

John Morton, the MU's General Secretary at the time, who represented the Union as an interested party at the 1980 tribunal, said that both organisations saw this as an important challenge and one which had to be repelled by whatever means they had at their disposal.

> The tribunal and the outcome of the tribunal did what I had hoped we could get it to do, which was to confirm that the arrangement between the Union

---

[34] A deal struck between PPL and the BBC in 1968 allowed all four of the BBC's national networks a combined weekly total of 82 hours of needletime.

[35] The BBC proposed cutting its orchestral provision in 1969, but was dissuaded from doing so by a mixture of pressure from the Union and government intervention. The issue was to return at the end of the 1970s, resulting in a strike by MU members at the BBC in 1980.

[36] Nineteen independent local radio stations launched in major cities between 1973 and 1975.

[37] Margaret Thatcher's Conservative government was elected in 1979.

[38] *AIRC v PPL* (unreported) 16 January 1986.

> and PPL was (a) legal, (b) moral and (c) equitable all round. It was the only arrangement that could be made, and that is a point that was misunderstood, and perhaps still is by many session players. They didn't have a right. They had no right, let alone the mechanism for establishing their entitlement to any recording, that didn't exist either. And the alternative to us having the collective payment would be for the record industry to keep it. That was the only real alternative. (*interview with author*, 20 January 2014)

However, 1980 marked a temporary victory for the Union, and PPL and AIRC continued to agitate both publicly and behind the scenes against the agreement. Their case was heard with increasingly sympathetic ears by a government that was heavily pro-business, and it was in this climate, and with moves afoot to further deregulate the radio market, that the Union's influence over the performance of recorded music was finally eroded.[39]

Phase 3: A New Position (1988 Onwards)

The primary mechanism for this was the MMC report on *Collective Licensing* (1988), which was ostensibly investigating PPL rather than the Union. Somewhat inevitably, the deal between the two was subject to renewed scrutiny and the subsequent acceptance of the report's recommendation that 'all performers should receive equitable remuneration, directly paid by PPL, specific to each recording's use in broadcasting or public performance' (1988: 39). This meant, 'the Union's controls over needletime, employment quotas and the policy of not allowing records to accompany live performance, all disappeared overnight' (Scard 1991: 8). For the Union, much of the next decade was spent trying to reposition itself among copyright stakeholders from a position of greatly diminished power.

When the findings of the report were accepted the following year by the government, the impact of this on the MU was visible in three main areas: financially, in the breakdown of industrial relations in the recording industry, and in its lobbying activities.

In purely economic terms, the growth of the recording industry meant that by 1987, the annual payment from PPL to the Union was £1.3 million and the Union also had built up in a 'Special Fund' a reserve of £5.1 million of unspent monies received from PPL. While the generally

[39] A detailed account of the lobbying of AIRC can be found in Stoller (2010).

cautious nature of the Union ensured there would be no immediate crisis, it did remove a substantial sum from the Union's annual income.

More problematic was a breakdown in the previously cordial relations with PPL. In the light of the MMC decision, PPL was in no position to, nor inclined to, defend the Union, as the outcome was of considerable potential benefit to the company. Indeed, the breakdown of industrial relations between the Union and PPL was immediately evident when a dispute broke out between both parties and the Department of Trade and Industry (DTI) as to who was best equipped to distribute the sums collected by PPL for the non-featured performers after 1989. The MU argued that it had the most accurate database of performers, but by the time this was agreed in 1994 the Union was faced with the considerable problem of allocating millions of pounds in revenue to individual musicians. As well as disputed claims among members and non-members as to who played on which tracks, it also served to place renewed focus and criticism on the way these funds had been handled in the past (Williamson 2014).

If the outcomes of the MMC report were mostly negative for the Union, the changes brought about by the CDPA began a rapid strengthening of the legal position of performers. Arnold notes that the Act granted performers 'statutory civil rights of action to prevent the unauthorised exploitation of performances' (Arnold 1997: 30), but these have subsequently been bolstered by a range of additions to it. The most important of these was a result of the Rental and Lending Rights Directive 92/100/EC (now Directive 2006/115/EC) that required member states to legislate on the basic levels of performer protection many of them (including the UK) had signed up to in the Rome Convention of 1961.[40] When the Rental and Lending Rights Directive was added to the CDPA in 1996, it gave performers in the UK a proprietary right for the first time and importantly granted them 'equitable remuneration' with the record producers.[41] Subsequent developments have further narrowed the gap between the rights afforded to performers and those for authors,

[40] The UK was one of several countries that signed the Rome Convention but did not legislate in its immediate aftermath. This was partly down to the wording of the Convention allowing the UK to interpret its existing protection of performers by criminal law as satisfying its requirements, and partly due to stagnation caused by lobbying from interested parties, notably broadcasters.

[41] Under the previous *ex gratia* agreements between the record companies and the Union, performers only received 32.5 per cent of income from use of sound recordings.

including the granting of moral rights to performers in 2006[42] and concessions, partly the result of lobbying by the Union,[43] in the wake of the extension of copyright term in sound recordings that were introduced to UK law in 2013 after the implementation of EU Directive 2011/77/EU.

In the period after 1988, the Union's focus moved from restricting public performances of recorded music to lobbying for legal recognition and greater remuneration for performers. Its gains in this regard were a result of a combination of the expertise and interest in the field of John Morton, and the ability of subsequent General Secretaries to work with other interest groups in the music industries both internationally and nationally.

The international outlook was reflected in Morton's work for the Union as a consultant after retiring as General Secretary in 1989. During this period he continued as President of the Federation of International Musicians (FIM) as well as working with the International Labour Organisation (ILO) and World Intellectual Property Organisation (WIPO). The MU has continued to play a leading role in FIM, and John Smith, the current General Secretary, followed Morton as its President.

At home, the Union had to cultivate a new relationship with the record companies and the increasingly powerful PPL, in the wake of the legislative changes between 1988 and 1996. One outcome of this was the MU's involvement in the formation of a new body, the Performing Artists Media Rights Association (PAMRA),[44] to distribute the funds collected on behalf of performers by PPL after the implementation of the Rental and Lending Rights Directive.

This new arrangement was accompanied by some old and some new problems. The perennial difficulties of matching payments to performers remained, while performers' representatives argued over the splits between featured and non-featured performers. This resulted in the International Managers' Forum (IMF) setting up a rival to PAMRA, in the form of the Association of United Recording Artists (AURA) in an

---

[42] This was a result of the Performances (Moral Rights, etc.) Regulations: http://www.legislation.gov.uk/uksi/2006/18/contents/made.

[43] The Union's successes included the setting up of a 'non featured performers fund' and a clean slate provision that makes record companies pay royalties to musicians after the 50th year of copyright protection and disallows the cross-collateralisation of such royalties against previous advances. See https://www. gov.uk/government/publications/copyright-in-sound-recordings/copyright-in-sound-recordings for a more detailed explanation.

[44] PAMRA was formed by the MU and Equity.

attempt to increase the share for featured performers. Despite the usual squabbling, these arrangements went some way towards formalising and professionalising the collection and distribution of monies for performers, and went some way to restoring the close working relationship between the Union and PPL. However, the organisations set up to implement them were not entirely successful. AURA was beset by allegations of fraud involving its former General Secretary, Peter Horrey (Williams 2004), and both it and PAMRA merged with PPL in 2006. This further solidified the relationship between the Union and PPL, and to accommodate the merger with the performers' organisations, PPL created a performers' board, on which the MU has two representatives.[45]

In addition, since 1989 the Union has become increasingly close to other music industries' organisations representing record companies, music publishers, collection societies and concert promoters with its involvement in the cross-sectoral lobbying organisations, British Music Rights and its successor, UK Music. Unsurprisingly, given the number of rights' holders involved, these organisations have been at the centre of campaigns to secure the extension of the copyright term on sound recordings. Despite failing to achieve the parity with the US term (95 years) they originally sought, the lobbying of music industries' organisations at EU level was ultimately successful, achieving a term extension despite commissions set up by the last two UK governments (Gowers 2006; Hargreaves 2011) recommending no change in the term length. An EU directive (2011/77/EU) approved in September 2011 duly extended the period of copyright on sound recordings to 70 years, and this became law in the UK in November 2013.

If the obvious beneficiaries of this change were the record labels, the Union was also able to lay claim to a positive outcome for non-featured performers, with a 'session fund' being created that ensured the Union's support for the extension bore some fruit for their non-featured performer members. The term extension was widely welcomed across the music industries (PPL 2011), and the MU's General Secretary, John Smith, chose to focus on the directive's 'acknowledgement of the important contribution that performers make to the European creative industries' (ibid) and its recognition of 'the current discrepancy that exists between the copyright regime and performers' rights' (ibid).

Although the final implementation of the directive admitted that performers' rights were still 'calculated slightly differently to the length of the term of copyright' (IPO 2014: 2), there is no question that the MU

[45] John Smith and Pete Thoms are the current MU representatives.

has played an important role, along with other music industries' organisations, in pursuing performers' remuneration and rights. From being a disinterested bystander in 1911, a century later the Union was central to both national and international campaigns on both performers' remuneration and copyright more widely.

I will finish by showing how the Union's journey through these three phases to its current position has had important internal ramifications and by reflecting on the way in which the Union's involvement with copyright has defined its relationship with employers in the music industries, making them more complex and less confrontational than in more traditional employer and Union relationships.

3. THE UNION PAYS A PRICE

Although the relationship with the major employers in the recording industry provided many benefits for both parties, it unsurprising that it triggered internal conflict at both the beginning and end of the period of operation of the 1946 agreement. In essence, the Union was conflicted both on what do with the payments from PPL, and 43 years later on how to deal with the loss of the same funds.

The former can be seen in Union conference reports following receipt of its first payment from PPL.[46] A lengthy debate over what to do with the funds ensued and the outcome was to shape a large part of the Union's operations for the next forty years. Two issues were at stake: whether to accept money from an employer and, in doing so, how to make use of it.

A primary consideration, when news of the PPL income reached members, was a fear of being seen as a 'yellow' union, which was described by Union official Tom Barton[47] as one 'that was bought by an employer because of certain considerations granted to the Union by the employer – possibly by grants made to Union funds': MU Report (1967: 17). While Barton eventually convinced himself that the receipt of employers' money was not compromising the Union, the bigger issue, still being discussed at Union conferences in the late 1960s, was how to distribute the funds.

---

46 PPL paid an advance of £15,000 against the still to be calculated amount due in 1951.

47 Barton was the Union's London organiser in the 1960s and a member of the Communist Party of Great Britain.

This was complicated by a number of restrictions PPL put on their use, the two most important being that the money could not be used for 'the purposes of furthering any trade dispute or for any purpose which may be contrary to or adversely affect the interests of PPL or its member companies' (*MU Executive Committee Report*, 1947: 23) and that only 5 per cent (later increased to 10 per cent) of the payment could be used for general administrative purposes. This meant that the Union had to be tactical in its use of the monies.

The Union's Executive decided that rather than distributing the funds to the musicians who actually played on the records in question, it would retain the funds and use them, in the words of another Union official, Stan Martin, 'for the benefit of all musicians' (Martin 1996: 16). The thinking behind this was that, in the early 1950s, the *minority* of members who were involved in recording were impacting negatively on the *majority* whose income derived primarily from live performance. This meant that the Union's eventual use of what became known as the 'phonographic fund' was determined by both internal and external factors.

Initially the funds were used to support a series of May Day Dances around the country and by way of contributions to various musical organisations including the Royal Philharmonic Orchestra, The Scottish Opera Society, and the Bournemouth Military Band. In 1959, a tactical decision was taken when the EC decided 'a large proportion of the Phonographic Funds should be utilised in the direct promotion of employment for members' (EC Report 1959: 16). Again influenced by the AFM,[48] the emphasis was to be on live performance and employment. These tentative steps were consolidated in 1964 when the Union advertised for an official to run what was then known as the 'Keep Music Live' campaign, a post that was held for over thirty years by Brian Blain. Interviewed in 2012, Blain reflected that his role was akin to that of running 'a very, very mini Arts Council, recycling money to musical activity of all kinds' (*interview with Martin Cloonan*, 18 December 2012).

Among the beneficiaries of this redistributive approach were the London Symphony Orchestra, the Royal Philharmonic Orchestra, and Ronnie Scott's jazz club, all of which, at various points, were under

[48] The AFM had set up a similar fund in the USA after their 1942–44 strike. The Recording and Transcription Fund 'raised money from the sale of recordings to underwrite free concerts for public consumption' (Roberts 2014: 37). In doing so, the Union's logic was that they would create work for unemployed musicians and bolster demand for live performances.

threat of closure. In doing so, it entrenched what was now known as the Music Promotion Committee (MPC) as an important part of the Union's business, and it established the MU as a major patron for some parts of the British music profession. By supporting places where large numbers of MU members worked,[49] the fund also did 'a good public relations job for the Union' (*interview with Martin Cloonan*) and served as a way of 'making the members more sympathetic to what the Union was about' (ibid).

For the period of its operation, the MU/PPL agreement and the services and funding that the Union could provide with it were hugely important in maintaining industrial relations across the music profession, meaning that it was important for both parties to ensure that the agreement was stable. Though this was continually threatened by government policy, legislation, technology, social change and economics, by voluntarily hitching their fortunes to each other in this way, significant disputes between the Union and the record companies were few and far between. For the purposes of dealing with the broadcasters[50] (at least publicly) the two parties maintained a united front.

Tellingly, while there were the inevitable disputes as to the most worthy recipients of the MPC funds, there was no evidence of any serious dissent among Union members and officials about the ethos behind the use of the PPL money either at conferences or in the Union's publications. It would appear that the public relations job worked, and for four decades the strategic use of the fund had also served to pacify some elements of the Union's membership.

It was only on the withdrawal of the PPL funds that sizeable numbers of individual members began to question the Union's prior use of them. This was accentuated by the previously mentioned problems in distributing to individual musicians, particularly when the new-found riches of some were detailed in the press (Wroe 1995). Having lost control over the public performance and broadcasting of records, a further consequence of recognition of performers in the CDPA and the MMC report was that, by having to pay out to individual members and no longer using the PPL funds for the collective good, the Union lost control over a large part of its own membership.

49 The highest density of MU membership has traditionally been in orchestras, often near 100 per cent.

50 Particularly with the advent of Independent Local Radio, whose management wanted to play as much music as possible while paying as little as possible for it – a very different stance to the BBC.

This was manifest in a series of challenges to the Union's leadership, the most visible example of which was the case of the session trumpet player Freddie Staff, who pursued a lengthy legal case against the Union, demanding access to its financial records. While this was eventually resolved in 2002 with no further action being pursued, it generated a considerable amount of bad press (Sweeting 2001, Lebrecht 2001), much of which implied or claimed mismanagement of the pre-1989 PPL funds.

Of course, the Union's leadership fiercely rejected the notion that there had been anything underhand in its handling of these payments, but this view was not shared by at least a sizeable minority of its members. This culminated in a major crisis when the incumbent General Secretary, Dennis Scard, was defeated in a leadership election in 2000, after his opponent, Derek Kay, had stoked discontent among members, claiming in his election material that the Union was bankrupt, and was being sustained by appropriating money given to compensate for the loss of work. Though Kay was ultimately prevented from taking office after the Executive Committee found him guilty of bringing the Union into disrepute for these and other claims surrounding the Union's finances, this resulted in a stream of bad publicity that had the Union characterised by *Guardian* journalist Adam Sweeting as 'a left-wing, doctrinaire organisation as secretive and tight-lipped as the KGB' (2001: 9).

While it has subsequently reorganised and been able to retain the membership levels of 2001,[51] it is a much-changed organisation from the one that was able to both control and generate income from the public performance of recorded music for much of the twentieth century. In 2014, the Union's main roles are engaging in collective bargaining with some of the larger employers (for example, the BBC and the Association of British Orchestras) and the provision of services and benefits for its many freelance members.[52]

CONCLUSION

This chapter has reflected on the role of the MU in developments in performers' rights and argued that its influence has been widely neglected in broader accounts of the expansion of musical copyright in the UK. By telling the story of the Union's interest intertwined with the development of performers' rights in three phases, it has shown how the Union used

---

51 In both 2001 and 2013, MU membership was just over 30,000.

52 These services include legal and contractual advice as well as low cost public liability, instrument and car insurance.

the moral case for performers' rights to achieve a considerable degree of power and control over both the recording industry and broadcasters before such rights were substantially recognised in UK law.

Throughout, it adopted a pragmatic approach to negotiations with the record industry and broadcasters, aware that this power was conditional not only on factors which applied to all trade unions (see Batstone 1988) but also some that were specific to the music profession, notably changes in public taste and the demand for both live and recorded music.

In working together the MU and PPL reached a series of agreements that not only controlled the use of recorded music but also ultimately strengthened the position of the musical performer in copyright law. The Union's campaigning for such recognition, both in a national and international context, was a major contributing factor, but for many years it was willing to subjugate the legal recognition of performers in order to maintain good industrial relations and protect the employment of live musicians.

Nevertheless, the role of the record companies in the advance of performers' rights should not be dismissed. While their motives were different from those of the Union, their need not to disrupt the industrial harmony in what had become a hugely profitable era for the recording industry[53] ensured that they too applied a common sense approach to negotiations.

Finally, it is worth noting that the weakening of the Union's negotiating position in recent years has not only been as a consequence of specific changes in broadcasting and copyright legislation but also as a result of the wider erosion of trade union powers and the privileging of the individual entrepreneur over the collective workforce under neoliberal governments across the last 35 years. In a profession where many workers are freelancers, it was perhaps unsurprising that such individualist notions had an intuitive appeal among many MU members.

For the British recording industry, the MMC report changed everything, and in doing so allowed those Union members who were more concerned with personal than collective gain to seriously challenge its ethos and leadership for the first time. Like other British trade unions in the post-1979 era, this meant the MU had to move towards a position that Ackers *et al.* describe as relying 'less on the collective context for Union

---

[53] With the exception of a few years prior to the introduction of CD players in the early 1980s, the British recording industry grew in economic value every year between 1963 and 1999.

activity and more on services that can be provided to individual members' (Ackers *et al.* 1996: 56).

Furthermore, the MU's historic experience of working closely with the employers in the recording industry made it an early adopter of the type of partnership and the co-operation with employers that characterised the 'new realism' of the British trade union movement under the leadership of John Monks. McIlroy describes this period as one wherein 'industrial relations and trade unions were no longer adversarial' (McIlroy 2009: 50) though perhaps in the case of the MU and the recording industry it was never really thus.

It is in this context that the MU's continuing role in the shaping of UK copyright legislation should be viewed. Its influence now is a result of an approach that allows it to frequently blur the boundaries between the interests of its members and those of other music industries' organisations. The Union has successfully aligned itself with the latter as a means of further advancing the rights of performers as part of a wider industrial relations and lobbying strategy. In doing so, it is pursuing a different type of collective approach from in the past, but significantly it is one that remains reliant on good industrial relations.

INTERVIEWS

Brian Blain, interviewed by Martin Cloonan. London, 18 December 2012.

John Morton, interviewed by John Williamson and Martin Cloonan. Dartford, 20 January 2014.

BIBLIOGRAPHY

Ackers P, Smith C and Smith P (1996), *The New Workplace and Trade Unionism* (London: Routledge).

Arnold R (1997), *Performers' Rights* (2nd ed., London: Sweet and Maxwell).

Barnard S (1989), *On the Radio: Music Radio in Britain* (Milton Keynes: Open University Press).

Barton T (1967), 'Phonographic Funds' in *Report of Musicians' Union Delegate Conference* (Musicians' Union).

Batstone E (1988), 'The Frontier of Control' in Gallie D (ed.), *Employment in Britain* (Oxford: Blackwell), pp. 217–48.

Board of Trade (1952), *Report of the Copyright Committee* (London: HMSO).

Boosey W (1911), 'The Gramophone and Its Claims' *The Times* (London, 4 May 1911) 7.

Clegg H, Fox A, and Thompson A (1964), *A History of British Trade Unions since 1889*, vol.1 (Oxford: Clarendon Press).

Cloonan M (2014), 'The Needle and the Damage Done: Some Reflections on Needletime' (IASPM UK and Ireland Conference, Cork, 12 September 2014).

Davison A (2012), 'Workers' Rights and Performing Rights: Cinema Music and Musicians Prior to Synthesised Sound' in Brown J and Davison A (eds), *The Sounds of the Silents in Britain* (Oxford: Oxford University Press).

Eames F (1934), 'A Performer's Rights' *The Times* (London, 27 March 1934) 10.

Ehrlich C (1989), *Harmonious Alliance: A History of the Performing Right Society* (Oxford: Oxford University Press).

Evans J (1966), *The Conways: A History of Three Generations* (London: Museum Press).

Gowers A (2006), *Gowers Review of Intellectual Property* (London: HMSO).

Greenfield S and Osborn G (2004), 'Copyright Law and Power in the Music Industry' in Frith S and Marshall L (eds), *Music and Copyright* (2nd ed., Edinburgh: University of Edinburgh Press), pp. 89–102.

Greenwood F (1929), 'Writing on the Wall' *Melody Maker* (London, 1 May 1929) 518.

Gronow P and Saunio I (1998), *An International History of the Recording Industry* (London: Cassell).

Hargreaves I (2011), *Digital Opportunity: Review of Intellectual Property and Growth* (London: The Stationery Office).

Humphries S (1934), 'Property in Music' *The Times* (13 April 1934) 10.

IPO (2014), 'Copyright in Sound Recordings' (https://www.gov.uk/government/publications/copyright-in-sound-recordings/copyright-in-sound-recordings) accessed 13 November 2014.

Laing D (2004), 'Copyright, Politics and the International Music Industry' in Frith S and Marshall L (eds), *Music and Copyright* (2nd ed., Edinburgh: University of Edinburgh Press), pp. 70–88.

Lebrecht N (2001), 'Discordant Saga' *The Telegraph* (London, 24 October 2001) 24.

Martin S (1996), 'Exploding a Myth' *The Musician* (March 1996) 16–17.

Martland P (1997), *Since Records Began: EMI, the First 100 Years* (Portland, OR: Amadeus).

McFarlane G (1980), *Copyright: The Development and Exercise of the Performing Right* (Eastbourne: John Offord).

McIlroy J (2009), 'A Brief History of British Trade Unions and Neoliberalism in the Age of New Labour' in Daniels G and McIlroy J (eds), *Trade Unions in a Neoliberal World* (London: Routledge), pp. 21–62.

Melody Maker (1929), 'Sensational Move to Protect Musicians' *Melody Maker* (London, 1 January 1929) 12.

Melody Maker (1947), 'MU Recording Sensation' *Melody Maker* (London, 17 May 1947) 1.

Monopolies and Mergers Commission (1988), *Collective Licensing* (London: HMSO).

Musicians' Report and Journal (1935), 'Performers' Rights' *Musicians' Report and Journal* (Issue 25) 4.

Musicians' Union (1947), *Executive Committee Report to Conference* (Musicians' Union).

Musicians' Union (1949), *Report of Proceedings of the Delegate Conference* (Musicians' Union).

Musicians' Union (1955), *Executive Committee Minutes July 3rd and 4th July 1955* (Musicians' Union).

Musicians' Union (1959), *Executive Committee Report to Conference* (Musicians' Union).
Musicians' Union (1967), *Report of Twelfth Biennial Delegate Conference* (Musicians' Union).
Peacock A and Weir R (1975), *The Composer in the Market Place* (London: Faber).
Phonographic Performance Ltd (2011), *British Music Industry Hails Extension of Copyright Term* (PPL).
Ratcliffe H (1955), 'Copyright Bill Dangers' *The Musician* (5 November 1955) 8.
Roberts M (2014), *Tell Tchaikovsky the News: Rock'n'Roll, the Labour Question, and the Musicians' Union, 1941–1968* (Durham: Duke University Press).
Robertson D (1911), 'The Copyright Bill: A Reply to Mr. Boosey' *The Times* (London, 2 May 1911) 10.
Scard D (1991), *Speech to Delegate Conference, Musician's Union, July 1991* (author's personal archive, 1991).
Shaw G (1911), 'The Copyright Bill: Composers and Compensation' *The Times* (London, 4 May 1911) 7.
Stoller T (2010), *Sounds of Your Life* (New Barnett: John Libbey).
Sweeting A (2001), 'Playing with Fire' *The Guardian* (London, 6 February 2001) Culture 9.
Taylor M and Towse R (1998), 'The Value of Performers' Rights: An Economic Approach', 20(4) *Media, Culture and Society* 631–52.
Thornton S (1995), *Club Cultures* (Cambridge: Polity).
Towse R (2004), 'Copyright and Economics' in Frith S and Marshall L (eds), *Music and Copyright* (2nd ed., Edinburgh: University of Edinburgh Press), pp. 54–69.
Wallis R (2004), 'Copyright and the Composer' in Frith S and Marshall L (eds), *Music and Copyright* (2nd ed., Edinburgh: University of Edinburgh Press), pp. 103–22.
Williams P (2004), 'AURA Makes Gains in Cash Recovery' *Music Week* (5 June 2004) 4.
Williamson J (2014), 'Cooperation and Conflict: The British Musicians' Union, Musical Labour and Copyright in the UK', 41 *MUSICultures* 73.
Witts R (2012), 'Needletime: The BBC, The Musicians' Union, Musical Labour and the Reform of Radio in the 1960s', 7 *Popular Music History* 241.
Wroe M (1995), 'Riches Drummed up for Musicians' *The Observer* (17 December 1995) 4.

8. How notice-and-takedown regimes create markets for music on YouTube: an empirical study

Paul J. Heald*

Not everyone likes notice-and-takedown regimes.[1] The Motion Picture Association of America and the Recording Industry Association of America together send out millions of takedown notices every month only to see infringing files re-uploaded at an undiminished rate.[2] The Digital Millennium Copyright Act (DMCA) provides immunity to a website that hosts infringing material as long as it has not directly encouraged the upload and promptly responds to a takedown request by the copyright owner.[3] Although reform of the system may be necessary to discourage some forms of piracy, any changes should preserve the portions of the regime that operate efficiently to facilitate new markets for creative goods.

In theory, notice-and-takedown regimes can lower transaction costs by facilitating communication between diffuse users and distant copyright owners. For example, an amateur cameraman may have recorded a live

* Thanks to my fabulous research assistants: Anne Lewis, Frank Madden, Laura Meli, Marissa Meli, Carolina Van Moursel, Carlos Ruiz, Marc Tan, DaChang Xie, and Xiaoren Xie, and for comments provided by Jill Crandall, Jason Mazzone, Arden Rowell, Christian Turner, and participants at the 2013 Intellectual Property Scholars Conference and the annual conference of the Society for Economic Research in Copyright Issues, especially Clive Bruton.

1 See Bruce Boyden, 'The Failure of the DMCA Notice and Takedown System: A Twentieth Century Solution to a Twenty-First Century Problem' (Center for Protection of Intellectual Property (December 2013)), http://cpip.gmu.edu/wp-content/uploads/2013/08/Bruce-Boyden-The-Failure-of-the-DMCA-Notice-and-Takedown-System.pdf (accessed 20 March 2014).

2 See *ibid.* at 3.

3 See 17 U.S.C. § 512(c)(1) (limiting liability to injunctive and equitable relief unless the service provider has actual or constructive knowledge, derives financial benefit, or does not remove infringing material).

television performance by French singer Jacque Brel in the early 1960s.[4] In the likely case that the performance is unavailable at any public outlet, the filmmaker would like to upload the performance on the internet, but how is he to clear the rights first? The television station likely erased the original videotape years earlier (if it was even recorded at all) and probably does not know that it owns any rights.[5] Internet databases make tracking down the owner of the underlying musical composition easier, but no compulsory license scheme offers the potential uploader an easy way to pay a royalty and all synchronization rights have to be negotiated directly with the distant copyright owner.

In the alternative, the amateur cameraman can accept the very low risk of being sued for copyright infringement and upload the recording to YouTube without seeking permission. The uploader will then await a response from a rights holder taking advantage of YouTube's content-filtering technology[6] who will be notified electronically almost immediately that its protected content has been uploaded. The notice facilitates three possible responses by the copyright owner who can: 1) Take the video down; 2) Leave the video up and monetize it via advertisement; or 3) Leave the video up without an advertisement. If one of the last two options is chosen by the copyright owner, then the public will have access to a previously unavailable work with the consent of the copyright owner, a response that can be programmed automatically without the constant need for the owner to review infringing uploads.

As applied to YouTube, the notice-and-takedown regime established by the DMCA has the evident potential to radically reduce transaction costs and thereby increase the availability of music to the public. In particular, the uploader is saved the cost of finding the rights holder, and negotiation costs are saved through the automated processes of the Content ID system. The Content ID system also lowers the rights holder's cost of monitoring infringement, while the ultimate consumer's cost of finding content is significantly lowered. In other markets, consumers must expend significant resources finding works, while those possessing

---

4 See, for example, Jacque Brel singing *Amsterdam*, http://www.youtube.com/watch?v=ZkZ_ihsn404 (accessed 21 March 2014).

5 See below, note 36 (providing examples of the poor archiving of shows from the 1950s and 1960s).

6 See 'How Content ID Works' (Google) https://support.google.com/youtube/answer/2797370?p=cid_what_is&rd=1 (accessed 4 August 2013) (explaining how YouTube software helps identify uploaded music that is subject to a claimed copyright and sends notice to participating owners).

copies of works must expend significant resources finding and communicating with rights holders. Instead of expensive searches and a room full of attorneys representing the interests of content providers, consumers, and content owners, YouTube can facilitate a three-way deal without any of the parties incurring the cost of direct communication and negotiation. And notably the system leaves the ultimate control with copyright owners who may choose to monetize and profit or to take down an infringing upload through an automated digital response.

In order to measure the potential of YouTube to increase availability, reduce transaction costs, and generate profits for content owners, the No. 1 US, French, and Brazilian hit songs for each year from 1930 to 1960 were identified and tracked as they appear on YouTube. The first ten uploads for each song were charted along with the identity of the uploader, type of upload, number of views, date of upload, and monetization status. Additional data from all uploads of 385 popular songs from 1919–1926 were compiled in order to ascertain the percentage of the songs present on YouTube, the average number of uploads, and the average number of views per upload. These two studies suggest that for websites like YouTube which have an automated content-filtering program, the notice-and-takedown regime of the DMCA fulfills its promise of reducing transaction costs to the benefit of consumers and copyright owners alike.

1. NOTICE AND TAKEDOWN ON YOUTUBE

For the time being, and despite copyright owners' ongoing efforts to modify the current law,[7] anyone with a computer and an Internet connection can upload infringing music on YouTube without rendering

---

[7] The most visible attempt by copyright owners was seen in the proposed Stop On-Line Piracy Act. See Mike Belleville, 'IP Wars: SOPA, PIPA, and the Fight over Online Piracy' (2012) 26 *Temp. Int'l & Comp. L.J.* 303, 31 ('Through a lobbying effort totaling over $91 million, the content industry, including the RIAA and MPAA, indicated to Congress that they were unsatisfied with the current state of copyright enforcement in the United States … presumably in response to lobbying efforts, two bills, PIPA and SOPA, were introduced in the House and Senate.'); see also Michael A. Carrier, 'SOPA, PIPA, ACTA, TPP: An Alphabet Soup of Innovation-Stifling Copyright Legislation and Agreements' (2013) 11 *Nw. J. Tech. & Intell. Prop.* 21; Dominic Rushe, 'Sopa Battle Hots Up as US Congress Debates Piracy Bill' *Guardian* (London, 15 December 2011), http://www.guardian.co.uk/technology/2011/dec/15/sopa-bill-congress-online-piracy (accessed 21 March 2014) ('According to figures compiled by the Center

the website liable.[8] Under either the Digital Millennium Copyright Act safe harbor provisions[9] or analogous common law rules,[10] YouTube appears to be neither directly[11] nor secondarily[12] liable for infringement

---

for Responsive Politics, the film, music and TV industries have spent more than $91m so far this year lobbying for the approval of the bill.').

[8] See *Viacom Int'l Inc. v. YouTube, Inc.*, No. 07 Civ. 2103, 2013 WL 1689071 (S.D.N.Y 18 April 2013) (granting Google summary judgment in lawsuit brought by Viacom suing YouTube for hosting infringing uploads). Although the Viacom litigation is still on appeal, much academic commentary has concluded that YouTube will prevail in cases where it lacks actual knowledge that uploaded material is infringing. Edward Lee, 'Decoding the DMCA Safe Harbors' (2009) 32 *Col.-Vla* 233; Jordan Sundell, 'Tempting the Sword of Damocles: Reimagining the Copyright/DMCA Framework in a UGC World' (2011) 12 *Minn. J.L. Sci. & Tech.* 335, 337; Jennifer M. Urban and Laura Quilter, 'Efficient Process or "Chilling Effects"? Takedown Notices under Section 512 of the Digital Millennium Copyright Act' (2006) 22 *Santa Clara Computer & High Tech. L.J.* 621; Andrey Spektor, 'The Viacom Lawsuit: Time to Turn Youtube Off?' (2009) 91 *J. Pat. & Trademark Off. Soc'y* 286, 290–91.

[9] See 17 U.S.C. § 512(c)(1) (limiting liability to injunctive and equitable relief unless the service provider has actual or constructive knowledge, derives financial benefit, or does not remove infringing material). Most cases applying the DMCA have found Internet service providers in positions analogous to YouTube to qualify for the DMCA safe harbor. See *Perfect 10, Inc. v. CCBill, LLC*, 488 F.3d 1102, 1114 (9th Cir. 2007); *UMG Recordings, Inc. v. Veoh Networks, Inc.* (UMG I), 620 F. Supp. 2d 1081, 1088 (C.D. Cal. 2008); *Io Group, Inc. v. Veoh Networks, Inc.*, 586 F. Supp. 2d 1132, 1148 (N.D. Cal. 2008); *Corbis Corp. v. Amazon.com, Inc*, 351 F. Supp. 2d 1090, 1110–11 (W.D. Wash. 2004). See also *Viacom Int'l. Inc. v. YouTube, Inc.*, No. 07 Civ. 2103, 2013 WL 1689071 (S.D.N.Y., 18 April 2013) ('But the governing principle must remain clear: knowledge of the prevalence of infringing activity, and welcoming it, does not itself forfeit the safe harbor. To forfeit that, the provider must influence or participate in the infringement.').

[10] For a discussion of the common law approach to liability for on-line platforms, see Alfred Yen, 'Third-Party Copyright Liability after Grokster' (2006) 91 *Minn. L. Rev.* 184; see also Brett White, 'Viacom v. Youtube: A Proving Ground for DMCA Safe Harbors against Secondary Liability' (2009) 24 *St. John's J. Legal Comment* 811, 814–21.

[11] *See Cartoon Network, LP v. CSC Holdings, Inc.*, 536 F.3d 121 (2d Cir. 2008) (finding cable company not liable for making system available for customers to copy programs remotely on its servers); *Religious Technology Center v. Netcom On-Line Communication Services, Inc.*, 907 F. Supp 1361 (1995) (finding on-line platform that provided open storage for uploaded material was not directly liable for infringement unless it committed a voluntary act beyond merely making space available); Spektor, note 8 above, at 290–91 (no direct infringement by YouTube).

[12] Since most cases hold that on-line platforms like YouTube qualify for DMCA safe harbor provisions, the application for other secondary liability

until it receives notice from a complaining copyright owner.[13] When it has actual knowledge[14] of infringement, it is potentially liable and has an obligation to take down the infringing upload.[15] YouTube, however, typically asks a question [paraphrased] of the copyright owner before taking down an infringing upload: 'Instead of having the infringing material taken down, would you like us to leave it up and insert an advertisement that will allow you to profit from subsequent views of the upload?'[16] To facilitate this sort of exchange, YouTube has developed its Content ID software[17] that helps it identify infringing music uploads, enabling it to present monetization opportunities to copyright owners.

YouTube, therefore, has the potential to be a low-cost intermediary between three types of parties: 1) those who possess copies of music in various forms (vinyl recordings and CDs; film or television clips; recordings of live performances); 2) those who want to hear that music; and 3) copyright owners who have not made the music available. YouTube transmits a signal to the market from someone who possesses a work that can be observed virtually costlessly by the copyright owner.[18] In cases where YouTube's Content ID service initiates contact with the copyright owner, a business opportunity is presented to the rights holder in such a fashion that an automated response can seal the deal[19] and

---

doctrines like contributory liability and vicarious liability remains underdeveloped. Commentators have made persuasive arguments that YouTube lacks the requisite mental state and control over the infringer to be held liable under historical principles of secondary liability. See Yen, note 10 above; see also White, note 10 above, at 811, 814–21 (discussing common law safe harbors as applied to YouTube).

[13] Since liability requires actual knowledge, it is possible that such knowledge could come from a source other than the copyright owner (for example, YouTube's own Content ID program).

[14] The Second Circuit has recently held that willful blindness establishes the requisite actual knowledge. See *Viacom Int'l Inc. v. YouTube, Inc.*, 676 F.3d 19, 28 (2d Cir. 2012); see also Case note, 'Copyright Law – Willful Blindness' (2012) 126 *Harv. L. Rev.* 645.

[15] See 17 U.S.C. 512(c) (2006) and cases cited above note 11.

[16] See *What Kind of Content Can I Monetise?* (Google), https://support.google.com/youtube/answer /2490020?hl=en-GB (accessed 4 August 2013) (explaining how videos can be monetized by content owners).

[17] See note 6 above.

[18] Either YouTube initiates contact via its Content ID program or the owner can find videos in systemized searches.

[19] 'How Content ID Works' (YouTube), http://www.youtube.com/t/contentid (accessed 4 August 2013) (listing the option to have all unauthorized uploads monetized).

initiate a stream of profits, circumventing the normally high transactions costs associated with music licensing.[20]

2. UPLOADING AND MONETIZATION OF NO. 1 SONGS

To see how and whether YouTube's potential to be a low-cost intermediary has been realized, a list of No. 1 songs from the US, France, and Brazil from 1930 to 1960 were collected and each song was tracked on YouTube.[21] Since all the musical compositions studied were published after 1923, they are (if properly renewed) all still protected in the US, as are all sound recordings of the compositions under a 1972 amendment to the Copyright Act.[22] The title of each song was entered into the YouTube search engine and the first ten search results retrieving the song were analyzed. Data was collected on the identity of the uploader, the date and type of upload, the number of views, and whether the upload had been monetized. It was assumed, as required by the YouTube terms of agreement,[23] that all monetization was conducted by the copyright owner. The data collected provides a snapshot of uploads as of May 2013, as conducted by researchers with IP addresses in the United States.[24] Like

[20] See Alfred C. Yen, 'A Preliminary Economic Analysis of Napster: Internet Technology, Copyright Liability, and the Possibility of Coasean Bargaining' (2001) 26 *U. Dayton L. Rev.* 247 (describing on-line platforms as reducing transaction costs).

[21] For a full list, see below Appendix A.

[22] See 17 U.S.C. § 301(c) (2006) (extending protection to pre-1972 sound recordings to the year 2067). In theory, federal protection for pre-1972 recordings depends on the existence of underlying state law protection that may vary from jurisdiction to jurisdiction. Since YouTube broadcasts in all 50 states, there seems little doubt that a YouTube upload of a pre-1972 recording implicates section 301(c).

[23] See 'Video Monetization Criteria' (YouTube), https://support.google.com/youtube/answer/97527?hl=en (accessed 4 August 2013) (stating that in order to monetize an upload, one must be able 'to provide documentation proving you own commercial rights to all audio and video content').

[24] Any conclusions, therefore, are limited to the US experience. Searching from Brazil for Brazilian No. 1 hits may well generate different search results. The copyright status of a song may vary from country to country, and therefore the IP address of the search may well affect search results. Importantly, some countries only protect sound recordings for 50 years, creating a much larger reservoir of public domain works whose availability may depend on the location of the listener.

the Heraclitean stream,[25] the content and status of uploads on YouTube is constantly changing, so the study catches a moment in time and freezes it.

Perhaps the most striking statistic to emerge from the data is that at least 95 percent of the videos appear to have been uploaded by non-owners/infringers.[26] Very few uploads seem to originate with the owner of the copyright in the underlying musical composition, sound recording, or film/television clip. Although it is impossible to tell for certain that 'wehavejoy,' an uploader who posted a video of Bill Haley's *Rock Around the Clock*,[27] is an infringer, a click on other videos posted by 'wehavejoy'[28] reveals a likely amateur who also has posted a video of his or her cute Yorkshire Terrier named 'Molly.'[29] This is absolutely typical. Only a handful of uploaders of hit music published before 1960 seem to be the copyright owners. Those who appear to be owners, like TheEdSullivanShow'[30] or 'BingCrosbyVevo',[31] not surprisingly, use more identifiable names to associate themselves with the legal owners of the material. Any measure of the percentage of unauthorized uploads can

---

[25] See 'Heraclitus' (Wikipedia), http://en.wikipedia.org/wiki/Heraclitus (accessed 8 August 2013). See also Jay Tidmarsh, 'Procedure, Substance, and Erie' (2011) 64 *Vand. L. Rev.* 877, 893 ('Reduced to its simplest expression, Heraclitus's view was that "all things flow." Perhaps the most vivid – and certainly the most quoted – statement of his position is that "you cannot go into the same water twice."').

[26] Viacom claimed in its complaint that 90 percent of uploaded copyrighted videos were infringing. See *Viacom International, Inc. v. Youtube, Inc.*, 676 F.3d 19, 28 (2d Cir. 2012).

[27] See 'Rock Around the Clock' (YouTube), http://www.youtube.com/watch?v=F5fsqYctXgM (accessed 4 August 2013).

[28] See 'wehavejoy', http://www.youtube.com/user/wehavejoy?feature=watch (accessed 4 August 2013) (home page of all uploads by 'wehavejoy').

[29] See 'Molly: Yorkshire Terrier' (YouTube), http://www.youtube.com/watch?v=KYU8dyAFecQ&list=UUQSU8yVbSz2ERAqnLq1LLw (accessed 4 August 2013).

[30] See 'Bill Haley and his Comets' (YouTube), http://www.youtube.com/watch?v=X31GQTS7C1c (accessed 4 August 2013) ('Rock-Around-the-Clock' posted by the 'EdSullivanChannel').

[31] See 'White Christmas' (YouTube), http://www.youtube.com/watch?v=aShUFAG_WgMm (accessed 4 August 2013) (showing 'White Christmas' posted by 'Bing CrosbyVevo'). According to Wikipedia, 'Vevo … is a joint venture music video website operated by Sony Music Entertainment, Universal Music Group, and Abu Dhabi Media with EMI licensing its content to the group without taking an ownership stake.' See 'Vevo' (Wikipedia), http://en.wikipedia.org/wiki/Vevo (accessed 4 August 2013).

only be an estimate (even legitimate-sounding uploaders might have adopted fake names or maybe Sony Music secretly uploads under names like 'calism23'[32]), but even a brief sampling of typical uploaders leaves little doubt that the job of uploading old music is primarily performed by non-owners. This is consistent with a study by Tim Brooks that found non-owners had digitized more historic sound recordings than copyright owners.[33]

The uploaded videos in the sample were made available to listeners in two different formats. Monetized uploads confront the listener with an advertisement which generates revenue for the content owner, while non-monetized uploads are available without advertisements. Figure 8.1 below depicts the percentage of monetized uploads.

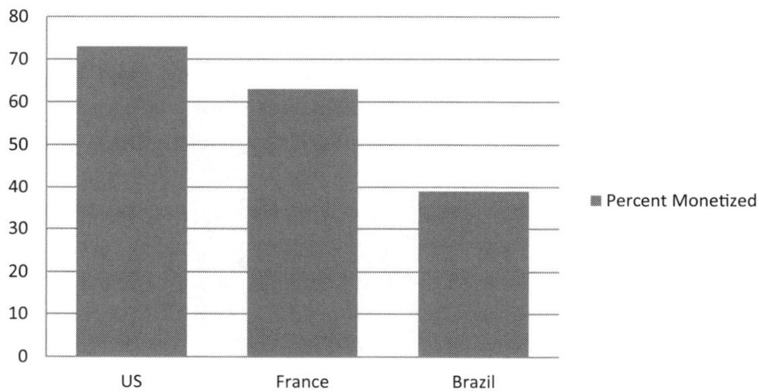

Figure 8.1 *US, French, and Brazilian 1930–1960 No. 1 songs: percent monetized*

Most infringing uploads of the US hits (73 percent) have been monetized by the copyright owner, but a large percentage have not. Twenty-seven percent of apparently infringing uploads of US No. 1 hits from 1930 to 1960 were not monetized and remained available and tolerated by the copyright owner(s). Notably, the non-monetized uploads are not primarily

[32] See 'calima23' (YouTube), http://www.youtube.com/user/calism23?feature =watch (accessed 4 August 2013) (showing home page of all uploads by 'calism23').

[33] See Library of Congress, *Survey of Reissues of U.S. Recordings* (Tim Brooks, 2005) 7–8 and 7, Table 4 (demonstrating that copyright owners had made only an average of 14 percent of popular recordings from 1890 to 1964 available on CDs, while non-owners had made 22 percent of them available to the public on CDs).

recent posts, too fresh to be undiscovered by the copyright owner. In the spring of 2013, the median upload date of the non-monetized subset was March 2009, while the median date for the monetized set was only two months earlier, January 2009. Four years of availability on YouTube is plenty of time for a copyright owner to detect an infringement. The non-monetized uploads appear, therefore, to be consciously tolerated.[34] And in many cases, more than one copyright owner appears to be tolerant. When a non-monetized upload is a television clip, for example, both the owner of the musical composition and the owner of the copyright in the video clip have the independent right to request a takedown.

Notably, US copyright owners seem to be more eager to monetize uploads than their French and Brazilian counterparts. This may be because French and Brazilian songs, although they have a strong presence on YouTube, do not attract nearly as many viewers as American hits, as illustrated in Figure 8.2 below. Many of the French and Brazilian videos may not be worth monetizing, although a simple email request would result in take down.

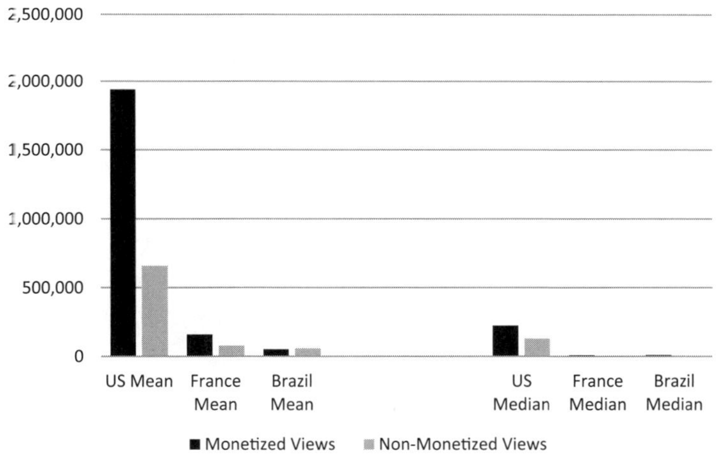

Figure 8.2 Number of views of No. 1 US, French, and Brazilian songs 1930–1960

[34] Of course, the works could be orphaned, in the sense that their copyright owner does not realize it is the owner, but this seems unlikely with chart-topping songs.

Whether an uploaded video has been monetized or not, it remains available to the listener, and further examination of the data shows the rich variety of forms in which the music is encountered by users. Figures 8.3 and 8.4 below depict the different sorts of uploads uncovered by the study and reveal different patterns of monetization by upload type and national origin of the hit song.

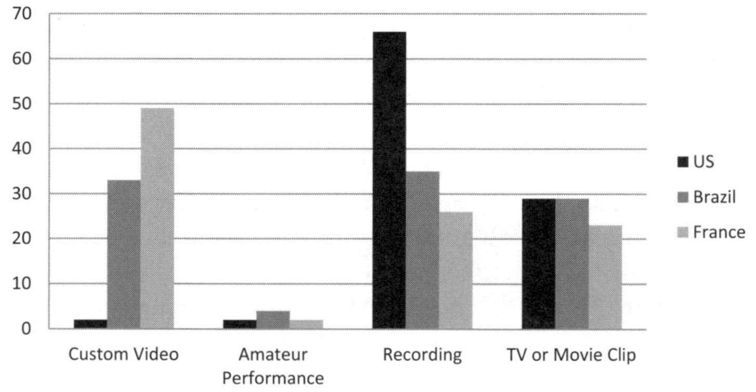

Figure 8.3 Monetized uploads by percent

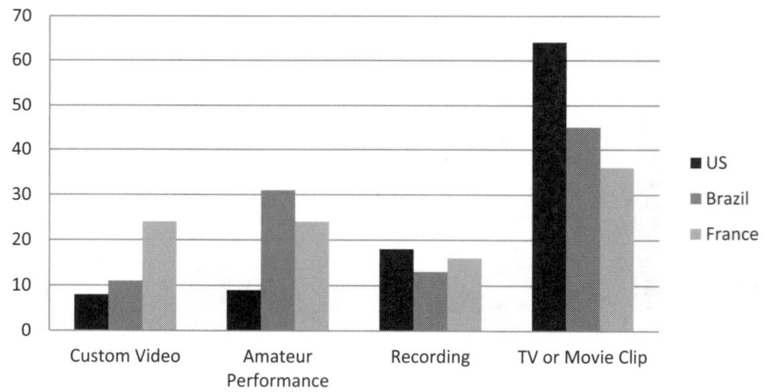

Figure 8.4 Non-monetized uploads by percent

The custom video category contains primarily amateur videos with copyrighted music in the background, including karaoke versions of the song. American copyright owners show little interest in monetizing these uploads or in monetizing amateur performances of their songs. French and Brazilian owners are more likely to monetize a custom video containing their music. American copyright owners focus on monetizing uploads of simple sound recordings, usually uploads of songs off vinyl albums or CDs accompanied by an image of the jacket cover, set of lyrics, or a picture of the artist.

More striking, perhaps, are the types of uploads that are typically *not* monetized, uploads which appear to be entirely tolerated examples of infringement. Figure 8.4 reveals that television and movie clips are the most common sort of non-monetized uploads of US, French, and Brazilian songs.

Two theories might explain the non-monetization of many television and film clips. First, in order for an upload to be monetized, YouTube states that the uploader must have rights to both the musical and visual aspects of a video.[35] This suggests that a television clip from a 1950s variety show cannot be legitimately monetized without the active cooperation of both the owner of the musical composition (probably a music publishing company) and the owner of the copyright in the visual performance (probably the originating television station, broadcasting network, or its assigns).[36] Because two copyrights are typically at issue, the cost of coordination may depress the rate of monetization. Of course, either owner has the right to take the clip down by sending notice to YouTube, but each owner independently might see a benefit in leaving the clip up. The owner of the copyright in the composition may welcome increased interest in the song via YouTube exposure, while the owner of the visual clip may be agnostic if it perceives no threat to its current profits.

In addition, many of the older television clips might be orphan works. For years, television stations did not routinely tape all live programming,[37] and when they did, they did not always archive copies.[38] For this reason, the technical owners of uploaded video programming may no

---

35 'What Kind of Content Can I Monetize?' (YouTube), https://support.google.com/youtube /answer/2490020?hl=en (accessed 4 August 2013).

36 YouTube does apparently sometimes allow a music copyright claimant to unilaterally monetize a video, even if it lacks ownership of the video content. See 'Can YouTube Force Ads on Your Video Content? Keep an Eye on Your Soundtrack' (Reelseo), http://www.reelseo.com/youtube-force-ads-on-your-video-content/ (accessed 4 August 2013) (discussing unilateral monetization); 'I'm Not a YouTube Partner, Why Am I Seeing Ads Next to My Videos?' (YouTube), https://support.google.com/youtube/answer/2475463?hl=en (accessed 4 August 2013) (providing FAQ on the phenomenon). Whether this only happens in the context of amateur uploads is unclear.

37 'List of Lost Television Broadcasts' (Wikipedia), http://en.wikipedia.org/wiki/List_of_lost_ television_broadcasts (accessed 4 August 2013) (listing many lost television shows and noting, for example, that '[a]lmost all of NBC's *The*

longer have their own copies of the works and may not even know precisely what they own. And most of the uploaded performances on YouTube do not provide an explanation of the source of the work, so copyright owners in video content (as opposed to musical content subject to Content ID) are not so easily put on alert that their works are being exploited.

Whether a particular upload is monetized or not, it is accessible to the public for free, which helps to counter the potential negative effect of copyright on availability.[39] Moreover, the work is often accessible in multiple forms, including uploads of music straight from CDs, digitizations of old vinyl recordings, and clips from television shows and films that are frequently more than 50 years old. Yet, despite YouTube's ability to revive and reanimate old works, it cannot make a work fully available. First of all, the music composition itself is not made available, just a recording of it. Moreover, videos containing music cannot be legally downloaded from YouTube by users, and potential listeners may have to wait through commercials in order to hear the music they desire. YouTube is not a particularly flexible platform for users, compared to CDs or digital downloads of music, but it clearly increases availability.

YouTube functions as an intermediary that lowers the cost of transacting over valuable cultural goods. Because the most efficient providers of the goods are often not the rights holders, notice-and-takedown law permits non-owners to signal their possession of the goods to both ultimate consumers and to rights holders without imposing liability on the marketing platform itself. YouTube notices the potential transaction to the copyright owner and cheaply facilitates a 'yes' or 'no' decision by the owner, who can then profit from the deal or refuse it at a very low cost. Although some intermediaries, for example real estate agents, raise transaction costs, the YouTube system lowers transaction costs and keeps some form of access to old music and performances publicly available.

Tonight Show with Jack Paar and the first ten years (1962–1972) hosted by Johnny Carson were taped over by the network and no longer exist').

38 See, for example, *Pacific and S. Co. v. Duncan*, 572 F. Supp. 1186 (1983), *aff'd in part, rev'd in part*, 744 F.2d 1490 (11th Cir. 1984) (plaintiff, television station WXIA-Atlanta, admitted to taping over or destroying all recordings of its newscasts).

39 See Paul J. Heald, 'How Copyright Keeps Works Disappeared' (2014) 11 *J. Empirical Legal Studies* 829 (demonstrating the negative effect of copyright on the availability of new editions of old books on Amazon.com and old music in movies).

3. UPLOADS OF POPULAR US SONGS FROM 1919–1926

The study described above relied on the list of No. 1 songs listed in Appendix A, and all of the songs were assumed to be under copyright.[40] As discussed, they are presently available in a wide variety of different forms on YouTube. But are older and more obscure songs equally available? And does the copyright status of the underlying musical composition have any effect on availability? To pursue these two further questions, a list of 385 popular US songs from 1919–1926 was generated and each song was queried on YouTube. Roughly half of the compositions (1919–1922) are in the public domain, and roughly half (1923–1926) are not. Seventy percent of the public domain compositions had uploaded versions on YouTube, while 77 percent of the copyrighted compositions from 1923–1926 had uploaded versions. This compares with the No. 1 hits from Brazil, France, and the US, which had a 97 percent YouTube presence. Age and popularity seem to affect availability on YouTube, although an average of 74 percent availability on YouTube of the songs from 1919–1926 is still quite impressive. By comparison, in the book market, only 27 percent of *New York Times* bestsellers from 1923–1932 are available in digital form in 2014.[41]

Finally, and consistent with the story told by the No. 1 hits, copyright law does not seem to pose an impediment to availability on YouTube. In addition to the greater availability (77 percent compared to 70 percent) of the copyright songs (1923–1926) over the public domain songs (1919–1922), the copyright songs averaged more uploads per composition. The public domain compositions averaged 9.8 uploaded songs per composition while the copyrighted compositions averaged 14 uploads. However, attributing the increased availability of songs from the period 1923–1926 to their copyright status is almost certainly premature. Previous data had suggested that songs on the more recent side of the 1923 divide have always been intrinsically more popular.[42] Indeed, the songs from the period 1923–1926 averaged 112,000 total views, while the songs from

---

40 Since massive hits are typically owned by large publishing houses that routinely registered and renewed their copyrights, it is highly unlikely that any of the hits studied are in the public domain.

41 See note 39 above at 852.

42 See Paul J. Heald, 'Bestselling Musical Compositions (1913–32) and Their Use in Cinema (1968–2008)' (2009) 6 *Rev. Econ. Res. on Copyright Issues* 31, 37 (studying 1,294 popular songs from 1913 to 1932 as they appeared in films released from 1968–2008 and finding that while songs from 1913–1932 were all

1919–22 averaged only 39,000 total views. Differential popularity best explains why a somewhat larger number of songs from the copyrighted set have a YouTube presence. In the YouTube market, copyright status may simply not be relevant to availability, at least for formerly popular songs of more than a certain age.

4. CONCLUSION

Economists are sometimes overly effusive in their praise of the wisdom of common law rules, but in the case of YouTube, established principles of secondary liability (as embodied in the DMCA) facilitate the development and creation of a more efficient market. Courts have so far usually held that market-making intermediaries are not liable for the maintenance of platforms that welcome infringers until those intermediaries have actual knowledge of the infringement.[43] In this way, the rules that encourage notice-and-takedown regimes help promote access to cultural works while leaving the ultimate decision in the hands of rights holders. These rules, however, are under attack as advocates push for a strict liability regime that would destroy the market just described.[44]

Congress should resist calls to dismantle platforms like YouTube which take advantage of current limits on secondary liability to create a marketplace that radically reduces the high cost of negotiating over rights to music and visual content. The access YouTube provides to valuable cultural products is far from perfect, but it provides a partial solution to the problem of disappearing works, at least in the music context. In any

---

under copyright, the songs from 1923–1932 were significantly more likely to appear in movie soundtracks).

[43] See note 10 above.

[44] See note 14 above. See also Steven Ward Gaches, 'Balancing Interests: The DMCA Debacle in *Viacom v. Youtube*' (2010) 19 *U. Balt. Intell. Prop. L.J.* 65; Amir Hassanabadi, 'Viacom v. Youtube – All Eyes Blind: the Limits of the DMCA in a Web 2.0 World' (2011) 26 *Berkeley Tech. L.J.* 405, 408; William Henslee, 'Copyright Infringement Pushin': Google, Youtube, and Viacom Fight for Supremacy in the Neighborhood That May Be Controlled by the DMCA's Safe Harbor Provision' (2011) 51 *IDEA* 607; Lior Katz, 'Viacom v. Youtube: an Erroneous Ruling Based on the Outmoded DMCA' (2010–11) 31 *Loy. L.A. Ent. L. Rev.* 101, 101; Philip Mazoki, '*Viacom International Inc. v. Youtube Inc.* and the Failings of the Southern District Court of New York' (2011) 30 *Temp. J. Sci. Tech. & Envtl. L.* 275, 309 (arguing against YouTube); Adam Shatzkes, 'The Destruction of an Empire: Will Viacom End YouTube's Reign?' (2010) 26 *Touro L. Rev.* 287, 287.

event, no new legislative initiative should proceed in the absence of concrete data testing the claim of copyright owners that their proposals make works more, rather than less, available to the public.

APPENDIX A

Table 8A.1 No. 1 hits from 1930–1960 from Brazil, France, and the United States

	Year
Brazilian No. 1 Songs	
Pra Você Gostar De Mim (Tahi)	1930
Tico-Tico no Fubá	1931
O Teu Cabelo Não Nega	1932
Alô Alô	1933
Cidade Maravilhosa	1934
Minha Palhoça	1935
Pierrô Apaixonado	1936
Carinhoso	1937
Pastorinhas	1938
O Que é Que a Baiana Tem?	1939
Dama das Camélias	1940
Canta Brasil	1941
Ai! Que Saudades da Amélia	1942
A Dama de Vermelho	1943
Atire a Primeira Pedra	1944
Maria Bethânia	1945
De Conversa em Conversa	1946
Copacabana	1947
A Saudade Mata a Gente	1948
Brasileirinho	1949
Pé de Manacá	1950
Vingança	1951
Lata D'Água	1952
Risque	1953
Terez da Praia	1954
Café Soçaite	1955
Conceição	1956

Mocinho Bonito	1957
Little Darling	1958
Estúpido Cupido	1959

French No. 1 Songs

Parlez-Moi D'amour	1930
Couches Dans Le Foin	1932
O Corse Ile D'amour	1934
Tout Va Tres Bien Madame La Marquise	1935
Marinella	1936
Mon Legionnaire	1937
Je Chante	1938
Le Soleil et La Lune	1939
L'accordeoniste	1940
Lili Marlene	1942
Douce France	1943
AH! Le Petit Vin Blanc	1944
La Belle de Cadix	1945
La Vie en Rose	1946
Maladie d'Amour	1947
Mademoiselle de Paris	1948
Ma Cabane au Canada	1949
Cerisier Rose et Pommier Blanc	1950
Comme un P'tit Coquelicot	1951
Ma P'tite Folie	1952
Le Gorille	1953
Le Petit Cordonnier	1954
Je Vais Revoir Ma Blonde	1956
Bambino	1957
Hello Le Soleil Brille	1958
Oui, Oui, Oui, Oui	1959

U.S. No. 1 Songs

Puttin on the Ritz	1930
Minnie the Moocher	1931
Night and Day	1932
Stormy Weather	1933
Moon Glow	1934
Cheek to Cheek	1935
Pennies from Heaven	1936
Sing, Sing Sing (with a swing)	1937
Begin the Beguine	1938
Over the Rainbow	1939
In the Mood	1940
Chattanooga Cho-Choo	1941
White Christmas	1942
Pistol Packin' Momma	1943
Swingin' on a Star	1944
Rum & Coca-Cola	1945
Prisoner of Love	1946
Chi-Baba, Chi-Baba	1947
Buttons and Bows	1948
Ghost Riders in the Sky	1949
Third Man Theme	1950
Too Young	1951
You Belong to Me	1952
Vaya Con Dios (May God Be with You)	1953
Mr. Sandman	1954
Rock Around the Clock	1955
Que Sera	1956
Jailhouse Rock	1957
Tom Dooley	1958
Marina	1959
Are You Lonesome Tonight?	1960

Let's Twist Again	1961
If I Had a Hammer	1963
Strangers in the Night	1966
Whiter Shade of Pale	1967
Hey Jude	1968
Get Back	1969

Index